BRITISH AND IRISH AU~~~~

Introductory critical studies

ALFRED TENNYSON

This book provides a valuable introduction for students and other readers of Tennyson's poetry and presents a challenging new account of its major themes and concerns.

Elaine Jordan examines Tennyson's uneasy position as a writer of the male middle-class ascendancy and shows how his poetry reveals ambivalent attitudes towards manliness, war, and nineteenth-century scientific rationality. In his early Idylls she finds him experimenting with different political attitudes, investigating the relationship between individual happiness and general progress; in his monologues he is caught between motion and stasis, calling into question the Romantic quest to integrate the language of self with its object; in *The Princess* he addresses contemporary debates on the role and status of women; his *In Memoriam* explores loss and relationship through images of the body and questions of language; *Maud* deals with images of masculinity and femininity in relation to violence and sexual love; and *Idylls of the King*, his most imperialist and most pessimistic poem, highlights his regard for intuition and vision in the face of scientific 'laws' of nature and society.

The study introduces these themes and shows how they relate to each other. By means of close and persuasive analysis of the poetry, Elaine Jordan argues that Tennyson's treatment of issues such as gender reveals the questioning of social life which underlies his art.

BRITISH AND IRISH AUTHORS
Introductory critical studies

In the same series:

ALFRED TENNYSON

ELAINE JORDAN

Lecturer in Literature, University of Essex

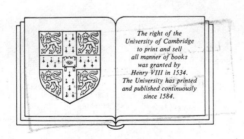

The right of the
University of Cambridge
to print and sell
all manner of books
was granted by
Henry VIII in 1534.
The University has printed
and published continuously
since 1584.

CAMBRIDGE UNIVERSITY PRESS

CAMBRIDGE

NEW YORK NEW ROCHELLE MELBOURNE SYDNEY

Published by the Press Syndicate of the University of Cambridge
The Pitt Building, Trumpington Street, Cambridge CB2 1RP
32 East 57th Street, New York, NY 10022, USA
10 Stamford Road, Oakleigh, Melbourne 3166, Australia

First published 1988

Printed in Great Britain at
the University Press, Cambridge

British Library cataloguing in publication data
Jordan, Elaine
Alfred Tennyson. – (British and Irish authors)
1. Tennyson, Alfred Tennyson, *Baron*
– Criticism and interpretation
I. Title   II. Series
821'.8   PR5588

Library of Congress cataloguing in publication data
Jordan, Elaine.
Alfred Tennyson.
(British and Irish authors)
Bibliography.
Includes index.
1. Tennyson, Alfred Tennyson, Baron, 1809–1892 –
Criticism and interpretation.   I. Title.   II. Series.
PR5588.J59   1988   821'.8   87-26789

ISBN 0 521 30822 4 hard covers
ISBN 0 521 31337 6 paperback

GG

To Matthew, Tom and Susanna,
and to my mother

And if I be, as truecast Poets are,
Half woman-natured, typing all mankind;
So must I triple-man myself and case
My humours as the caddisworm in stone,
Or doing violence to my modest worth
With one long-lasting hope chain-cable-strong
Self-fixt, inmoor in patience, till I die.

Unpublished lines, 1839
(Printed in Christopher Ricks, *Tennyson*, p. 161)

. . . a man solitary and sad, as certain men are, dwelling in an element of gloom, – carrying a bit of Chaos about him, in short, which he is manufacturing into Cosmos! . . . He had his breeding at Cambridge, as if for the Law, or Church; being master of a small annuity on his father's decease, he preferred clubbing with his mother and some sisters, to live unpromoted and write poems. In this way he lives still, now here now there; the family always within reach of London, never in it; he himself making rare and brief visits, lodging in some old comrade's rooms. I think he must be under forty, not much under it. One of the finest looking men in the world. A great shock of rough dusty-dark hair; bright-laughing hazel eyes; massive aquiline face, most massive yet most delicate, of sallow brown complexion, almost Indian-looking; clothes cynically loose, free-and-easy; – smokes infinite tobacco. His voice is musical metallic, – fit for loud laughter and piercing wail, and all that may lie between; speech and speculation free and plenteous: I do not meet, in these late decades, such company over a pipe! – We shall see what he will grow to. He is often unwell; very chaotic, – his way is thro' Chaos and the Bottomless and Pathless; not handy for making out many miles upon.

Carlyle to Emerson, August 1844 (*The Correspondence of
Emerson and Carlyle*, ed. J. Slater, New York, Columbia
University Press, 1964, p. 363)

Contents

Preface

Work on this book has fascinated and instructed me, and I have
hoped that in following up what captured my attention it would
also interest readers. Though I have drawn gratefully on a wide
range of works on Tennyson, I have not given a bibliography of
these: works mentioned in the notes provide a sufficient starting
point for further reading. One can almost always find something
even in books which are antipathetic: in writing we are dependent
on others even as we become convinced that only our own way of
going about things will do.

My main enterprise has been to re-read the poems: to listen to
them and then come back from that immersion to try and com-
municate my sense of what they were and how they worked. No
such reading is ever entirely innocent and open. My individual
response in the England of the 1980s is coloured by this moment
and place, and must also encounter what I can recover of Tennyson in the 1830s or 1860s, for example – very different moments
in his long career.

In pursuit of his range of interests in the current of the nineteenth century I have been enlightened by work which crosses the
boundaries of the literary. Poetry is a special discourse, but not a
restricted one. I have tried to make available to students the
results of my reading, not only in the specific studies of the *Tennyson Research Bulletin* or in Isobel Armstrong's survey of critical
responses to poetry in the light of Victorian aesthetics, *Victorian
Scrutinies*, but in studies ranging from printing technology and
publishing practice to political and legal changes in the status of
the middle classes and of women. Tennyson's distaste for the
Manhood and Beauty model of men and women, and his serious
concern with what women could be, have engaged me particularly; I hope this will not prove to be too much at odds with my
sense of how erotic his writing is.

Knowing how much Tennyson's love of pictorial art informed
his poetry, and how much he admired Turner, I looked at
Turner's paintings and became convinced of significant affinities
between the older painter and the poet, as they expressed in their

different media their response to the age. Work on Turner by John Gage, Ronald Paulson and Mordecai Omer was very exciting here. Their commitment to their art, their investigation of its powers and problems in their time, is accompanied by shared influences in their reading in mythological scholarship and spiritualism or theosophy. I came to see that what looked like minor eccentricities of thought – the sort that feed into 'alternative' cults still – were elements in a major historical transition from the dominance of religious ways of thinking to the dominance of science.

John Killham's pioneering *Tennyson and 'The Princess'* offered a base for thinking about this transition, which carried with it rethinking of society and of the role of women. All this was elaborated by W. D. Paden's *Tennyson in Egypt* (1941), and by A. J. Busst, E. S. Shaffer and Barbara Taylor in their respective works which are mentioned in the notes of this book; finally clinched and made coherent to my mind by unpublished work of Gareth Stedman Jones, which he has kindly allowed me to cite. Tennyson seems to me modern, sceptical and rationalistic; but his sisters and brothers, especially Mary and Frederick, were fascinated with spiritualism, entering the Swedenborgian Church of the New Jerusalem. Spiritualism, like mesmerism and phrenology, was a form by which older religious and ethical habituations tried to adapt to the materialism of science. Tennyson's poetry, addressing common human experience of desire and death, is another mode of adaptation, enquiry and endurance, immensely influential and to me undoubtedly better. In studying the effects of scientific enquiry on nineteenth-century ideas, imagination and writing, I have learned much from Gillian Beer, W. F. Cannon, Walker Gibson and from Tess Cosslett's book *The Scientific Movement and Victorian Literature*, Harvester Press, 1982, as well as the book she edited, *Science and Religion in the Nineteenth Century*, Cambridge University Press, 1983.

I would like now to express my gratitude to friends and colleagues for their encouragement and advice, and for odd passing comments that provoked further thought according to my own fancy: especially to Leonore Davidoff, Ludmilla Jordanova, Angela Livingstone, David Musselwhite, Gabriel Pearson and Harry Tait. My thanks to Sylvia Sparrow, who helped with that archaic business of typing, and to Terry Tostevin and all the library staff at Essex University for their friendliness and patient help; also to the librarian of Trinity College, Cambridge, for per mitting me to examine manuscripts of *In Memoriam* and *Maud*; and finally to the Tennyson Research Centre, Lincoln, for quotation from the unpublished 1848 Lincoln proofs of *The Princess*, by permission of Lord Tennyson and the Lincolnshire Library Service.

My greatest debt is to Christopher Ricks, both for his scholarship and his critical intelligence. When I was an Oxford undergraduate, having come from the very different world of a northern girls' grammar school, he showed me that being clever was not incompatible with common human affections; my original work on Tennyson's manuscripts was under his supervision; and his generosity has been continued even when increasingly we have disagreed. He has animated my thinking – pointing out, for example, that 'Cyril' in *The Princess* is an anagram of 'lyric', which was far from a petty point for my reading, especially when supported by the lines in the 1848 proofs to which he drew my attention, and which now conclude my account of *The Princess* in Chapter 3. For this and for other information, insights and admonitions I am grateful.

A chronology of Tennyson's life and major publications

1809   Born at Somersby, Lincolnshire, on 6 August

1816–20   Pupil at Louth Grammar School

1827   *Poems by Two Brothers* published by Jacksons of Louth

1827–31   At Trinity College, Cambridge

1829   Beginning of friendship with Arthur Henry Hallam, b. 1811

          In June, awarded the Chancellor's Gold Medal for his prize poem, *Timbuctoo*

          In October, elected to the undergraduate debating society, the 'Apostles'

1830   Publishes *Poems, Chiefly Lyrical*, in June

1831   Death of his father, in March

          Leaves Cambridge without taking a degree

1832   Severe review of *Poems, Chiefly Lyrical* by 'Christopher North' in *Blackwood's Magazine*, in May

          Hallam's engagement to Emily Tennyson recognized by Hallam's family

          Publishes *Poems* (dated 1833)

1833   Harsh review of *Poems* by J. W. Croker in *Quarterly Review*

          In September, the sudden death of Hallam, while visiting Vienna

1834–6   Love for Rosa Baring

1836   Marriage of his brother Charles to Louisa Sellwood, and the beginning of Tennyson's love for her sister Emily, whom Tennyson had met in 1830

1837   In May the Tennysons move from Somersby to High Beech, Epping, in Essex

          His engagement to Emily Sellwood recognized by both families

1840   Engagement broken off, partly for financial reasons

          The Tennysons move to Kent, first to Tunbridge Wells and in 1841 to Boxley, where Park House, near by, the home of the Lushingtons, was to provide the setting for *The Princess*

1840–1   Invests his inheritance of about £3,000 in a mechanical wood-carving scheme promoted by his doctor, which fails finally by 1843

1842   Publishes *Poems*, in May. The first volume took poems from *1830* and *1832*, with some written *c*. 1833; the second, new poems. Also published in America, by Ticknor

1843–4   Hydropathic treatment for 'hypochondria' near Cheltenham, where the family has now moved

1845   Granted a Civil List pension of £200 per annum, on the grounds that his poetry is unlikely to become popular

1847   Publishes *The Princess*, in December

1849   Renews correspondence with Emily Sellwood

1850   Publishes *In Memoriam* anonymously, at the end of May
Marries Emily in June
Appointed Poet Laureate in November, succeeding Wordsworth who had died in April

1852   Birth of his son Hallam; a first son had been stillborn, in 1851
Publishes *Ode on the Death of the Duke of Wellington*, in November

1853   Moves to Farringford, Isle of Wight, which he buys with the proceeds of *Maud* in 1856

1854   Birth of his son Lionel

1855   Publishes *Maud, and Other Poems*, in July

1859   Publishes *Enid, Vivien, Elaine* and *Guinevere*, in July

1862   Publishes *Idylls of the King* with a Dedication in memory of the Prince Consort (d. December 1861), in January
In April, first audience with Queen Victoria, at Osborne, Isle of Wight

1864   Publishes *Enoch Arden, and Other Poems*

1865   Death of his mother, in February

1868   The foundation stone of his second home, Aldworth, at Blackdown in Surrey, is laid

1869   Publishes *The Holy Grail and Other Poems*, in December (dated 1870)

1872   Publishes *Gareth and Lynette* volume. With the Imperial Library *Works* (1872–3), the *Idylls of the King* with a new Epilogue: *To the Queen* are complete except for *Balin and Balan*, written 1874

1875   The publication in June of *Queen Mary* inaugurates Tennyson's career as a playwright. It was produced the next year, with Henry Irving, who also produced and acted in *The Cup* (with Ellen Terry) and *Becket*, in 1893

1879   Publishes *The Lover's Tale*, the first authorized edition of this much-pirated early poem

1880   Publishes *Ballads and Other Poems*, in December

1883   Accepts a barony, taking his seat in the House of Lords in March 1884

1885   Publishes *Tiresias, and Other Poems*, in November

1886   The death of his son Lionel at the age of thirty-two, returning from India
            Publishes *Locksley Hall Sixty Years After*

1888–9   Severe rheumatic illness

1889   Publishes *Demeter and Other Poems*, in December

1890   Records some poems, with the assistance of Edison

1892   Dies at Aldworth on 6 October
            The Death of Oenone, Akbar's Dream, and Other Poems published posthumously

A note on sources

I have drawn extensively on the notes to individual poems in Christopher Ricks, *The Poems of Tennyson*, Longman, 1979 (referred to as Ricks, *Poems*).

For biographical information I have relied largely on three books:

Charles Tennyson, *Alfred Tennyson*, Macmillan, 1950.

Christopher Ricks, *Tennyson*, Macmillan, 1972.

Robert Bernard Martin, *Tennyson: The Unquiet Heart*, Faber and Faber, 1983.

Information which does not appear in the notes is drawn from these sources. Within my text I cite line references for the published poetry unless the poems are short ones, and refer the reader to pages in the Ricks edition for all manuscript extracts, which are given in his notes to the poems. This edition has now been revised in three volumes (1987), to include material from the Trinity College manuscripts which could not originally be quoted; but I assume that the one-volume edition which I have used will be adequate for readers of this book, and accessible.

Introduction

SOMETHING OF THE LIFE

Tennyson lived from 1809 to 1892. The third son among eleven children of a Lincolnshire clergyman, he worked only as a poet and became wealthy by poetry. His work inherited gratefully from the past, weaving past writing into the new by allusion. At a time when the usefulness of studying the Greek and Roman classics in an industrial economy was being queried, he kept them within literary consciousness. His extensive knowledge came first from his father, who educated him at home between the ages of ten and seventeen, when he went up to Trinity College, Cambridge. From his father's library came the encyclopaedic information that went into poems like *On Sublimity*, published in 1827 in *Poems by Two Brothers*. His father, Dr George Clayton Tennyson, predicted that Alfred would be a great poet, but was also the source of deep anxieties.

The rectory at Somersby was crowded, its eleven rooms housing 23 people, family and servants, in 1824. In a sonnet to Tennyson's mother on her husband's death, Arthur Hallam addressed her as 'Oh woman tried in danger and in pain'.[1] Her husband had been the danger to her; his drunkenness and violent rages told on the health of them all. Foreign travel was prescribed for him; Alfred, taking responsibility, felt that the younger sons would benefit by removal from the brooding atmosphere. Insanity, alcoholism and the epileptic seizures, to which the father was also subject, were feared to be hereditary; one son was confined to an asylum.

Their paternal grandfather had made money by the law and become quite a substantial landowner. He clearly preferred his second son, Charles, to George, the elder. The Somersby family always spoke of a disinheritance; though this is not strictly accurate, the story dramatized the complex bad relations between father and elder son, and excused the son's hatred of his profession, especially when his younger brother prospered in the law and politics. Old George Tennyson expected his sons to work as he had

1

done, and wanted his three elder grandsons educated for similar professions, which they dodged. The family grievance reflects the more general problem of what the functions of education and the educated classes were in the nineteenth century: a problem Tennyson addressed in *The Palace of Art* and which, as a discussion of the values of work and leisure, runs through the 1842 *Poems*. Refuge from toil is a kind of death in *The Lotos-Eaters*, but *Ulysses* suggests there might be more than one kind of work. For Dr George Tennyson and his sons art and learning were values in themselves – for the old man, it seems, such notions were above their class.

The second son, Charles, took over his father's house, Bayons Manor, and converted it into a magnificent Gothic building; he later took the name d'Eyncourt, as if he were creating an aristocratic tradition for himself, though he had entered Parliament on the Radical side. His pretensions and his success, which felt as though it were at the expense of the Somersby Tennysons, provided some of the animus for Tennyson's many poems which attack the thwarting of young love by pride based on land and money: *Locksley Hall*, *Edwin Morris*, *The Flight*, *Maud*, *Aylmer's Field*. A resentful sense of financial and social inferiority was intensified by Tennyson's love in the early 1830s for the wealthy Rosa Baring, whose beauty may have been the model for the 'Rose in roses' of *The Gardener's Daughter*. The grandfather's economic power over the Somersby family was felt keenly; on his death in 1835 the bequest to Alfred did not give him the means to travel which he wanted. George Clayton Tennyson died in March 1831. Alfred, who had left Cambridge to help his mother, wanted to return and take his degree, but the grandfather saw no point if he would not commit himself to the Church. Tennyson's father had left debts, to which the three sons at Cambridge added, and there were still all the younger children to be started out in life if possible. The poet's long years of combined domesticity and bachelor wandering were under way.

At Cambridge, Tennyson had formed the friendship with Arthur Hallam which has been taken as the major emotional relation of his life. The eldest child of the historian and literary scholar Henry Hallam, Arthur was widely recognized as a warm and attractive personality, and as very able, especially in debate. Gladstone, a close friend at Eton, retained an ideal view of him sixty years after his early death. Tennyson in *In Memoriam* presented him as a potential statesman; Gladstone saw him as a literary man. His work included a theodicy (a work justifying 'the ways of God to man') and translations from Italian poetry. Although Gladstone could describe him as an emanation from another, less darkly chequered world, he was as much subject to depression and doubt as Tennyson: the two friends supported each other, within a group of mutual friends. Hallam became engaged to Tennyson's sister Emily. He died suddenly in Vienna, on 15 September 1833, at the age of 22, from a brain haemorrhage caused by the abnormal enlargement of an artery. A local clergyman wrote of Tennyson in early 1834, 'Hallam seems to have left his heart a widowed one', foreshadowing *In Memoriam*'s imagery. But Tennyson went on writing: *Ulysses* in October 1833, and the fragments of elegy which became *In Memoriam* – XXX, IX, XVII, XVIII, XXXI–XXXII, some lines of LXXXV, and XXVIII.

Early in 1838 Tennyson became engaged to Emily Sellwood, the sister of his brother Charles's wife, but the engagement was suspended in 1840. His financial situation was doubtful, and Charles's marriage had broken down because of his addiction to laudanum; but this was not all. When Tennyson proposed again in 1848, Emily refused him on the grounds that the worlds of religious thought in which they moved were too different. At this time of the Evangelical movement, the revival of an enthusiastic religion of personal commitment, Christian women often stressed their independent relation to God, unmediated by priest, father or husband: marriage could interfere with meditation and charity, the duties of a spirit which had to answer for itself before its maker. The tone of the correspondence which survives between Tennyson and Emily is intensely spiritual; once they were married in 1850 she encouraged him in studies of the mysteries of pain, the virtues of sacrifice for a high good, marking passages for him to read, in works which suggest the masochistic side of idealization, especially of service to nation and Empire. She was the niece of Sir John Franklin, whose ill-fated Arctic expedition of 1845 provided a painful example of dedication and disaster.

In 1837 the Tennysons had been obliged to leave Somersby. At the first of a succession of new homes Tennyson came under the influence of a doctor, Matthew Allen, who persuaded him to improve his financial prospects by investing in a scheme for mechanical wood-carving. By early 1843 this scheme had failed completely, though most of the money was recovered on insurance when Allen died in 1845. In spite of their critical success the slow selling 1842 *Poems* looked unlikely to redeem the family fortunes. One of those poems, written in 1833, was the monologue of St Simeon, who martyrized himself on a pillar. Edward FitzGerald records Tennyson reading this aloud 'with grotesque Grimaces, especially at such passages as "Coughs, Aches, Stitches, etc.", laughing aloud at times' (Ricks, *Poems*, p. 542).

During the 1840s Tennyson's physical and mental health were bad; later he called it hypochondria. The treatment he went in for was the water cure, which aimed to encourage the circulation of the blood and the excretion of impurities; most dramatically the internal and external application of water produced 'crises', eruptions of boils. Tennyson wrote with rather Simeon-like pride of the remarkable quantity of his crises. At best the treatment had real virtues in that it took the whole person, their mental state and social situation, into consideration, and avoided the use of drugs in order to cure the body through its own natural resources: a thoroughly Romantic treatment.

Tennyson's most acute anxieties had eased by 1848. In 1845 he accepted a Civil List pension which he had twice refused, not liking the connotations of 'pension' and expecting hostile criticism, which duly came. Even when poetry had made him both popular and rich, Tennyson kept this pension: a sense of grievance and anxiety about money was one legacy from his grandfather. The major work of these years was *The Princess*, which had been discussed with Emily Sellwood before their estrangement. When it came out in 1847 the critical response was cool and puzzled, but it sold well. In March 1850 half a dozen copies of *Fragments of an Elegy*, the trial edition of *In Memoriam*, were sent to friends, and a copy was lent to Emily Sellwood. Soon after the publication of *In Memoriam* in June, they were married, rather hurriedly; no member of Tennyson's family was there, and even his mother 'did not know of it till it was done'. At Emily's request they went first to Clevedon in Somerset, where Hallam was buried. Tennyson said that his wedding was the nicest he'd ever been at, and wrote to a mutual friend, Sophie Rawnsley: 'We seem to get on very well together. I have not beaten her yet' (Ricks, *Tennyson*, p. 208). Later he said: 'The peace of God entered into my life when I married her.'

This middle year of the century was the turning point for Tennyson. The wide admiration for *In Memoriam* made him the strongest candidate to succeed Wordsworth as Poet Laureate. The remaining forty-two years were ones of domesticity and friendships, and extraordinarily sustained work. They had two sons: Hallam, born in 1852, who devoted his life to his father, taking over as secretary when his mother's health failed; and Lionel, born in 1854, whose death at 32 is mourned in *To the Marquis of Dufferin and Ava* (1889). It has been questioned whether Emily Tennyson's piety and loving care for 'dearest Ally' were good for his poetry, but this can hardly be fairly answered. Why blame the woman? She was not as strait-laced as she has been made to seem: the nonsense writer Edward Lear adored her and she visited George Eliot, whose liaison with G. H. Lewes made many respectable women reluctant to receive or visit her. Earlier, she had no qualms about the relation of Elizabeth Siddall to Dante Gabriel Rossetti – his model, student, and later wife. When Moxon's *Illustrated Edition* of Tennyson's poems was being planned in 1855, Rossetti told a friend that Mrs Tennyson had written to the publisher 'declaring that she had rather pay for Miss Siddall's designs herself than not have them in the book'. However, these designs were not included in the end, except in so far as they influenced Rossetti's own work.[2] Elizabeth Siddall's passion for Tennyson's poetry is typical of young artists and writers at this time. That she and Rossetti also went on a pilgrimage to Clevedon suggests that *In Memoriam* had made Hallam a minor saint.

After 1869, when the *Holy Grail* volume was added to the *Idylls of the King*, a younger generation including Swinburne and J. A. Symonds, who had come to Tennyson's work through the admiration for it of fathers and teachers, were finding the poetry oppressive and dishonest, though Symonds in particular kept up a reverential attitude in his personal contacts with Tennyson.[3] Opinions were mixed about the *Idylls*, but Tennyson's popularity and sales increased. In December 1883 he accepted a barony, taking his seat in the House of Lords in March 1884. He had turned down lesser honours three times since the offer of a baronetcy in 1865, only accepting it now as an honour to Literature rather than to himself, he maintained. His informal title, 'Poet of the People', marked his own consciousness and that of others, of how his poetry could make for national cultural unity: Alexander Strahan, for a time one of his publishers, wrote in 1870 of the need for Literature to 'strike our grappling-iron in the working-people's soul, and chain them, willing followers, to the car of advancing civilization'.[4] I doubt if Tennyson would have liked that image, though he was himself capable of thumpingly reactionary statements, as of more generous and sceptical withdrawals: with the liberal Gladstone or the Irishman William Allingham, he adopted a wilfully antagonistic pose. As he aged he tended towards pessimism about advancing civilization and especially democracy, but 'freedom' remained an ideal.

In the 1840s the continuity of his later work would have seemed incredible. Besides selections and collected editions there were new volumes in 1880, 1885 and 1886; *Demeter and Other Poems* in 1889; and, posthumously, *The Death of Oenone* in 1892. In 1875, at the age of 66, he had turned to the theatre, with *Queen Mary* – a work whose original version, based on the historical writing of J. A. Froude, displays hostility to Roman Catholicism, the Oxford Movement and subsequent High Church Anglicanism, but whose acting version toned this down to a more general distaste for religious intolerance.

Since I do not intend to deal critically with the plays I will say something of them now, in tribute to Tennyson's late energy and readiness to take risks with his reputation. From the 1840s, developments in stage lighting and machinery had made possible spectacular productions with heroic dramas and acting styles to suit. Tennyson was a great reader of his own poetry, in more or less intimate groups; his voice can still be heard on recordings made in 1890, some of them in support of what Kipling ironically called the 'charge' of the Light Brigade, the impoverishment of Crimean War veterans. Henry Irving told him, 'You are a good actor lost.' It was Irving's star performances which made theatre a major cultural focus in the 1870s; Tennyson saw his famous *Hamlet* in 1874, and Irving acted in *Queen Mary*, which was neither a disaster nor very successful. Henry James wrote that although individual scenes were richly worked it remained 'a dramatised chronicle, without an internal structure'. *Harold*, on the last Saxon king, was less unwieldy but was not acted; it was published in 1876. *Becket*, completed in 1879 but not published until 1884, was considered too long and too expensive to produce; but Irving had one of his greatest successes in it, the year after Tennyson died. *The Falcon*, from a story by Boccaccio, followed in 1879; *The Cup*, acted in 1881 by Irving and Ellen Terry, was Tennyson's first success on the stage. A classical story of marriage and murder, it had a huge cast, and grandiose costumes and sets whose historical accuracy was verified by the British Museum. *The Foresters*, on the Robin Hood story, was a popular success in America after Tennyson's death. The last play, *The Promise of May*, in Lincolnshire dialect, Tennyson's only published work in prose, was a total failure in 1882. Tennyson's bid to fill in the gaps left by Shakespeare in the national chronicle did not come to much in the end.

Reminiscences of Tennyson in later life are full of a fascination with 'genius', with coming near the mystery of greatness which his recalcitrance and impressive physical presence did little to dispel. But when the genius is a contemporary, people fear being taken in by a conceited pose. What is emphasized about Tennyson instead is his simplicity, his unguardedness, his indifference to conventional behaviour, and his geniality, the gift of 'bestowing *himself*'. Broadly, the summary of James Knowles, journalist and architect of Aldworth, will do for a late-Victorian view of Tennyson: 'An immense sanity underlay the whole – the perfection of common-sense – and over all was the perpetual glamour of supreme genius.'[5] A more intimate memory was recorded by Tennyson's grandson Charles:

a very powerful old man, and a man who still had a lot of life in him . . . a strangely-dressed old man, very much intent on his own business and his own life, and very conscious that he has a lot of work to do and doesn't meant to let anybody stop him from doing it.[6]

'TYPING ALL MANKIND'

When Tennyson's first mature volume came out in 1830 the boom in poetry publishing, with the great success of Scott and Byron, was fading. During the post-revolutionary wars with France the expensiveness of paper had given an advantage to shorter volumes of poetry, but cheaper production methods were being developed; and as innovations in printing such as the power press and the stereotyping process also reduced costs, poetry was rivalled by long prose works and by the new periodicals carrying serials and short stories. From the 1820s, Annuals were popular, intended as Christmas gifts for ladies: 'picture books for grown children', the poet Southey called them. Tennyson like other poets reluctantly published in *The Gem*, *The Tribute*, *Friendship's Offering* and *The Keepsake*. Assumptions about the audience for these Annuals had their effect on the poems that were written, or at least on those that were accepted.[7]

The price of individual volumes of poetry remained high; a much smaller and more educated readership was assumed for them. The publishers required their poets to share the losses as well as any profits, and those who could not guarantee their publishers in this way, such as Hood, Darley and Beddoes, had to seek other means of support. Wordsworth tried to keep his prices low, to reach as wide a public as possible, and so did Tennyson once he was established in mid century. We can see a division in Tennyson's work between the more trivial of the lyrics and, say, the classical monologues, but *The Princess*, *In Memoriam* and *Maud* do not fit this pattern, while *Enoch Arden* and *Idylls of the King* challenge the novel by their appeal as stories of marriage and its deviations. They were Tennyson's greatest financial successes, and among the most popular poems of the period, with other narrative poems such as the *Ingoldsby Legends* and Elizabeth Barrett Browning's *Aurora Leigh*. They share with contemporary narrative painting and drama the aim of pictorial 'realization': to produce both strong emotion and a sense of actuality in effects or 'situations' which would influence moral and social consciousness.[8] Guinevere lying at Arthur's feet is a theatrical situation of that kind, which Edward Lear thought would be too strong for the prudish. Effects in the theatre were directly modelled on paintings, for example the tableau recalling Wilkie's 1815 painting *Distraining for Rent* in Jerrold's play *Rent Day* (1832). When Walter Bagehot criticized *Enoch Arden* (1864) for its application of an ornate style to a 'dismal' story of people it would be 'horrid to meet' he was echoing the opposition of Scott and Coleridge to sentimental Jacobinism (revolutionary or radical sympathy) in painting, fiction and the theatre. In drawing attention to the working class as a subject for art and demanding respect as well as sympathy for them, Tennyson's poem stands in a long humane tradition.

A poet's work is not wholly determined by its audience, nor can the ways in which an audience impinges on a poet's work be reduced to economics, technology and publishing practice. But these things clearly had their effect on the choices and anxieties of a beginning poet, quite as much as the reviewing to which frequent attention has been paid in Tennyson's case. The review by Arthur Hallam of Tennyson's *Poems, Chiefly Lyrical*, in *The Englishman's Magazine*, August 1831, begins defensively with the assertion made by Wordsworth and others, that popularity was not the test of poetry; Hallam's anxiety relates to the whole climate in which Tennyson's poems came out. The Tory J. W. Croker boasted notoriously that he would kill off Tennyson as he had killed off the 'Cockney' poet Keats, with whose poetry and radical politics he associated Tennyson's 1832 *Poems*. Tennyson published no volume for ten years after 1832; and when the *Poems* came out in 1842, earlier poems which were reprinted had been impressively revised.

In fact the early volumes were generally well received, and not just because Cambridge friends were promoting Tennyson's work. Reviewers' assumptions about the status of poetry differed considerably from the wariness of publishers. One sample review, interesting in itself, is John Sterling's of the 1842 *Poems* in the *Quarterly Review*, LXX, September 1842.[9] Sterling had been an influence on the Cambridge debating society, the Apostles, of which Tennyson and Arthur Hallam were members in their time. His view of *Morte d'Arthur* is likely to have been one of those which stopped Tennyson from carrying on with Arthurian material at this stage; he said it was 'jewel-work' without strong human interest: 'The miraculous legend of Excalibur does not come very near us, and as reproduced by any modern writer must be a mere ingenious exercise of fancy.'

Like many reviewers of the period Sterling does not isolate Tennyson's work within a distinct sphere of literature but views it historically and politically, in relation to the 'state of the nation'. Tennyson's way is being prepared by judicious counsel, to be the national poet. Sterling writes in full consciousness of Britain's world power, and of the situation produced by the 1832 Reform Act, with an enlarged electorate addressed by newspapers and journals:

it is a great thing that the whole country must at least be willingly deceived if it is to be gained over – must seem to itself rationally persuaded . . . Within a year after the Election in an English village, its result is felt in the more or less cost of food and clothes in Kaffir huts, and in the value of the copper saucepans trafficked at Timbuctoo for palm-oil and black babies.

(While at Cambridge Tennyson had won the Chancellor's medal with a poem on Timbuctoo – a vision poem which mourned the diminishment of fantasy into fact.) Just as Hallam had boldly placed Tennyson's first volume in relation to Dante and Shakespeare and to the Romantic poets, allying him with Shelley and Keats as poets of sensation, so Sterling reviews the contenders, Scott, Byron, Crabbe, Wordsworth, in 'the poetic representation of our age', this 'huge, harassed and luxurious national existence' in which both 'severity of conscience in the best minds' and 'the fierceness of the outward struggle for power and riches' might absorb those energies which produced a Shakespeare or a Milton. But their art throve on the conflict of their times. Sterling's own writing has point and energy in his condensed account of Protestant capitalism:

The power of self-subjection combined with almost boundless liberty, indeed necessitated by it, and the habit of self-denial with wealth beyond all calculation . . . The death-struggle of commercial and political rivalry, the brooding doubt and remorse, the gas-jet flame of faith irradiating its own coal-mine darkness – in a word, our overwrought materialism fevered by its own excess into spiritual dreams – all this might serve the purposes of a bold imagination.

Sterling's insistence that women constitute a major part of the new public deserving representation is significant for Tennyson's sense of his destiny as poet; the point was made also by W. J. Fox in his review of the 1830 *Poems*. In 1837 a woman, Victoria, had become the sovereign head of state. Reviewing the first four *Idylls of the King* in 1859, Gladstone was to call Tennyson 'the poet of woman': 'he has studied, sounded, painted woman in form, in motion, in character, in office, in capability, with rare devotion, power and skill'.[10]

With the attainment of political power by the middle class, the possibility of a place for women in public life was beginning to be imagined and debated. Capitalism's dream of individual enterprise needed adaptation to fit the economic dependency of women; this was most often done by celebrating their 'moral culture' and private influence, but men committed to reform do show a sense of women as a specific interest group. Although Hallam had argued that a fit audience for the poetry of Tennyson, Shelley and Keats would be small because of the effort of intellectual and moral sympathy required, this was a way of sending out a challenge and an invitation. Ideas like Sterling's, that Tennyson should speak to and for a reformed England, were more frequent. The Christian Socialist Charles Kingsley has the hero of *Alton Locke, Tailor and Poet* (1850) enthuse at length about Tennyson's poetry, in Chapter VI: 'This is what I call democratic art – the revelation of the poetry which lies in common things.' With such definitions of his destiny and constituency we can see why Tennyson's first published poem of any length was one on women's powers in relation to social ideals, *The Princess*, and not an Arthurian romance.

Presuppositions about gender appear in an equally important but different light in some lines which Tennyson wrote in 1839.[11] I use 'gender' to mean cultural assumptions about masculinity and femininity, rather than biological differences of sex. The lines were

10

unfinished and unpublished, so that I do some violence to Tennyson's privacy in raiding them for an epigraph, and in substantiation of my argument. My justification lies in his lifelong concern with these problems, which shape his work in ways significant for modern debates about gender. Tennyson's apologia is private but haunted by fear of judgement by others. To be a 'popular property' would 'yield my feeling organism pain/Thrice keener than delight from duest praise'. His sense of Art, 'clear as conscience to the moral man', is at risk. Why *should* he:

> Sane mind and body, wish to print my rhyme,
> Fame's millionth heir-apparent? why desire
> (If like a man that hath his sense compact
> I write a clean fair hand) the public thumb
> Of our good pamphlet-pampered age to fret
> And sweat upon mine honest thoughts in type,
> The children of the silence?
>
> (Ricks, *Tennyson*, p. 161)

I do not want to use these lines to confirm the old story that Tennyson at his best was simply at odds with the requirements of 'the Age'. It is equally true that he had a strong sense of public responsibility, like the leading lights of his Cambridge contemporaries. This is not something to be deprecated; it is part of Tennyson's significance as a writer of the male middle-class ascendancy. During the 'ten years' silence', his friends were urging him to publish, accusing him of waywardness and laziness. From these lines it is clear that he was also under internal attack over putting his thoughts into type. Metaphors of Tennyson manufacturing and reproducing his work as a familiar product with a known market are found not only in Marxist criticism but also from Carlyle, FitzGerald, Gerard Manley Hopkins and T. S. Eliot. Here in 1839 such reproduction is contrasted not only with the 'clean fair hand' of a conscientious student, but also with the female power of giving birth to 'children of the silence'. 'Typing', in the extract I have chosen as an epigraph, is consequently used in a different sense. In natural philosophy of the late eighteenth and early nineteenth centuries 'type' meant the fixed general structure of a group of animals or plants, or an individual embodying the distinctive characteristics of such a species (*Oxford English Dictionary*, sense 8). In Protestant theology 'types' were symbolic; for example, events and persons in the Old Testament were understood to prefigure those in the New Testament and in subsequent history (*Oxford English Dictionary*, sense 1). Both meanings were important in nineteenth-century thinking; they suggest fixed patterns within a total scheme, rather than the changes and differences of evolutionary biology. Tennyson presents the poet as the type of full humanity:

> And if I be, as truecast Poets are,
> Half woman-natured, typing all mankind;
> So must I triple-man myself and case
> My humours as the caddisworm in stone,
> Or doing violence to my modest worth
> With one long-lasting hope chain-cable-strong
> Self-fixt, inmoor in patience, till I die.
>
> (Ricks, *Tennyson*, p. 161)

The whole passage is rich in mixed metaphors and confused feelings; to simplify and paraphrase, the writing self includes the female, but publication would call for manliness as armour. The alternative is to coil up in immobility, weathering contemporary unacceptability in the hope of posthumous fame when not the person but the poems may be judged.

I want to give some time to thinking about this claim for the poet's androgyny, or double gender: the term is made up from the Greek words for 'man', *andros*, and 'woman', *gyne*. John Killham's *Tennyson and 'The Princess'* related ideas about androgyny to early socialism and campaigns for women's rights; they have a bearing in fact upon all Tennyson's work, and the ways in which it has been received. His stature as a major poet has always been in question, and peculiarly vulnerable to mockery. It is reasonable to assume that Sterling and Gladstone, seeing him as the poet of woman and as addressing the Woman Question, did not think of the position from which he wrote as being 'half woman-natured'. A physical hermaphrodite is regarded as freakish, disturbing to culturally accepted norms of what is feminine and what is masculine. But the notion of androgynous consciousness has a long history; the intense nineteenth-century concern with manliness is only one extreme in a continuum of discussions about being human. Significances given to the androgyne are varied, not stable. Virginia Woolf in *A Room of One's Own* (1929) appealed to Coleridge's assertion that the minds of great poets were androgynous, neither masculine nor feminine but both. Longfellow's mid-nineteenth-century American hero Hiawatha was significantly posed between two friends, the 'very strong man, Kwasind' and the gentle Chibiabos:

> He the best of all musicians,
> He the sweetest of all singers,
> Beautiful and childlike was he,
> Brave as man is, soft as woman,
> Pliant as a wand of willow,
> Stately as a deer with antlers.
>
> (*The Song of Hiawatha* VI, 20–5)

To claim feminine qualities for an artist seems to call manliness into question, so that uses of androgyny tend to reassert a fixed distinction between masculine strength and feminine softness, insisting that there is no loss of manliness but an incorporation of the feminine. Sandra Gilbert and Susan Gubar in *The Madwoman in the Attic* claim that writing, especially of poetry, has been felt to be peculiarly masculine: if the pen is equated with the penis, no wonder women have felt excluded from writing, or freakish when they do write. But the gross assertions which they quote are obviously produced by anxiety, fending off the possibility that to be a writer is to be effeminate. Why else should these men need to protest the masculinity of their work? In such conflicts it is assumed that to be feminine is to be really inferior, to be unworthy of respect, reflecting the long-established relation of women to power in society.

The image of the androgyne has entered into Western religious, political and philosophical thinking; in English literature it is found, for example, in the work of Edmund Spenser and of Shelley, whose *Witch of Atlas* is a compendium of hints for Tennyson's poetry. The witch makes for herself a companion, Hermaphroditus, with whom she opposes all limits: monarchies, religions, and institutions such as marriage, playing out the powers of fantasy to liberate love and pleasure. Mystical and occult traditions of thought accepted the divine as androgynous, while the symbol of Christ as mother and husband, producing his bride the Church through the wound in his side, was orthodox theology, 'typed' by Adam giving birth to Eve. The cultural values built on such images were important to Tennyson across his whole career. He praised the 'man–woman' in Christ, 'the union of tenderness and strength', and made this the attribute of Hallam in *In Memoriam* CIX, 17. At the end of *In Memoriam*, Hallam is the type of a 'crowning race' like that prophetically imaged in the marriage that concludes *The Princess*:

> . . . seeing either sex alone
> Is half itself, and in true marriage lies

> Nor equal, nor unequal: each fulfils
> Defect in each, and always thought in thought,
> Purpose in purpose, will in will, they grow,
> The single pure and perfect animal,
> The two-celled heart beating, with one full stroke,
> Life. (VII, 283–90)

The problem with marriage as an image of androgyny is that it too easily reconfirms the oppositions which Tennyson did to some extent want to overcome. Even talking about individuals who combine qualities which are usually attributed to the different genders has this effect of reconfirming opposition, though Tennyson went on valuing such types, as with the wife in *Locksley Hall Sixty Years After* (1886) who has the 'charm of woman' and the 'breadth of man'. *On One Who Affected an Effeminate Manner* (1889) is more nervous:

> While man and woman still are incomplete,
> I prize that soul where man and woman meet,
> Which types all nature's male and female plan,
> But, friend, man–woman is not woman–man.

Hallam and Christ must not be imagined as *effeminate*! A late notebook jotting reads 'Men should be androgynous and women gynandrous, but men should not be gynandrous nor women androgynous' (Ricks, *Tennyson*, p. 218). In his chapter on *In Memoriam* Christopher Ricks spends some time distinguishing androgyny as morally desirable from 'anything tawdry': a sign of the anxiety associated with gender-crossing once it descends from ideal symbolization to practice. Effeminacy is now strongly associated with homosexuality. Ricks is convincing about Tennyson's lack of self-consciousness as to any homosexual implications of his friendship with Arthur Hallam. I would want to call the friendship an 'unclassified affection' (a phrase from Virginia Woolf's *To the Lighthouse*) whose indeterminate quality is one of the strengths of *In Memoriam*.

In Shakespeare's *Antony and Cleopatra* Caesar calls Antony womanly because he enjoys the company of women rather than of soldiers and statesmen (IV, 1–10). From one nineteenth-century viewpoint, writing, and all work from behind a desk or counter, could be seen as unmanly compared to military occupation or the outdoor activities of gentry, yeoman and peasant. A poet not seeking public employment might seem to be aligning himself with women, especially as 'nature' (the great subject of poetry) and a culture drawing its criteria from feeling and refinement, were both imagined as feminine. The response of his old friend Edward FitzGerald to Tennyson's work is an interesting index. 'Fitz' liked no poems after 1842, especially not *In Memoriam*, which he considered both morbid and mechanical. Five years before it was published he wrote that Tennyson should have gone horse-riding and not wilfully protracted his sorrows. He wanted heroic poems of Tennyson; thought he should have translated Aeschylus; wanted him, it seems, to be manly. For seventeen years between the death of Hallam in 1833 and his marriage in 1850, Tennyson's way of life was like FitzGerald's whole life, 'a kind of genteel vagrancy', in George Darley's words (Martin, *Tennyson: The Unquiet Heart*, p. 288). For Tennyson this became a misery of anxiety and ill health. It just suited FitzGerald, whose attempt at marriage was brief and disastrous, as his comment on being offered blancmange at his wedding breakfast, 'Ugh! congealed bridesmaid', may suggest.[12] His deepest affections were given to younger men with less wealth and education than himself.

'Fitz' can stand for the opposite of the demand made by Sterling. For FitzGerald Tennyson's status as a poet was compromised by a betrayal of bachelor solidarity in associating with women; from this point of view Tennyson's marriage to Emily Sellwood could be felt as effeminate. This mildly scurrilous speculation is worth entertaining because of its affinity with a persistent element in the critical evaluation of Tennyson's work, which makes for doubts about his 'stature'. Douglas Bush parodied the early twentieth-century consensus about 'the taming influence of a wife who ruled his spirit from her sofa', but in pointing out that 'the husband and wife and widow business' in *The Death of Oenone* is not a 'Victorian' importation but even more present in the sources (Ovid and Quintus Smyrnaeus) he concedes that 'Tennyson's notions of love do revolve too much around the ring and the cradle; there is enough evidence against him in this respect'.[13] To write much about marriage seems to constitute some kind of criminal charge, though there is no advocacy of alternative arrangements for childbearing and child care. *In Memoriam* values marriage positively, as a model of relatedness, not a negative necessity.

The *Critical Heritage* volume on Tennyson has many examples of distaste for his writing as feminine: 'sugar sweet, pretty-pretty, full of womanly talk and feminine stuff' (1879).[14] We do not know what a notion of the feminine might be that has not been touched by masculine fantasy and privilege in discourse, social practices and institutions. Writing as a woman, I do not want to insist that Tennyson is really very manly; nor that his writing is immune from consideration in terms of assumptions about gender, when these are present in his language and in ours. One option is to welcome aspects of his work as 'feminine', without seeing this as weakness: *In Memoriam* is not a unity, not altogether a phallic monument, but woven together, valuing the hand's touch, its rhythms making a new fabric out of old elements to recover the value of the lost friend in the continuity of life. Although the Prologue begs forgiveness from the 'Strong Son of God' for 'these wild and wandering cries', the value of *In Memoriam* is that it is not 'one' but 'indeterminately other', as Luce Irigaray has defined the feminine; working in the spaces between fixed oppositions.

The weaving of *The Lady of Shalott* can be taken as an emblem of Tennyson's work. But the androgyny which both *The Princess* and *In Memoriam* hold out as an ideal gives place to a violent opposition of masculinity and femininity in *Maud*, while in *Idylls of the King* idealized masculine power is doomed by materialism and the female, although Arthur as a human ideal still incorporates the feminine. Part of the reason for this change may lie in the association of androgyny with Utopian socialism, becoming less theoretic with the European revolutions of 1848; and with the descent of ideals about women to specific reforms in their legal and civil status. One way of resisting demands for a voice in public life was to idealize women's influence in the house, and such idealization has denigration of deviance as its other face. The sufferings of Enid and Elaine, the devoted heroines of the *Idylls*, have little effect compared to the damage attributed to the adulterous Guinevere and to the cynical materialist Vivien. In the 1830s and 40s bourgeois men could identify themselves with the spirit of reform, and could envisage reconsideration of women's relation to public life. But in mid century the old reformist ideals of freedom and change sounded differently, from a working class challenging established middle-class interests. New demands from women were associated with claims from those whom the bourgeois, with a stake in the country through business or the privilege of education, felt to be unqualified. Anxious and angry resistance to new insurgencies can be found in Dickens's letters, as much as in Tennyson's writing.

The claim of Utopian socialism to bring about enlightenment in society had roots in occult religion such as the theosophy of Jacob

Boehme, whose influence W. D. Paden has seen in the imagery of Tennyson's early poems. The 'socialists' based their claims on a science of the natural world which in its supposed comprehensiveness retained much of the character of theosophy's claims to such knowledge, founded on esoteric writings on the divine nature. In German science, philosophy and literature there was also a fascination with what forces might unite all forms of life and with gender as a unity manifested in different structures; in the work of Goethe, for example, with his curiosity about what botanical and human forms had in common, of Hegel, and of Friedrich Schelling, who like Fourier in France took from Boehme the idea of a universal bisexual divinity seeking incarnation. For the socialists the androgynous Adam of the occult tradition became a symbol of the whole of mankind considered as an individual, endowed with a single mind, pursuing its single destiny throughout all the events of universal history.[15]

The fragmentation of fallen humanity into differently sexed individuals was to be restored to a whole. Social equality and the emancipation of women went together in the arguments of the St Simonians in France and the followers of Robert Owen in England – both attracting public notice around 1830. They opposed the existing political economy (the competitive right of individuals to amass and inherit property) and valued socially purposive work and co-operation. The St Simonians considered women as more developed than men in the supreme value of loving; on the other hand, none could be found advanced enough to take on the role of Female Messiah. Though such ideas brought the St Simonians into disrepute, their repercussions can be felt throughout nineteenth-century literature, not least in the work and the status of George Eliot. As Barbara Taylor has shown in *Eve and the New Jerusalem*, Owenite writers of the late 1830s and early 40s were discussing the nature and classification of 'man-power' and 'women-power'.

Tennyson was aware of these ideas. Moderate versions of them were put into practice by his friend F. D. Maurice in association with another friend, Charles Kingsley, and the Christian Socialists, whose paper Maurice edited for a few weeks. He helped found Queen's College, London, in 1848, to provide for the more advanced education of women as governesses; and founded the Working Men's College in 1854, of which he was principal. The idea of the universe as a bisexual organism continually coupling can be paralleled in Charles Kingsley's letters to his fiancée, and

INTRODUCTION

for another friend, Coventry Patmore, marital intercourse was an
image of the bisexual God:

> Female and male God made the man;
> His image is the whole, not half;
> And in our love we dimly scan
> The love which is between Himself.
> (*The Angel in the House*, Canto VIII, 'Preludes', IV, 1854–6)

The phrase 'Angel in the House' has been taken to describe the
ideal wife, but in Patmore's poem it means marital sex. He and
Kingsley show how definitions of the divine, the natural and the
human as both female and male quickly retreated from notions of
advancing women to equal social status, to the safer idea that
woman (at her best) was already infinitely superior and best
celebrated in the sacrament of marriage, typing the love of God.

When Hallam praised Tennyson as a poet of Sensation he was also
valuing him for his power of sympathy – 'the faculty of sharing
and understanding the situation of another person by being able
to change places with him in imagination'. That definition is given
by Isobel Armstrong in *Victorian Scrutinies: Reviews of Poetry
1830–1870*. Her introduction gives a good sense of how important
'sympathy' was in this period as a term uniting literature with
ethics. Humanitarian philosophy in eighteenth-century Britain
had made moral understanding dependent on an act of imagination, an idea which influenced German philosophy and the 'higher
criticism' of the Bible. In *Kubla Khan and the Fall of Jerusalem* E. S.
Shaffer has shown how these ideas were developed, re-entering
English intellectual life through the influence of Coleridge and
later George Eliot. Higher criticism mediated between philosophy
and literary criticism, subjecting the Christian scriptures to close
analysis not as the revealed word of God but as texts imaginatively
produced in particular historical circumstances, for the purpose of
advancing certain beliefs. The prophets and the gospel writers
were imperfect and biased mediums for beliefs which were nevertheless valuable, though 'accommodated' to the understanding of
particular periods. This was a way of thinking which saw human
consciousness as developing and advancing spiritually, even when
orthodox Christianity itself was rejected. The Bible was harmon-
ized with other mythologies, as itself a mythology. The notion of
'accommodation' became particularly important to liberal
Anglican theology, on which Maurice had a strong influence. The

18

whole mental set is important for appreciating Tennyson's dramatic and classical monologues, with their sense of partial insight: his Ulysses, for example, is an advanced type impatient of the conditions of his time and of the 'savage race' for whom his son will work in a more patient manner.

This intellectual atmosphere also produced Tennyson's sustained interest in comparative religion, seen for example in *The Higher Pantheism* (1867), *Vastness* (1885), *The Ancient Sage* (1885), *Akbar's Dream* (1892) and *The Making of Man* (1892). He saw no important difference between his own broad Christianity and the code of morals of Akbar, the sixteenth-century Mogul emperor, whose tolerance and hatred of religious persecution he admired, contrasting it with the Tudor monarchs. There are two things often said about Tennyson: that he was no intellectual, and that in his later work he took themes suggested to him as if at random. The poems I have cited are not great poems but they are not uninteresting. It may be that Tennyson glimpsed the possibility of being a world poet, an English Goethe, addressing his time with philosophical breadth. His poetry is not of a kind to achieve this, but these late poems show how his intelligence responded to the currents of thought in which he moved, persistently querying in ways which related to the deepest concerns of his poetry. *Akbar's Dream* sees the divine as immanent, symbolized in and through the world, but *The Higher Pantheism* entertains a possibility which King Arthur feared at his worst moment, that this world is one made by a lesser God (*The Passing of Arthur*, 1869, 9–17). As in the heresy of the Gnostics, natural signs (earth, stars, the body) are signs not of the divine, but of division from it; signs *between* human existence and meaning. Tennyson's best poetry explores the tension between metaphors which reach for unity, different signs connecting with each other within a meaningful universe which language can express, and metonymy, by which the sign, a part intended to stand for a whole, is revealed as part of a chain in which meaning is endlessly displaced elsewhere. It is often said of the nineteenth century that the yearning for meaning which religion had roused and perhaps satisfied was displaced on to literature: Matthew Arnold's 'The future of poetry is immense' suggests this role for literature in explaining humanity to itself. Tennyson's poetry works movingly with the consequent anxieties, as I shall suggest in chapters 1 and 2.

Coleridge was a strong influence on Tennyson's group at Cambridge, even though the reviewers do not list him as a poet to be contended with: Julius Hare, chaplain and classics tutor at Trinity, called him 'the great religious philosopher to whom the mind of our generation in England owes more than to any other man'.[16] The broader influence of Wordsworth's poetry gave 'Feeling' a value in itself, as a touchstone of being human. It is hardly necessary to demonstrate Tennyson's pervasive appeal to feeling as evidence: it was through the sympathetic imagination of a poetry of sensation that feeling was to be communicated. The obvious rider that 'Feeling' as a value must exclude many forms of feeling as damaging, is tacit.

Cartesian philosophy had split mind and body ('I think, therefore I am'). In the latter half of the eighteenth century the influence of Rousseau was important in bringing the bodily sense of touch into thinking about consciousness and being human. This coincides with the entry into the main current of philosophy of explicit consideration of the human as both female and male. A significant instance is Feuerbach, whose *The Essence of Christianity* was published in an English translation by Marian Evans (George Eliot) in 1854. His account of the I/Thou relation – awareness of self produced by awareness of another – argues that this is most lively when it is between women and men. Feuerbach also had been studying Jacob Boehme, whose opposed principles (light and dark, male and female) Feuerbach thought would be properly considered by 'pathology' – the study of the passions or emotions. The error lay in considering such oppositions as a matter for theology rather than for anthropology, pathology and psychology which, he writes, had more claim to the name of theology than theology itself. This replacement of metaphysical thinking by what was claimed to be science is found in all the Utopian socialists.[17] I cite Feuerbach not in order to argue a direct influence on Tennyson, but rather to indicate the tendencies of German thinking and the connection made between claims to divine knowledge and claims for science. Feuerbach was an influence on George Eliot, Marx and Freud; like Coleridge he is a key figure in the passage from theological to psychoanalytic thinking. Ideas of relatedness and isolation, and of the sense of touch, are beautifully engaged in *In Memoriam* XLV, which I will discuss in chapter 4.

In one instance at least Feuerbach offers an interesting analogy to a reported saying of Tennyson. Feuerbach takes up the idea that accounts of miracles may be 'true' without being factual, in order to redefine fact.

As fact is every possibility which passes for a reality, every conception which, for the age wherein it is held to be a fact, expresses a want, and is for that reason an impassable limit of the mind. A fact is every wish that projects itself as a reality.[18]

Tennyson's poetry is interested in desire, in 'limits of the mind' and in the power of projection, whether in images or in dramatic impersonation. He said in 1869 that if he had to leave one wise saying to the world it would be:

'Every man imputes himself,' meaning that a man, unless he is very sane indeed, in judging of others, imputes motives, etc. which move himself. 'No man can see further than his moral eyes will allow him.'

Memoir II, 476

THE GROUNDS OF BELIEF: SCIENCE, RELIGION AND POLITICS

The nineteenth-century split between religion and science has been exaggerated. The idea that essential spiritual truths had been accommodated to fit different and successive phases of human culture sat easily with scientific ideas of unity and development. Although Darwin's theory of the mechanism of evolution by means of natural selection entailed a view of change which was random and not purposive, this point was not always clearly taken. Darwin's own language in *The Origin of Species* (1859) shows him struggling to distinguish his account from already available metaphors and meanings, as Gillian Beer has shown.[19] Tennyson read popularizations of science such as Robert Chambers's *Vestiges of the Natural History of Creation* (1844), as well as the great geologist Charles Lyell, whose work was an influence on Darwin. Lyell held to the 'Uniformitarian' view, that the scientific laws presently operating had always done so: this gradualism fitted with political Reform. 'Catastrophism', the alternative view, could seem to entail revolution as necessary to change. The significance of Tennyson's work in relation to science is not a matter of the knowledge shown about this or that phenomenon or hypothesis, but of his imaginative negotiation of changes in ideas about the world and time; he was frequently quoted by scientific writers. The propagandists of science, Huxley and Tyndall, testified to the depth and accuracy of his scientific understanding – though they did have an interest in claiming a writer of his stature and influence for their advocacy of the hard rational truths of science.[20]

In 1829 Tennyson and Hallam voted in an Apostles debate

against the argument from natural theology, that an intelligent First Cause (that is, God) could be deduced from the phenomena of the universe: a proposition which had no place for revelation or for intuition. The natural theologian Paley was required reading for Cambridge undergraduates, producing both the terms of debate and ingrained recalcitrance. Paley's universe was essentially static, random items being picked out to demonstrate a God who was a designer of a machine. This did not suit either liberal theology or scientific thinking from the 1830s, since both of these stressed development according to providential or natural laws:

> The old order changeth, yielding place to new,
> And God fulfills himself in many ways . . .
>
> (*The Passing of Arthur*, 408–9)

Tennyson's tutor at Cambridge was William Whewell (the inventor of the terms 'Uniformitarian' and 'Catastrophist') who played a major part in revising natural theology towards an understanding of development. He added a sense of history to the perpetual change suggested by Lyell's *Principles of Geology* (1830–3), which Tennyson read in 1837. This fitted both the biblical idea of a world with an origin and an end, and the apparent evidence of astronomy and geology, which Tennyson called the 'terrible Muses'. Although crucial aspects of his evidence were later disproved, Whewell's work was vital for keeping scientific rationality in touch with the historical thinking of liberal theologians. He retained the idea of God as a designer, working through the secondary agencies which could be scientifically studied; but his God was also capable of 'Creative interference' – that is, of miracles. This, surprisingly, filled a real intellectual gap. Lyell had deliberately avoided any account of origins, because to do so would have challenged Genesis, and therefore he gave no explanation of why the fossil population of one geological stratum was adapted to that stratum but not related to the adapted populations of succeeding strata: an observable fact which enabled the Catastrophists to argue for a series of special creations in each new era. Observation means little without theory, and a Christian world view was part of the very means of thinking for most scientists. Whewell sought not a random inexplicable world, but an intellectually acceptable continuity. He argued that where secondary observable phenomena were not scientifically continuous with other secondary causes, they could then be thought of as continuous with the First Cause. This

definition of miracle as divine intervention after the original creation filled the gap left by Lyell: it was the strongest available
hypothesis, since the origin of new species could not be explained
by any scientific law then known. Nevertheless, Whewell
emphasized separation between natural historical development
and the history of human activity and consciousness: they could
be connected only by the belief that both pointed to a First Cause,
which could not be proved in either case.[21]

That gap between consciousness and natural laws was the
space in which Tennyson's poetry worked. Tess Cosslett has
argued that the world view of Huxley and Tyndall may
in part have been formed by Tennyson's early poetry, responding to the sense of wonder and living growth in the work
of writers such as Whewell. It is important to keep this
sense of interplay between literature and science, not assume
the poet's dependence on 'facts' produced by scientists. Lyell
had a classical education like Tennyson's, and wrote with
respect of Ovid's speculations in *Metamorphoses* about physical
origins and changes. Scientific hypotheses need imagination.
The 'organic unity' of both poets and scientists was an 'ideal
construction', as Huxley said, not a simple 'transcript of facts':
science, morality and poetry all called on intuition. Tennyson
shared with scientists a belief in evolutionary progress limited by
laws, and a conviction that the ground of human values
lay in a world with an origin and a purpose, which were not
scientifically demonstrable. To this Tennyson added his emotional
conviction of immortality.

One poem which explores grounds of belief and their consequences is *Lucretius* (1868). The Roman philosopher has a dream of
his own atomistic philosophy, which reads as Catastrophism speed-
ed up into nightmare:

> A void was made in Nature; all her bonds
> Cracked; and I saw the flaring atom-streams
> And torrents of her myriad universe,
> Ruining along the illimitable inane,
> Fly on to clash together again, and make
> Another and another frame of things
> For ever . . .   (37–43)

Later the philosopher sets his 'golden work' (the *De Rerum Naturae*
which Tennyson's poem adapts) against a vision of human extinction, when 'momentary man' shall pass:

> And even his bones long laid within the grave,
> The very sides of the grave itself shall pass,
> Vanishing, atom and void, atom and void,
> Into the unseen for ever . . .   (255–8)

However Lucretius is not securely materialist and atheist. One of the poem's major questions is what he may mean by Gods as opposed to Nature; it is one I will take up again in later chapters. He has inherited the idea of Gods and needs such an idea to endorse his ideal of philosophic life, sane and secure, 'centered in eternal calm'. Tennyson's poem is based on the legend that Lucretius was poisoned by a philtre given him by his wife to reawaken his passions. Deranged, he feels himself suffocated by sensuality. He has written that if Gods exist they are without care (as he wishes to be) and therefore careless of human desire and suffering: why then should he care for the Gods? If there is no transcendent ground for value, why care for life? In a catastrophically changing world power is without restraint. Lucretius' inherited values are threatened by the value-free atomistic snowstorms of his philosophy:

> 'How should the mind, except it loved them, clasp
> These idols to herself? or do they fly
> Now thinner, and now thicker, like the flakes
> In a fall of snow, and so press in, perforce
> Of multitude, as crowds that in an hour
> Of civic tumult jam the doors, and bear
> The keepers down, and throng, their rags and they
> The basest, far into the council-hall
> Where sit the best and stateliest of the land?'   (164–72)

Yoking exploration of grounds for value to questions of politics and power, *Lucretius* shares a concern with limits with the other classical monologues, *Ulysses*, *Tithonus*, *Tiresias*, and *Oenone*, as well as *The Lady of Shalott* and *Mariana*; they also suggest impatience with gradualism, in so far as it is experienced as the condition of life, as boredom.

Tennyson wrote a number of political poems in the early 1830s. The unpublished *Hail Briton!* ends with a warning image of tyranny ('The coarse extremes of Power and Fear') exemplified in Czarist Russia's dominance over Poland. The secret political police of Czar Nicholas I had established Russia in Europe's imagination as a police state. The inexorability of this power, under which 'knowledge dreads to hear/Her footsteps falling in the street', is imaged in snow, like that in *Lucretius* because it jams doorways.

24

It is unlike the power in *Lucretius* in that it is not anarchic and mobile. As the citizens are silenced the Czar's power grows 'step by step':

> And gathers like the silent snows
> And binds in fetters like the ice.

Tennyson was always keen on the responsibility of liberal Britain towards the struggles of European nations against the old empires: Poland, Hungary, Italy, Greece, the Balkan states. (He had less sympathy for the Irish and for blacks in the West Indies.) Internally, freedom as he understood it was a middle-class value: although he had sympathy and respect for the unlearned and working poor, 'freedom' for mobs in rags changed its meaning, putting workers and all at the mercy of the debased language of 'demagogues': democracy would lead to populist tyranny. The preference of the political poems is for gradual reform according to the precedents set, for example, by Hampden before the English Revolution of the 1640s. But the unpublished *I loving Freedom for herself* and *Love thou thy land . . .* (1842) acknowledge that history does change violently:

> For all the past of Time reveals
>   A bridal-dawn of thunder-peals,
> Wherever Thought hath wedded Fact . . .
>
> Oh yet, if Nature's evil star
>   Drive men in manhood as in youth,
>   To follow flying steps of Truth
> Across the brazen bridge of war – . . .
>
> Not yet the wise of heart would cease
>   To hold his hope through shame and guilt,
>   But with his hand against the hilt,
> Would pace the troubled land, like Peace . . . (50–2, 73–6, 81–7)

The political poems express Tennyson's desire for peaceful change not crisis, a concern which bleeds into other poems. *The Progress of Spring*, written probably in 1833, is on the face of it a delicate and erotic notation of the coming season:

> The ground flame of the crocus breaks the mould,
>   Fair Spring slides hither o'er the Southern sea,
> Wavers on her thin stems the snowdrop cold
>   That trembles not to kisses of the bee:
> Come Spring, for now from all the dripping eaves
>   The spear of ice has wept itself away,

INTRODUCTION

And hour by hour unfolding woodbine leaves
    O'er his uncertain shadow droops the day.
She comes! The loosened rivulets run;
    The frost-bead melts upon her golden hair;
Her mantle, slowly greening in the sun,
    Now wraps her close, now arching leaves her bare
        To breaths of balmier air;

Up leaps the lark, gone wild to welcome her . . .   (I. 1–14)

But the political concerns of the poem's last two stanzas are not
arbitrarily tacked on. When Tennyson published it in 1889 he
prefaced it with a poem to his daughter-in-law's aunt, Mary
Boyle, which recalls the rick-burnings of the 1830s by agricultural
labourers, whose employment was threatened by new machinery;
he had helped put out such fires near Cambridge. The sane consolation of Mary Boyle, who was mourning the death of a woman
friend, is more attractive than the suspiciousness about 'lowly
minds' maddened by 'tonguester tricks' (*To Mary Boyle*, 33–4).
But his imagery of spreading fire transmuted into the generative
warmth of spring was already political: radicals like Richard
Price, Tom Paine and Blake had used such images for the spread
of libertarian ardour from America to France, and, as they hoped,
to England. Natural observation in *The Progress of Spring* is infused
with ideas of gradualist hope:

for – while my hand exults
    Within the bloodless heart of lowly flowers
To work old laws of love to fresh results,
    Through manifold effect of simple powers –
I too would teach the man
    Beyond the darker hour to see the bright . . . (VII, 83–8)

Politics enters Tennyson's poetry directly, and is implied by
underlying ways of thinking. This is true of science also, and I
want to end with one characteristic mode of assimilation and
modification. Throughout his life Tennyson wrote vision poems,
envisaging all the past and all the future, 'all these old revolutions
of earth' (*Vastness*, 1885). In the 1832 version of *The Palace of Art*
the soul contemplates foetal evolution according to the latest
theory, and a note adds lines about 'the results of astronomical
experiment'; similar material appears in the lectures on *The
Princess*. Walker Gibson has compared the poet's stance in such
passages, including some lyrics of *In Memoriam*, to the speaking
position and syntax of Lyell and Darwin. The scientists argue a

26

case to their audience in a way that stresses intellectual activity: 'I may conclude that . . . We shall discover that . . .' What may be discovered about the past from the interpretation of present signs is given in the dependent clauses – by implication, their conclusions are open to argument and reinterpretation. In Tennyson's visions the discoveries are the main statements, presented as if directly experienced, so that the speaker's position within the poem is a magical one: 'he stands where no one can stand, unrestrained by space or time, and he watches things happen that no one can watch'[22]:

> There rolls the deep where grew the tree.
>   O earth, what changes hast thou seen!
>   There where the long street roars, hath been
> The stillness of the central sea.
>
> The hills are shadows, and they flow
>   From form to form, and nothing stands;
>   They melt like mist, the solid lands.
> Like clouds they shape themselves and go.
>
> (*In Memoriam* CXXIII)

The truth which this prophet reveals is that of nineteenth-century science. But while giving 'Knowledge' the force of revelation in this way, Tennyson kept the notion of 'Reverence' as a restraining concept (as in *In Memoriam* CXIV). His work showed fascination with attempts to find a scientific ground for human values but also maintained conservative scepticism.

1

English Idyls

> – And here, methought he seemed to grasp
> A pair of shadowy compasses, with these
> To plant a centre and about it round
> A wide and wider circle
> (*The Golden Year*, manuscript, *c*. 1839, Ricks, *Poems*, p. 717)

EARLY POEMS

Selecting and ordering Tennyson's poetry for discussion is a critical statement in itself, in the first place about the difficulty of ordering it. When a study is structured along the lines of this one, by the chronology of the longer poems, it becomes difficult to find an appropriate place for the shorter poems, which range from trivial to major achievements: the 1830 Song, *A spirit haunts the year's last hours*, *Break, break, break* (1842 *Poems*), or *Crossing the Bar* of 1889. I have allowed my studies of lyrics in *In Memoriam* and *The Princess* to stand in for full analysis of Tennyson's lyrics and lyricism, in which poetic language and rhythm face the unorganized character of time and the material world. It is characteristic of Tennyson's work that forms and themes recur, with variations and back-answers; some poems were revised over time and published thirty or fifty years 'late'. For example, *Tithon* (1833) became the *Tithonus* of 1860, while *Tiresias*, begun at the same time, appeared in 1885. Some poems are written as sequels: *The Death of Oenone* (1892) matched *Oenone* (1832), *Locksley Hall Sixty Years After* (1886) started from two lines dropped from *Locksley Hall* (1842). These are like the *In Memoriam* lyrics which were written as 'pendants' to others (for example LIX to III),[1] and this matching suggests comparison with painters like Turner, who wished paintings to be hung together as contrasts or variations on a theme. The process of reconsidering earlier work is intrinsic to Tennyson's mentality as a writer. High finish in the style goes along with a persistent troubled return, circling back to the same, but seen otherwise.

The classical poems, the other dramatic monologues, and the

English Idyls of 1842, can be seen as homes, places from which to speak in the 'psychic homelessness' of these years, the 1830s and 40s. The early poems, read all together, are inordinate and disorderly, veering between an artificial intimacy haunted by Remorse without a cause in which Memory turns to Despair, and apocalyptic visions of the historically or geographically remote, stealing fire from 'the fountains of the past' (*Ode to Memory*, 1830). There is much experiment with metres and rhythms – odes, sonnets, the wreathing seven-syllable *Anacreontics, Leonine Elegiacs*, and *The Kraken*, a sonnet but for its fifteenth line in which the sea beast rises roaring to its death. At the age of twelve Tennyson had translated the first 93 lines of Claudian's epic *Rape of Proserpine* into heroic couplets, and one of the best and most surprising of his early works was written when he was fourteen, *The Devil and the Lady*, a verse comedy from a medieval story, in Jacobean style with Byronic overtones. The husband who has summoned the Devil to guard his young wife Amoret from suitors is an aged Magus, rancorous and desiccated. A phrase of his was borrowed for *Lucretius* in 1868 (265, 'Passionless bride, divine Tranquillity'):

> When couched in Boyhood's passionless tranquillity,
> The natural mind of man is warm and yielding,
> Fit to receive the best impressions . . .
>   'Tis like the seaplant
> Which in its parent and unshaken depths
> Is mouldable as clay, but when rude hands
> Have plucked it from its billowless Abyss
> Unto the breathings of Heaven's airs, each gust
> Which blows upon't will fix it into hardness.
>
>   (III, ii, 176–86)

The quietude of depth and the danger of surfacing is a chord early struck and long maintained in Tennyson's work. This adolescent writing assumes the roles of old man and devil, contemptuous and knowing about naive hopefulness. In a third scene added to Act I (probably not much later) the Magus contrasts the fair tapestry of life seen by inexperience to

> The dark reverse of it,
> The intertwinings and rough wanderings
> Of random threads and wayward colourings   (40–2)

– he claims never to have been hopeful himself, at his gayest. Woven through the play are fear of youth as vulnerable, and fear of ageing: the mask of age is adopted as a premature defence, becoming deliberately what the boy fears he may harden into. Charles Tennyson noted the significance for all Tennyson's work of the Latin motto in the earliest manuscript of the play, which means 'Hope nourishes youth and poesy, abuse represses and injures it.' But all this is rather vigorously and enjoyably engaged in – there's a strong sense of power and play as well as fear. The gloom and grimness are side-effects of energy aggrieved at limits, such as death.

Tennyson is a great poet of anxiety, and also of serenity:

> In the afternoon they came unto a land
> In which it seemèd always afternoon.
> All round the coast the languid air did swoon,
> Breathing like one that hath a weary dream.
> Full-faced above the valley stood the moon;
> And like a downward smoke, the slender stream
> Along the cliff to fall and pause and fall did seem.
>
> (*The Lotos-Eaters*, 1832, 3–9)

My main decision in ordering his poems has been to take the 'English Idyls' together as a first major work, one which attempts and achieves serenity. In writing the Idyls he found his peculiar forms and themes, which illuminate understanding of *The Princess*, *In Memoriam* and *Maud*. He did not move on according to the classical pattern from the apprentice work of pastoral to tragedy and epic, because the poetry of landscape was his mode, Romantically *sui generis*. He wanted to call the *Enoch Arden* volume of 1864 *Idylls of the Hearth*; had he done so this would have made his claim on the form more evident. Portrait and landscape description, and some degree of story, are subordinated to mood, as Hallam said in his review of 1831 in *The Englishman's Magazine*. The mood suffuses the poem and is also its still point of inwardness, though this may widen into social and political concern. But there is really no fixed point: the self is questioning, doubled or multiply refracted, tending to both optimism and pessimism, aware of the dark reverse of the fair surface.

In this the Idyls catch up themes of earlier poems; including those which explore the divided mind with considerable intensity. In the unpublished but very interesting *Perdidi Diem* (meaning 'I have lost a day', *c.* 1830) and *Pierced through with knotted thorns of barren pain* (*c.* 1832), morbidity is rather enjoying itself; their juxtaposition of sublimity and physical dread derive from the early *Armageddon*:

dark ourselves and loving night,
Night-bats into the filtering crevices
Hooked, clinging, darkness-fed, at ease.

(Perdidi Diem, 15–17,*

So with *Supposed Confessions of a Second-Rate Sensitive Mind Not in Unity With Itself* (1830) which seeks and fails to erase its self-concern. The 154 octosyllabic triplets of *The Two Voices* (1842) would, but for the length of the poem, get the struggle for a form in these earlier poems too neatly under control. The 'self' struggles wearily against a tirelessly negative voice whose optimistic twin only speaks up near the end; only a change of mood really, and the self has already resisted the temptation to suicide:

Whatever crazy sorrow saith,
No life that breathes with human breath
Has ever truly longed for death.

'Tis life, whereof our nerves are scant,
Oh life, not death, for which we pant;
More life, and fuller, that I want.

(The Two Voices, 394–9)

One argument of the pessimistic voice is a perennial one of Tennyson's that idealism with its notions of God and immortality is only a projection, an imputation of human desire:

Who forged that other influence,
That heat of inward evidence,
By which he doubts against the sense? . . .

That type of Perfect in his mind
In Nature can he nowhere find.
He sows himself on every wind.   (283–5 and 292–4)

The second-rate sensitive mind had feared to embrace 'Idols' (179–80), forgeries of error; the 'soul' in *The Palace of Art* (1832 and 1842) gives up whole galleries of pictures she has idolized. In the latter poem a family problem – old George Tennyson making sure his sons made their own way in the world – is transformed into a fable of the larger problem, the function in the nineteenth century of a class educated in the humanities: whether its knowledge and skill should be a storehouse for use, or a superior prospect on the world below. The question of work, and of whether art and literature are idleness, haunts the Idyls – Tennyson pronounced the word 'Eye-dyl' so that phrases such as 'Tears, idle tears' (from *The Princess*) and 'It little profits that an

ALFRED TENNYSON

idle king' (from *Ulysses*, which was published with the 'English Idyls') tend to attach the notion of idleness to Idyl: idleness produced idols, the fetishistic forms so mistrusted by the Protestant spirit. Love as the theme of art and literature may be merely a matter of idealized pictures, offering a moment out of time, a respite; or the forms of art may be the true business of consciousness in the world, relating self to objects of desire.

PICTURES OF LOVE

The climax of *The Princess* (1847) is a kiss:

> She turned; she paused;
> She stooped; and with a great shock of the heart
> Our mouths met: out of languor leapt a cry,
> Crown'd Passion from the brinks of death, and up
> Along the shuddering senses struck the soul,
> And closed on fire with Ida's at the lips.
>
> (VII, 12–17, 1st edition)

The *Quarterly Review* commented: 'The *shock* of this meeting is communicated to the nerves of the reader, and not pleasantly. The last three lines are as obscure as the others are inharmonious.'[2] The lines were revised:

> She turned; she paused;
> She stooped; and out of languor leapt a cry;
> Leapt fiery Passion from the brinks of death . . .
> My spirit closed with Ida's at the lips.
>
> (VII, 139–43, 3rd edition)

On one level *The Princess* is an Idyl in which the story and songs often embedded in classical idylls have taken over nearly all the space. The first reading of the kiss is truer to the feeling of those Idyls which celebrate love, the mutual influence of sensuality and emotion in response to another, as the source and end of art.

The concern is also with constraints, limits and difficulties; one limit is that they are all from a male point of view. Along with *The Gardener's Daughter* which was published as an 'English Idyl' in 1842 I am going to discuss some of the 1832 poems and *The Lover's Tale*, beloved by friends but withdrawn by Tennyson after having it printed in 1832 (it was published in 1879 with a conclusion which had earlier been published separately). Arthur Hallam thought Tennyson was mad not to publish *The Lover's Tale*; he was strongly sympathetic to the value Tennyson put on love in relation

32

to art. Tennyson said that *The Lover's Tale* was 'very rich and full'; and that 'allowance must be made for abundance of youth . . . The poem is the breath of young love' (Ricks, *Poems*, p. 300). The same sense of abundance running to excess is found in comments on *The Gardener's Daughter* and, tacitly, in the number of lines suppressed either after first publication or from manuscripts. Formal containment was a problem: *The Palace of Art* was a series of word-pictures which in spite of its neat quatrains had no necessary limits, no principle of exclusion; even in 1832 Tennyson was reserving to footnotes extra stanzas of no less quality and interest than those in the main text, because the poem was 'already too long'. To a later friend, James Knowles, he defined the artist as one 'who recognizes bounds to his work as a necessity, and does not overflow illimitably to all extent about a matter'.[3] Manifestly, as a poet of love he has difficulty respecting limits: it is significant that he could express the problem not in terms of a single impulse taking its own form (as in another image of the short poem being like a rind of fruit flung on the floor) but as a need to check something otherwise illimitable. Fluidity, flowing, influence, are important phenomena for Tennyson's early poetry; throughout his work he sought forms which could contain, while leaving 'A hint of somewhat unexprest' (*Whispers*, in Ricks, *Poems*, p. 556). Though his work seems peculiarly 'finished' in one sense, it avoids the complete closure which suggests death.

Being over-abundant is not necessarily the innocent putting into words of upsurging passion. It can be over-artfulness. This is the kind of criticism that *Edwin Morris* makes of the earlier *The Gardener's Daughter*.[4] Edwin is a poet described by a landscape painter or amateur sketcher; his celebration of his love is adapted from manuscripts of *The Gardener's Daughter*. The painter comments:

> Were not his words delicious, I a beast
> To take them as I did? but something jarred;
> Whether he spoke too largely; that there seemed
> A touch of something false, some self-conceit,
> Or over-smoothness: howso'er it was,
> He scarcely hit my humour.   (71–6)

The painter suggests, possibly, that artful language itself is 'cathected' (invested in because lit up and charged with sexual energy, in Freudian terms): his love is cherished as an attribute of himself quite as much as it is a response to the loved one.

Alberti, the Italian Renaissance architect and theorist, said that the inventor of painting was Narcissus, the youth described by Ovid (for example), who fell in love with his own image on the surface of a pool, while Echo, the nymph who loved him, mourned nearby and was doomed to echo his self-love. This myth has been used in many ways, not least by Tennyson. The lovers of *The Gardener's Daughter*, *The Lord of Burleigh* and *Edwin Morris* are all artists; 'The Lake' is the subtitle of *Edwin Morris*. These Idyls are concerned with aesthetic representation as much as with men's love of women. Edwin's description of his beloved makes her sound like Echo, although it is he who echoes her name:

> Her voice fled always through the summer land;
> I spoke her name alone. (67–8)

Some excess of sexual feeling in *The Gardener's Daughter* was suppressed, for example the two manuscript versions of lines 185–208 which include kisses poured:

> Incessantly, like flakes of soft light
> Melted from lip to lip, and from my heart
> Sank, fused in hers now growing one with mine.
> (Ricks, *Poems*, p. 517)

The downward sinking there may be contrasted with the upward striking of the original kiss in *The Princess*: each closes in unity, mutual fusion. In the published version of *The Gardener's Daughter* the marriage of a friend helps instead to produce a verbal covenant under gray cathedral towers beyond the encircling trees: man-made structures which offer spiritual consent to passion.

One parallel to this sort of decision about what to publish and what to withhold can be seen in Tennyson's continual republication of *The Miller's Daughter* while never again after 1832 reprinting *The Hesperides*, which modern criticism has found the more interesting poem: T. S. Eliot, for example, praised its rhythmic originality. *The Miller's Daughter* is contained in regular stanzas and celebrates courtship and marriage sanctioned by parental consent. *The Hesperides* has the irregular and complicated metre and rhyme scheme which Tennyson tried to avoid after 1832; it is a song of unfallen sensuality. Hesperus, his daughters and a dragon guard golden apples whose theft would heal 'the old wound of the world':

> If ye sing not, if ye make false measure,
> We shall lose eternal pleasure,
> Worth eternal want of rest. (23–5)

Although Hanno, the heroic voyager of the poem's blank verse beginning, apparently pays no attention to the song, even in those first lines there are the compound words ('lotusflute', 'bloombright', 'cedarshade') which Tennyson came to see as a youthful affectation, a vice of luxuriance not even disciplined by the hyphen, and which seem like the nearest thing to Gerard Manley Hopkins before Hopkins. They run through the poem ('honeysweet', 'redcombed'), clustering toward the end:

> But when the fullfaced sunset yellowly
> Stays on the flowering arch of the bough,
> The luscious fruitage clustereth mellowly,
> Goldenkernelled, goldencored,
> Sunset-ripened above on the tree.
> The world is wasted with fire and sword,
> But the apple of gold hangs over the sea.
> Five links, a golden chain are we,
> Hesper, the dragon, and sisters three,
> Daughters three,
> Bound about
> All round about
> The gnarlèd bole of the charmèd tree.   (99–111)

One problem with *The Hesperides* may have been that its concern with art and feeling is not fully framed by narrative (nobody knows where Hanno goes) nor by a speaker who can put it in perspective.

In spite of doubts and withdrawals, Tennyson wanted to write about love as a force that fuses persons and the world, the self and the other-than-self that defines it, involving art, nature and time. In his 1831 review Hallam expressed a hope that Tennyson's poetry would bring 'our over-civilized condition of thought into union with the fresh productive spirit that brightened the morning of our literature' – with that curious reversal by which dead precursors were seen as youthfully vigorous, and modern artists prematurely aged:

> For we are Ancients of the earth
> And in the morning of the times.
> *(The Day-Dream, 1842, 19–20)*

One model was in the Hellenic idylls of Alexandria in the third century BC, although his favourite Theocritus treated sexual love much less spiritually than Tennyson. In Theocritus' fifth idyll the herd buggering his beloved is not so much goatish (the classical

Renaissance analogy for human lust) as an inspiration to the goats. The term 'idyll' originates in the word for 'little picture', *eidyllion*; *eidos* in Greek means 'shape, form, figure, species'. The Alexandrian idyll is a literary form self-consciously concerned with the handling of form, especially with framing devices which distance its material. Literary and scholarly, it shows already the anxiety of influence, playing like a disrespectful child with material from the epic tradition, incorporating lyric songs, the contest of ritual mime, and dramatic dialogue between characterized speakers. The idyll was from the start a medley, as Tennyson was to call *The Princess*, but a medley within limits produced by certain repeated elements which made it recognizable as a form or 'kind'. Theocritus, in particular, takes material from heroic narrative and uses it against its original nature to explore the psychology of feeling, especially of sexual love: the gods of his idylls are those for which epic had little time, the deities of witchcraft and love, Hecate, Eros and Aphrodite. Love mainly presides over Tennyson's Idyls; but there is a comic supernatural episode in *Walking to the Mail* and *The Hesperides* is a sort of spell.[5]

The subtitle of *The Gardener's Daughter* is 'The Pictures'; its protagonists are painters. Modern landscape painting was another form which Tennyson had in mind, and late twentieth-century analysis of the work of Claude Lorraine, Turner and Constable offers analogies to Tennyson's Idyls which are as interesting as those with the Alexandrians. In *The Experience of Landscape* Jay Appleton suggested that the aesthetic pleasure of foreground refuges (woodland, for example) and distant prospects (sky, sunsets) in landscape painting of the late seventeenth to early nineteenth centuries derives ultimately from the need of primitive hunters to see without being seen; the fascination may also be associated with the account given by psychoanalysts of the young child's pleasure and guilt in observing its parents making love. Such associations are not necessarily reductive, but can enrich a sense of how landscape idylls engage desire and disturbance, incorporating primitive feeling in sophisticated art.

Ronald Paulson, in *Literary Landscapes: Turner and Constable*, makes much of the origins of Turner's graphic experiments, suggesting for example that his swirling vortices derived from his father's name and work as a barber – 'vortex' comes from 'vertere', to turn; the barber's pole had a red streak winding round it. The meditative trances that Tennyson recorded were produced by repetition of his name, in which 'son' would be the turning point. Although their social backgrounds were quite different the family experience of both Tennyson and Turner was coloured by the violent moods of a parent; Turner's mother was finally committed to Bedlam, the hospital for the insane. There were more conventional connections between them; and in seeing an influence from Turner on Tennyson's work I am interested in what Lawrence Gowing has called the 'unconscious response to the cultural matrix'.[6] Both were concerned with the Romantic problem of translation between nature, poetry, and painting: with working immediate sensual experience into a more intellectual and collective symbolism. In terms of the result, the circling quality of Tennyson's verse, its reluctance to reach a final end, can be compared with the way in which Turner's work in contrast to Constable's leaves something to be guessed – the sublimity of the spire of Salisbury Cathedral is suggested by not showing the whole of it, for example.

Tennyson and Turner were both guests at the breakfast and dinner parties of the old poet Samuel Rogers, which brought new and leading figures in artistic and intellectual work together, although I do not know that they actually met there. Turner's engravings for Rogers's *Italy* (1830) were responsible for the immense success of that volume; during the 1830s he illustrated Rogers's *Poems*, Byron, Scott, Milton, Tom Moore and Campbell's *Poetical Works*, brought out by Tennyson's publisher Moxon in 1837. Turner's two versions of *Sinai's Thunder* in that edition may have influenced the conclusion of *In Memoriam* XCVI, a poem which shares Turner's concern with the relations of light and dark:

> And Power was with him in the night,
> Which makes the darkness and the light,
> And dwells not in the light alone,
>
> But in the darkness and the cloud,
> As over Sinai's peaks of old,
> While Israel made their gods of gold,
> Although the trumpet blew so loud.

I believe that Tennyson alluded to paintings as he alluded to poems; that the end of *In Memoriam* CIII, to take only one example, has Turner's effects in mind, and that the figure on the shore and the symbolism of the evening star, in other *In Memoriam* lyrics and in *Break, break, break* and *Crossing the Bar*, may be associated with paintings by Turner such as *The Evening Star*, exhibited in 1830.

Tennyson's father collected paintings on his travels in Italy; he wrote a treatise (unpublished) on oil painting. Tennyson himself admired the colour and rich elaboration of Italian painting, and also Dutch domestic interiors and landscapes; he visited several public and private collections. On his first visit to Paris he noted especially a *Narcissus and Echo*, possibly the one by Claude, and the painting called 'La Maîtresse de Titien' – one of the works which in the 1860s provoked Edouard Manet's explorations of what it meant for the fully dressed bourgeoisie to admire classic nudes. Hallam knew that Venetian colourist Titian to be a favourite of Tennyson's, and thought their imagination and style akin; the art critic Ruskin saw a kinship between Turner and Titian. Hallam in his last letter urged Tennyson to rival Titian's Danae, and this was very likely attempted in 'Now sleeps the crimson petal', in *The Princess* VII, 161–74. Tennyson acknowledged that the autumn scenes of *The Gardener's Daughter* were taken from the background of a Titian: landscape offered a more veiled expression of erotic emotion, but erotic affect is not necessarily the less powerful for being veiled. As for Turner, Tennyson certainly saw his paintings as well as his illustrations, for example at an exhibition he went to Manchester to see in 1857, and in the 1880s William Allingham records him seeing the world in the light of Turner:

Tennyson spoke of the 'sea of silver mist' seen at early morning from his windows at this season – also of the effect of mist spread over the wide green woodland and the sun shining on it – 'incredible! Turner would have tried it'.[7]

In subject matter *Oenone* and *The Hesperides* could have been influenced by Turner's *Goddess of Discord Choosing the Apple of Contention in the Garden of the Hesperides* (1806). *The Vision of Sin*, one of Tennyson's 1842 *Poems*, was acknowledged to be inspired by Turner's *Fountains of Fallacy* (1839) – a painting now lost – but *The Fountain of Indolence* of 1834 seems equally suggestive for the poem's images of languid voluptuaries awaiting a fountain, 'Sleet of diamond-drift and pearly hail', which ejaculates to 'low voluptuous music' and 'woven in circles':

> Ran into its giddiest whirl of sound
> Caught the sparkles, and in circles,
> Purple gauzes, golden hazes, liquid mazes,
> Flung the torrent rainbow round.
>
> (*The Vision of Sin*, 29–32)

Tennyson said that his poem represented the soul of youth given up to pleasure and becoming cynical, but the words and the rhythms, recalling those of *The Hesperides* and trying to catch the excitement of Turner's vortices of haze and light, can hardly escape the contradiction between the viewer's pleasure and critical judgement which is exposed by Manet's nudes, when he reworks Bathsheba illicitly seen naked by King David, or Susanna ogled by the Elders, into the modern courtesan *Olympe*, unwrapped for observation like the bunch of flowers her admirer has sent, or into the *Déjeuner sur l'herbe*, where the replacement of generalized flowers by a hat and a muslin dress let the viewer know that this is not a safe classicizing nude, but a picture of a woman who has taken her clothes off. As practitioners, and as observers of earlier art, Manet and the Tennyson of the 'English Idyls' share an interest in what ancient models and the taste for them can mean in the nineteenth century; the displacement of erotic interest into landscape may seem more inhibited, more 'Victorian'; Manet's interest is certainly more conscious and witty; but it is not absolutely certain which is the more erotic.

The imaginative models for Tennyson and Turner are Romantic as well as classical: they share a fascination with the sea, its extent, its 'perpetual motion and irresistible force'. They laid claim to authenticity, attempting to present natural images in their own right, for their own sakes (Turner had himself lashed to the mast in his sixties to observe a storm which he thought he might not survive); but both were curious about fusion and influence, things at their most fluid – the sea, the sky with its light and clouds, solid rocks seen through mist, swirling vortices with the sun for centre. Turner's last words were said to have been 'The sun is God.' In his study of Tennyson's early poems W. D. Paden claimed that Tennyson was fascinated by the idea of sun worship; it has been said of both the poet and the painter that they were influenced by theories of the origin of religion in the work of Boehme, the theosophist, and of the mythological scholar Jacob Bryant, who argued that the belief in many gods derived from misunderstandings of stories about the one original father–god, the sun. Values associated with the natural world (the apparent object of their work) were mixed with assumptions about the origin of those values, whether in mythology/religion or as described by science (by optics for Turner, by astronomy and geology for Tennyson). But these assumptions were mixed with feelings about the father: 'the sun' as the supreme source is compromised by the verbal pun 'son', as an alternative source of energy and value. Such oppositions (light and dark, right and wrong, father and son, father and mother, masculine and feminine) have traditionally shaped ways of living, feeling and thinking. The work of Turner and of Tennyson uses and disturbs them, exposing their ambivalence. Contemporaries like Hazlitt and Carlyle saw Tennyson and Turner themselves as godlike beings of genius who produced an ordered cosmos out of chaos; as in Turner's famous final touches to apparently formless canvases.

Tennyson's 'English Idyls' should be read in the light of Titian's glowing colour and female forms, the landscapes of Claude and Turner, and the image of Narcissus. His own studies of solitary women like *Mariana* and *The Lady of Shalott* are also recalled, with images of enclosed places like islands in water, or of reflections in mirrors or on water. In the Idyls these are framed by some account of male friendship, and by retrospect – the days described are infolded in the orbit of memory. This sense of benign maternal enclosure is intensified by memories of the woodland refuges of landscape painting, as some lines rejected from *The Gardener's Daughter* make clear:

> On either side the figure where one caught
> A glimpse of landskip crisp with shining woods
> And summer bolts . . .   (Ricks, *Poems*, p. 510)

Such refuges are defined by their limits, for example by distant prospects glimpsed beyond: sea and sky, dawns and sunsets, are pictured in some of the loveliest lines, like those from the manuscript of *The Lover's Tale* which were taken for the conclusion of *The Princess*, 111–15:

> Till gradually the powers of the night
> That range above the region of the wind
> Deepening the courts of twilight, broke them up
> Through all the silent spaces of the worlds
> Beyond all thought, into the Heaven of Heavens.
>
>   (Ricks, *Poems*, p. 303)

The lines that end *Love and Duty* (1842; a poem which may relate to the breaking of Tennyson's engagement, but which can be seen as an Idyl without a frame) are of this kind and, again, were adapted for *The Princess* III, 1–2:

> Then when the first low matin-chirp hath grown
> Full quire, and morning driven her plow of pearl
> Far furrowing into light the mounded rack,
> Beyond the fair green field and eastern sea.
>
>   (*Love and Duty*, 95–8)

These scenes, charged with emotion, are also given definition
by the idea of the city:

> Not wholly in the busy world, nor quite
> Beyond it, blooms the garden that I love . . .
>
> (*The Gardener's Daughter*, 33–4)

In *Edwin Morris* the painter comes from and returns to the 'dust
and drouth' of London life'; the repeated phrase frames the Idyl.
In *The Lover's Tale* 'all the separate Edens of this earth / . . . centre
in this place and time' (540–1). The country refuge, whether by
cavern and lake or by the quiet bay, 'like to a quiet mind in the
loud world' (7), represents inwardness. The eyes of the beloved
are the extremest depth, like something for the lover to drown in:

> You cannot find their depth; for they go back,
> And farther back, and still withdraw themselves
> Quite into the deep soul, that evermore,
> Fresh springing from her fountains in the brain,
> Still pouring through, flood with redundant life
> Her narrow portals.   (*The Lover's Tale*, 77–82)

The woman's soul here is also a metaphor for the lover's own feelings: in the manuscript lines it is his own image he worships in her
eyes – until, shockingly, he sees the image of another man there,
'There in my realm and even on my throne' (582). In the manuscript of *The Miller's Daughter* the lover wishes to be her mirror, but
also to be the song she sings and the book she reads; so in the
manuscript of *The Gardener's Daughter* she 'reads' her lover's
glances. The notion of eyes as windows through which a person's
self can be seen is a common one; so is the notion that it may be
the gazer's self which is really seen, while he himself becomes a
picture or a book to be read. As such ideas emerge and then disappear from the texts anxiety is evident, both about being observed
oneself and as to whether another can be truly seen.

These Idyls are interesting and moving not so much because of
their idealism and the sober decency of their sentiments, but
because of the repeated images which they share in common. Certainly they offer the aesthetic pleasure of the picturesque, but that
pleasure is strongest in the exploration it allows of emotion. I have
fused their specific narratives, shapes and characters because
really I think that is the best way to come at them – they tell the
same story. The superabundant lines of the manuscripts are part
of this story, in the way that preliminary sketches by a painter may
help in understanding the effect he was seeking.

The language flows and circles until it reaches a point of refuge: the self seen in a woman's eyes, or the woman herself like Eve in Milton's Paradise before the fall. As allusion to *Paradise Lost* suggests, what is desired may be a point of absolute security and satisfaction; but that is always elusive. *The Lover's Tale* is one of loss, and loss is also the outcome of *Edwin Morris*. In *The Lord of Burleigh* and *The Gardener's Daughter* the girl marries the lover but dies, the 'idol' of youth becoming the memory of age. Lines rejected from *The Gardener's Daughter* at the point of engagement are suffused with images of autumn which recall both the 1830 song, *A spirit haunts the year's last hours* and Keats's great *Ode to Autumn*: 'sallower gleams', 'when the swath-rake cleared', 'sleepy autumn nodding rode', together with luscious images of fatly ripe fruits – lines which were later to seek a home in *Audley Court* and still be refused admission:

> Every musky gust
> Tumbled the mellow pear: the apple boughs
> O'er burdened bowed, loaded with rosy globes
> Brushing the fat black mould . . .

(Ricks, Poems, pp. 519, 707)

Marriage, sexual maturity and fulfilment are at once imagined as leading on to death: not a death of attrition into skeletal bones but one of composting, becoming rich food for further fruition. The same feeling informs the engagement of the Prince and Ida:

> and all the rich to-come
> Reels, as the golden Autumn woodland reels
> Athwart the smoke of burning weeds. Forgive me,
> I waste my heart in signs: let be.

(The Princess VII, 335–8)

Even in *The Miller's Daughter* where the married lovers survive to re-encounter, from his perspective, the scenes of first love, the meeting of eyes is not entirely direct and unequivocal. It is prefaced by his sighting of the girl's image reflected in water and wavering (76–8). The closing claim of *The Miller's Daughter* is for two spirits made one, but its closing image is of a sunset reflected on to a window and from there on to water, touching the sullen pool below into illusory fire (235–46).

The notion of women's eyes as homes of security that can renew themselves, springing up in fountains, is found in *Isabel* (1830), *Supposed Confessions of a Second-Rate Sensitive Mind* (1830) and in *In Memoriam* XXXII. In the Idyls the one who suffers the greatest loss, in *The Lover's Tale*, is also the one who most insists on an original sense of security. Edwin Morris claims that his love for nature is of the same age as himself and that his love for the girl is twin-sister to this (though 'of different ages'!): these lines are borrowed from ones in the manuscript of *The Gardener's Daughter* which in turn were taken from a passsage in *The Lover's Tale* (139–280) describing how

> my love
> Grew with myself – say rather, was my growth,
> My inward sap, the hold I have on earth . . .   (159–61)

so that they lie in the cradle together with only one mutual parent, his mother, folding each other like the perfume in the folded petals of a rose:

> So what was earliest mine in earliest life
> I shared with her in whom myself remains.   (241–2)

So strong a denial of differences carries its own danger within it. What the ultimate cradle of security may be is suggested by the last lines of *To J. S.* (1832), which Tennyson addressed to James Spedding on the death of Spedding's brother:

> Sleep till the end, true soul and sweet.
>   Nothing comes to thee new or strange.
> Sleep full of rest from head to feet;
>   Lie still, dry dust, secure of change.

The Lover's Tale, so long unpublished, became a storehouse of elements used in other poems: the lover's death-like swoon and deranged but prophetic visions prefigure those of the Prince in *The Princess*, and the image of Ida as music to the Prince's words is suggested by the manuscript, 15–16, 'my heart beat / Time to the melody of her's' (Ricks, *Poems*, p. 304); a fusion of love, landscape and music which is also echoed in *Edwin Morris* immediately after the lines about love of nature and the beloved as twin-sisters:

> To some full music rose and sank the sun,
> And some full music seemed to move and change
> With all the varied changes of the dark,
> And either twilight and the day between.
> (34–7, taken from the manuscript of *The Gardener's Daughter*,
>   Ricks, *Poems*, p. 709)

If this sense of a harmonious natural world also recalls 'the Sun in Western cadence low' of *Paradise Lost* X, 92, that only confirms

ALFRED TENNYSON

the high degree of literary mediation in these poems which seek
to explore the experience of love – the relationship in itself cannot
be verbalized very directly. *The Lover's Tale* is the most extensive
of these explorations of desire which cannot be satisfied without
losing its nature, so that poetry or painting becomes the nearest
thing to lasting fulfilment. An infolding like the petals of a rose is
one image from *The Lover's Tale* which was always important for
Tennyson: charged with erotic energy, it also represents complex-
ity, because the female body, natural objects or the writing self
may all be the object of desire. In *The Gardener's Daughter* the
speaker's friend has painted his beloved:

> those eyes
> Darker than darkest pansies, and that hair
> More black than ashbuds in the front of March.   (26–8)

'Love' is the given the credit for this portrait, and for the rival one
which the speaker is to paint. The verbal portrait of the gardener's
daughter, pinning back flowers like Milton's Eve, is the centre of
the Idyl; manuscript lines dwell more on her breasts and on her
lips like 'ripe anemones', kissing each other. She is certainly felt
both as an art object and as an object in nature, warmly and
tenderly felt, but as with the beloved's eyes in *The Lover's Tale* the
object is also the self which can surge up like a fountain:

> Sweeter than all, the moments that I spent
> In watching how her pure and virgin soul,
> (That hoarded all its odour in itself,
> Deep blooming fold in fold by slow degrees)
> Opened before me, till she read and knew
> The meaning of my glances . . .
> (*The Gardener's Daughter*; manuscript, Ricks, *Poems*, p. 517)

In the published text this is replaced by an image of the two lovers
'mutually enfolded', encircled by the arms of Love, and shadowed
by the cathedral towers (210–13). The folded rose that opens up
its secret delights is a miniature of the garden refuge itself. Variations of this language of folded petals and inscribed leaves in still
gardens, of blooming and the surging of springs from deep wells,
are found where Tennyson's emotions are deeply engaged, in *In
Memoriam* XLIII, for example.

For all their evocation of inwardness enclosed in painting and
poetry the frames of the Idyls remain conscious of the nineteenth
century; they have been called a middle class of poems for middle-
class readers. The love affairs usually remind us of class divisions

by crossing them; the gardens are part of the estates of great houses. Class-consciousness forms part of the 'hindrance' (the city, death, autumn) that helps define the limits of the refuge; it stands in for forbidding parent figures, who are otherwise absent, as if the lover and beloved could exist in themselves, open to and folded in each other. In *Edwin Morris* the family does rise in a body to disrupt the lovers' embrace: but only cousins, aunts, uncles, pugs and poodles are mentioned. The mood here is hardly solemn: *Edwin Morris* distances the obsessional theme of money-marriage, wryly transforming the god of love into 'a lawyer's clerk / The rentroll Cupid of our rainy isles' (102–3). The painter revisiting the lake remembers his lost love without resentment because she was part of the refuge, part of the past fresh days, one only of his visions of the lake:

> While the prime swallow dips his wing, or then
> While the gold-lily blows, and overhead
> The light cloud sn.oulders on the summer crag.   (145–7)

The Idyls are sketches of surface images which both suggest and withhold depths; images of desire for a condition before and after life. In *In Memoriam* deep emotion drowns poetry (XIX, XLIX) which can offer at best:

> Short swallow-flights of song, that dip
> Their wings in tears, and skim away.   (XLVIII)

XVI asks if sorrow only seems to take:

> The touch of change in calm or storm;
> But knows no more of transient form
> In her deep self, than some dead lake
>
> That holds the shadow of a lark
> Hung in the shadow of a heaven?

In Memoriam takes several lines and images from manuscripts of the Idyl period, and encloses many 'idylls', as in the setting of the 'bounded field' of love within the 'eternal landscape of the past' in XLVI. The poet of the love Idyls is a Narcissus seeking his own image. Because this goal is folded back into his origin in the woman's body its environs are no place for an adult to stay. Later Idyls move onward and outward, and the poet of love is left as an Echo commemorating the quest of Narcissus, which survives in poetry.

In so far as these Idyls are about love for specific women my

45

account should be framed by *Dora* and by *Locksley Hall* (1842). *Dora* like *The Miller's Daughter* is taken from a story by Mary Russell Mitford, and attempts Wordsworth's simplicity in praising the devoted love of women – for a man, for each other, for a child – that heals the divisions of masculine harshness. *Locksley Hall* in contrast damns the girl who has submitted to marriage for money, and fantasizes escape to exotic Edens where 'the passions' can be free and 'some savage woman' will 'rear my dusky race' (167–8 – a colonialist fantasy that haunted Tennyson's writing from time to time). Neither the sentiment of *Dora* nor the invective of *Locksley Hall* is in tune with the feeling of the characteristic English Idyl, whose fusion of classical form and modern landscape provides the perfect medium for Tennyson's writing of love and love of writing. It is easy to see, however, that he could then feel enough was enough, or too much. The later Idyls are briefer and more pointed.

THE WIDENING COMPASS

I have written of the love Idyls as if they were an involuted mass; the appropriate treatment for the Idyls of friendship is more 'distinct in individualities' (*The Ante-Chamber*, 27). The individual needing to make his way in the world takes precedence over Romantic unity, its swamping and confusing of the self. The Longman annotated edition of Tennyson prints the poems in order of composition, and this is useful for seeing what could have been written first and for relating the poems to the life – which Idyls were written at Torquay or at Llanberis, for example; they breathe the spirit of holiday with its disembarkations from sea trips. But since I want to consider these Idyls in relation to each other as a sequence, and not all were printed together in 1842 (*The Golden Year* came out in 1846, *Edwin Morris* in 1851) I have followed Robert Pattison's *Tennyson and Tradition* and discussed them in the order in which Tennyson finally put them, with the exception of *Edwin Morris*, whose refining and revaluation of the love Idyls makes it a significant turning point. As Pattison says, Tennyson's arrangement of his poems under different headings is one guide to his own sense of them. He did not offer critical prefaces or manifestos; his comments on how his poems should be read, often arising from what he thought were misunderstandings, are recorded by family and friends, informally.

In *Locksley Hall* love is a brief episode that stops or reverses time like a work of art:

Love took up the glass of Time, and turned it in his glowing hands;
Every moment, lightly shaken, ran itself golden in sands.   (31–2)

This is like the memory of love in *Edwin Morris*, but *Locksley Hall* is more like the other Idyls I am about to discuss in that its sense of time expands beyond personal memory, reaching back to pre-history and forward to aerial trade and warfare; ultimately to universal peace in 'the Federation of the world' (128) – always one of Tennyson's visions. Not the inward fold of love but the sense of having social responsibilities informs these Idyls, which consider from a moment of leisure the classical opposition between the requirement to work and the desire for ease. The speakers of the Idyls are at ease: as figures in a landscape they differ from the eighteenth-century gentleman surveying his property, nor are they agricultural workers. They are very much of the nineteenth century, on leave from city work in a countryside which has become a national resort, as if open to all. Some degree of class difference is engaged in most of the Idyls, suggesting the shift in economic power from inherited land to industrial and commercial wealth. In *Edwin Morris* the Tudor mansion is now owned by cotton millionaires from Merseyside, who reject the gentlemanly but impoverished suitor. In *Audley Court* the great house is up for rent and old Sir Robert's books for sale; and in *Walking to the Mail* a similar mansion is to be sold, its owner Sir Edward gone abroad for fear of what might happen after the 1832 Reform Bill.

Within the framing landscapes the Idyls take the form of discussion between men friends. Some of these are, apparently, mere acquaintances, especially in *Walking to the Mail* – it is not that homo-eroticism has replaced heterosexuality as the focus, but that the poems are turning from love to the business of the world, a male preserve. *The Gardener's Daughter* can be seen as the founding experiment for all these poems, and *The Ante-Chamber* which Tennyson would not have printed with it because he thought the poem was already full enough, offers a composite portrait of Tennyson (as friends said) and Hallam, split into one friend with a luxurious fancy and one who took more interest in the varieties of political and social life. The manuscript of *The Gardener's Daughter* evokes a tenderness for youth and friendship which disappears later: the speaker like the Prince in *The Princess* is mildly bisexual, the down

47

on his lip like that on a quince-leaf, his 'girlish curls' wantoning in 'sunny rings', and the friends are likened to playful foals that

> Sometimes idly stand
> Musing together in the shade, and each
> Sleeking for love the shoulder of his mate.
>
> (Ricks, *Poems*, p. 509)

It looks as though Tennyson were trying to make the young men as physically attractive as the girls they love, as much part of the natural world; but he did not persist, although something of this reappears in *The Princess*. What survives in the late Idyls is the sense of public interest, all shadow of effeminacy removed.

In *Edwin Morris* the discussion is still about love; it is in this sense that it reviews and concludes the earlier Idyls. Edwin the poet represents the idealization of love and the artistic narcissism that attends this. The speaker is more down-to-earth, and while he claims to put no less a value on love, like Hamlet's mourning it is something that 'passes show'. He has 'a wayward modern mind / Dissecting passion', and this later seems like a forewarning of his loss in the face of the realities of modern economics. Counterpointing these two is the fat curate Edward Bull who insists, with a traditional sense of hierarchy like that of the King in *The Princess*, that woman was made for man's use and not to be idolized. The other two find him a joke, not worth answering, yet he is not quite alien to the speaker in his belief that 'love' is produced by art, an unreal and threadbare theme (17–49). The answer to this is in the loveliness of the conclusive visions of the lake, of love and art: but the doubt has been given voice. This partly tacit quality gives Tennyson's Idyls their particular form: the arguments are not exhaustively put and answered but lightly juxtaposed, sometimes suggested by a song or a story or bit of gossip, and framed by prospects of a wider natural world, a longer span of time, which can be read as answering the dispute, but partly set it aside. The degree of open-endedness recalls the policy of the Cambridge Apostles, of listening with as much tolerance and understanding as possible to diverse opinions; though obviously some opinions would not have come within the pale.

Audley Court is exemplary in its apparent innocence of all tendentiousness. 'Francis' arrives by sea, the friends picnic, talk local and national politics and go home; we are not told what position each took about the Corn Laws, only that they were in dispute but ended up laughing. Since Francis is a farmer's son, the only protagonist of the Idyls who is given a specific relation to the land-scape in terms of either property or work, we can assume he was for a policy of protection and that the speaker, a gentleman of leisure at least for the time, must have been a liberal, for free trade. The friendship mildly crosses class boundaries, akin to the cross-class marriages of the love Idyls where propertied and artistic leisure woos the working man's daughter, or artistic educated poverty is rejected by new wealth; the burden of it all is the bourgeois desire for national harmony. The two engage in a Theocritean singing match. Francis's song rejects the claims of love and of all public service, clerking or soldiering:

> Be shot for sixpence in a battle-field,
> And shovelled up into some bloody trench
> Where no one knows? but let me live my life.   (40–2)

The speaker's song leaves all options for work aside, but though he sings of his own beloved, folded in her sister's arms, he has taken the original from a book (bought at 'Sir Robert's' sale). The Idyl places the need for a choice of life within a lovingly detailed English scene, from the emblematic picnic pasty whose contents are like fossils of the rock, to the final homegoing prospect, step-ping down beneath the moon:

> till we reached
> The limit of the hills; and as we sank
> From rock to rock upon the glooming quay,
> The town was hushed beneath us: lower down
> The bay was oily calm; the harbour-buoy,
> Sole star of phosphorescence in the calm,
> With one green sparkle ever and anon
> Dipt by itself, and we were glad at heart.   (81–8)

Donald Hair is surely right when he says that this suggests the spirit of *The Princess*: holiday and pastime producing a mood of generous mental pleasure, in which imagination may be released, new possibilities conceived.[8]

Walking to the Mail, however, may produce a more negative and pessimistic judgement. It is modelled on Theocritus's fourth idyll which deflates the pretensions of love, drawing comparisons between human and animal sexuality. Tennyson does not imitate this particular kind of cynicism directly, but it does affect form and theme, and the metamorphosis of Niobe, the mythical mother mourning her dead children, into a pig. This Idyl is a dialogue between the liberal John and the Tory James, whose name reappears in *The Golden Year* and who has a counterpart in the Tory member's elder son in the Conclusion to *The Princess*. James has no faith in progress because he takes a low view of human nature, as only to be controlled by law and discipline, although those who are 'great' by birth have 'manners' which fit them like a second nature. He compares Chartism, the agitation for a working-class voice in government (fear of which is said to have driven 'Sir Edward' abroad) to his own rebellions and cruelties as a schoolboy. He has already told a comic story of a tenant farmer flitting (moving house) to get away from a haunting, only to find the ghost packed up with his furniture, so that he returns home to live with it:

> but, sir, you know
> That these two parties still divide the world –
> Of those that want, and those that have: and still
> The same old sore breaks out from age to age
> With much the same result. (68–72)

The other story he tells is more enigmatic: how he and his schoolfriends stole a pregnant sow, hiding her at the top of their college tower, and took the piglets, presumably to eat. There's a curious painfulness, of which he seems unconscious, in the details of dragging the animal from her 'warm bed' up the 'corkscrew stair', and since they are neither found out nor punished the story hardly proves that 'there was law for us; / We paid in person' (77–8); rather, it takes pleasure in the memory of petty crime and triumphant cruelty.

The Idyl tells three stories which tacitly reflect on each other to support James's case, or give evidence of his attitude to people: the ghost, the pig, and Sir Edward Head's marriage to a cottager's daughter. She is remembered by John as idyllically full and sweet, like a pear, like a white privet flower, but described by James as, ten years on, 'like a butt, and harsh as crabs' (in manuscript, 'like a fungus bloated white – / And harsh as verjuice', Ricks, *Poems*, p. 702). As in *The Lord of Burleigh* this cross-class marriage has not prospered. In so far as a position can be guessed behind this Idyl, it is like the speaker of *Edwin Morris* in his most suspicious and anti-idyllic mood, or like the 'morbid devil' in Sir Edward's blood 'That veiled the world with jaundice' (13–14). The souring of the cottager's daughter to what she always really was, in James's view, is matched by his mock-tragic description of the pig:

> Large range of prospect had the mother sow,
> And but for daily loss of one she loved
> As one by one we took them – but for this –
> As never sow was higher in this world –
> Might have been happy: but what lot is pure?
> We took them all, till she was left alone
> Upon her tower, the Niobe of swine,
> And so returned unfarrowed to her sty.   (85–92)

It is James's attitudes which are displayed at length. John responds rather generally, that intelligent men don't see things so much in black and white, that ruthless judgement is childish ignorance; and as if in agreement the mail-coach which is presumably to carry them back to the world of business appears, pulled by horses of unequally mixed colour, 'three pyebalds and a roan'.

The appearance of one-sidedness in *Walking to the Mail* would be worrying if it were the last Idyl: there seems little defence against James's projection of his own malice on to a view of society. John's desire for tolerance has no backing but good will. Similarly the 'free trader' of *Audley Court* is just espousing an opinion, having no stake in the matter that we know of, whereas Francis's position of individualism and protectionism is rooted in his role in agricultural production. *The Golden Year* restores optimistic possibilities. Like *Edwin Morris* it has three figures, the speaker who simply provides a perspective on the others, the choleric old James, and Leonard who:

> lived shut up within himself,
> A tongue-tied Poet in the feverous days   (9–10)

– days which require some response to the desire of the 'have-nots' for more, though the speaker presents this most unsympathetically as wanting to be crammed with food like a herd of animals, but not to be estimated as a herd. Tennyson is clearly trying out different political attitudes that were possible for himself, without resting satisfied with any; generosity and suspicious contempt at war. Like the over-fanciful or self-indulgent artists of *The Ante-Chamber* and *Edwin Morris* Leonard is a projection of aspects of his self-image as a poet. Full of doubts, feeling himself born too late, he has nevertheless written a prophetic song of hope, which the speaker remembers along with the past summer day. The song imagines humanity more equal in ability and in the distribution of wealth. Leonard's future peaceful federation of the world when 'all men's good' will be 'all men's rule' is very obviously here the moral notion of the British Empire, with the Press, free trade and the 'mission of the Cross' flying together; but the limits of the ideology don't derogate from the value of imagining a world free from militarism and competition. Leonard's song contrasts the individual life moving day by day to age with the cycles of progress:

> And human things, returning on themselves
> Move onward, leading up the golden year.   (25–6)

Old James won't have this: his critique of fantasies of idyllic pasts and futures pre-empts Raymond Williams's in *The Country and the City*:

> Old writers pushed the happy season back, –
> The more fools they, – we forward: dreamers both . . .   (65–6)

He accuses Leonard of being out of time with the pace of modern life (a concern shown already in *Walking to the Mail* which contrasts the changes of seasonal time with timekeeping, the need to meet the coach's fixed schedule), and like the social critic Thomas Carlyle insists that the golden age is always present to 'him who works, and feels he works' (72). The comparison of him to an oaken stock 'o'erflourished' with clematis, and his own analogy of the seedsman who must sow as well as dream of golden harvests, aligns him with the local patriotism of Francis (oak being the British symbol). In fact they can be seen as belonging less to the world of pastoral idyll than to that of Virgil's *Georgics*, the Roman poetry of patriotism and agricultural admonishment.

In keeping with the mode of the Idyls, which is elliptical and suggestive, not dogmatic and certain, the published poem simply juxtaposes Leonard's song and James's answer, which could be captured both for radical and for reactionary politics. It thus offers two idylls, one of ideas and one which turns the spirit of the form against itself by implying that leisure leaves room for unresolved anxieties, so that work is the happy life. But in the manuscript there is an important passage in which Leonard questions his own position before James speaks, from which I have taken the epigraph for this chapter because it focuses the concerns of all the Idyls, illuminating also the classical monologues: *Ulysses*, for example, moves out from refuge while suggesting that there is more than one sort of work, that heroic dreaming like Leonard's may be work too. Leonard's unpublished musings suggest that general progress and individual happiness are two different things: individual happiness being the kind of centre, the still point of refuge, which the love Idyls were concerned to gain. Modern astronomy has brought new ideas of time and motion which may produce an overwhelming need 'To fix a point, to rest.' Though humans are by nature restless, always moving on may cost the sense of identity – everything may be gained but a central and secure sense of self. The answer to his restless and unhappy thinking is hinted by the image of the compasses which the speaker attributes to Leonard, replacing the song's notion of onward cycling with that of a fixed centre, the self, deliberately planted, with widening circles inscribed around it:

> '. . . will it come or, being come,
> Be felt as gain? this age of ours is gold
> To much before it; yet no happier we,
> Nor may our sons be happier than ourselves.
> O grand old sires, who wagged their beards in hall
> And laughed and let the world go round, nor knew
> The noiseless ether curdling into worlds
> And complicated clockwork of the suns.
> Motion: why motion? were it not as well
> To fix a point, to rest? again, it seems
> Most adverse to the nature of a man
> To rest if there be any more to gain.
> And there is all but what he is: no rest:
> Why then, to be resolved into the all.
> That will not do, being to lose myself.
> What else?' – And here, methought he seemed to grasp
> A pair of shadowy compasses, with these
> To plant a centre and about it round
> A wide and wider circle: and while he mused
> Came James, his business ended, and resumed . . .

(Ricks, *Poems*, pp. 716–17)

Clearly this Leonard is heir to Hamlet. These unpublished lines are emblematic of the English Idyls, moving from the centre of the self (never in fact quite fixed, always split into reflections and represented images) to the wider social and political context of the later Idyls. I have tried to show how literally Tennyson worked with such images – of surface and depth as reflection and drowning, of infolding, of refuge and prospect, of centre and circle (and line).

The Golden Year as published closes with one of the most marvellous prospects in the Idyls, making the poetry of uncertainty

into a shapely piece of art. It is a frame and not a frame, closure
for the moment but no closure, since it evokes a continuing work
which is also destruction. The poem begins in memories of the
Welsh mountains: its close, though in the past tense, evokes the
immediate present of the noise of work, which is not, however, a
single effect but redoubled in echo. The phrase 'from bluff to
bluff' may be recognized as a verbal habit of Tennyson's (compare
James's 'from age to age' in *Walking to the Mail*, and 'From rock
to rock' in the closing passage of *Audley Court*): it is a graphic grammar of repetition and enclosure, in strong contrast to Leonard's
restlessness in seeking a point of rest ('To fix a point, to rest? again
it seems . . .'). Quarries for the nineteenth century suggested not
just ongoing production, but discovery of the past, for example of
the fossils which provided that conceit in *Audley Court*, the pasty
with its lower layers to be excavated in one of the most basic
human pleasures and needs. The blasting and buffeting of the final
strong but multiply-meaning image contrasts with the refusal
within the Idyl to hammer home its points too finally:

> and, high above, I heard them blast
> The steep slate-quarry, and the great echo flap
> And buffet round the hills, from bluff to bluff.

2

Monologues and metonymy

> Motion? why motion? were it not as well
> To fix a point, to rest? again, it seems
> Most adverse to the nature of a man
> To rest if there be any more to gain.
> And there is all but what he is: no rest . . .
>
> > (*The Golden Year*, manuscript, *c.* 1839,
> > Ricks, *Poems*, p. 717)

> I live not in myself but I become
> Portion of that around me.
>
> > (Byron, *Childe Harold* III, 72, 1816)

Tennyson's Idyls reworked the problems posed by Romantic idealism: desire for unity with the world imaged in nature or in woman, focused on a speaking self which was no sooner represented than betrayed as divided. Wordsworth wrote of past days

> Which yet have such self-presence in my mind
> That sometimes, when I think of them, I seem
> Two consciousnesses, conscious of myself
> And of some other Being.   (*The Prelude*, 1850, II, 30–3)

The differences between imagination, reality and language, and the will to make them one thing, produced the power of Wordsworth's writing. He suspected all ways of seeing that interposed between the mind and nature, 'landscape' as well as classical and traditional allusions and forms. Coleridge was both more sceptical and more desperately assertive of ideal unity, seeking to 'realize' it through the traditional narrative form of the ballad, through exotic visions, through fragments implying a lost whole, the paradisal unity which in Wordsworth's writing was ordinarily available, a 'simple produce of the common day' (Preface to *The Excursion*, 1814, 55). Tennyson shared Coleridge's uncertainty about access to truth, freely using the 'ready-mades' of the classics and landscape. The second wave of Romantic poets in England, the generation of Byron, Shelley and Keats, questioned the Real and the Ideal, and Tennyson pursues this questioning, acknowledging the inauthenticity of poetry, which could still offer at the least sheer pleasure or an illusion of consensus about experience, while still exploring the self in its reflected, refracted representations.

'Refract', derived from the Latin *refrangere*, 'to break', means in physics, according to the *Oxford English Dictionary*, to break the course of light and turn it out of the direct line; especially, to deflect at a certain angle at the point of passage from one medium into another of different density. For example, sunlight onto window glass onto water, and thence onto the retina of an eye; and, finally, a sense impression such as this into words. It means both 'to reflect', to throw back the same image, and 'to break up, impair'; suggesting both reflected truth in which the real and its representation are one, and the impossibility of such reflection. *The Lady of Shalott* (1832; 1842) is about reflection, about mirror images and meditation; like Coleridge's *The Ancient Mariner* it tends to make a mockery of the intellectual reflection it provokes. Its fascination is that of rhythm as well as picture, and this is intensified in some of the revisions, changing, for example, the merely pretty

> The líttle ísle is áll inráiled
> With a róse-fénce, and óvertraíled
> With róses . . .   (28–30, Ricks, *Poems*, p. 355)

to the haunting trochees, reversed then reasserted, of

> Bý the márgin, wíllow-véiled,
> Slíde the héavy bárges tráiled
> By slów hórses . . .   (19–21)

Modern criticism has interpreted the Lady in psychoanalytic terms, as imprisoned libido unable to find expression in a utilitarian age, as the poet's Jungian anima, his feminine self turning from inner creativity to be crushed by confrontation with the real world. Looking backwards, she can be related to 'one of those nymphs occupied in weaving, whom Porphyry explained as human souls about to be born into the world', or to the Fates who wove destinies and cut the thread of life, or to Shelley's *Witch of Atlas*.[1] 'Text', as we have often been reminded in recent years, means etymologically 'something woven', from the Latin *tectere*, 'to weave', and Tennyson used weaving to describe his own process of working, as when he spoke of weaving the *In Memoriam* lyrics together. Rather than finding associations for the figure of

56

the Lady alone, it is important to look at how her poem is worked.

In an image from *The Devil and the Lady*, I, 3, which I quoted in Chapter 1, the 'dark reverse' of life is imagined as more real than the fair tapestry of youthful art and imagination. Commentators on *The Lady of Shalott* have noted that weavers did use mirrors so that, working from the reverse, they could also see the effect on the right side. I find it hard to see the Lady's mirror in this way; the poem mentions only its reflection of the world, and could it be placed so as to show both the view from the window and its representation on the tapestry? The Lady is multiply distanced from the world, not only by her work, the mirror and the window, but because her castle is on an island in a river. She knows nothing of the world personally, and it knows only her name: 'art' and the world are quite separate, though mutually curious. This distance and her refuge are broken by the image of Sir Lancelot, on whom the sun shines so that all the colours of his accoutrements glow. He resonates sound also, in the ringing of his armour and in his song, 'Tírra lírra' – silly, but repeating the poem's dominant rhythm, imposed perhaps by the name of the metropolis, Camelot, to which the river flows. All this artistry in the real world appeals to the Lady who is already 'half sick of shadows' at the sight of young lovers; these shadows are the reflections of which she weaves an image. To match this doubling within her room Lancelot's image, catching the light of the sun, is reflected both directly and from the river. It's all too much, and the excess provokes the poem's crisis, where the enchantment of the trochaic rhythm surrenders to a doom-laden iambic pace, except at the climax:

> She léft the wéb, she léft the loóm,
> She máde three páces thróugh the róom,
> She sáw the wáter-lily bloóm,
> She sáw the hélmet ánd the plúme.
>   She loóked dówn to Cámelót.
> Oút flew the wéb and flóated wíde;
> The mírror crácked from síde to síde;
> 'The cúrse is cóme upón me', críed
>   The Lády of Shalótt.   (109–17)

It is not simply that, as in *The Kraken*, imaginative art and the realities of the surface life are incompatible: what is dramatized is the strain of mediation, of perceiving and representing in different media. In 1842 Sir Lancelot's final musings replace the Lady on the right side of a tapestry: ' ''She has a lovely face.'' ' In 1832 she did not gain even this much recognition, as the 'well-fed wits at Camelot' puzzled over the inscription borne by her corpse, ' ''this is I, / The Lady of Shalott'' '. No one has commented on what seems to me a curious fact, that in a poem about a Lady with a mirror, the traditional emblem of vanity, the Lady herself is never imaged in the mirror, saying 'this is I'. It is always the real world outside the room, outside the Lady's self, which is reflected – emotion in her splinters the mirror and tears the weaving up (an image of a great piece of weaving ripped up which recurs both in *The Princess* and in *Idylls of the King*). Selfhood is silent in *The Lady of Shalott*; things not said are significant by their absence in several poems which I discuss in this chapter.

Though the Lady's face itself becomes 'glassy' as she foresees her fate, neither she herself nor 'the dark reverse' are ever seen in her mirror. The strongest visual effect of the poem is of parallel lines, running always towards the city, an effect which is particularly marked in the first and last Parts of the poem and intensified by the lay-out of the poem on the page as well as by its aural effect. In each stanza the first and the last four lines have the same rhyme, whose onward drive is not seriously checked by the looping-in of the fifth and ninth lines:

> On either side the river lie
> Long fields of barley and of rye,
> That clothe the wold and meet the sky;
> And through the field the road runs by
>   To many-towered Camelot;
> And up and down the people go,
> Gazing where the lilies blow
> Round an island there below,
>   The island of Shalott.   (Part I, 1–9)

> Under tower and balcony,
> By garden-wall and gallery,
> A gleaming shape she floated by,
> Dead-pale between the houses high,
>   Silent into Camelot.   (Part IV, 154–8)

Though I have said 'looping-in' to evoke the weaving effects of rhyme and repetition, the poem's linear drive, with long fields and road, river banks and buildings, as 'life in the real world', represents that which was always passing through and beyond the mirror, so that it could not find its equivalent in the Lady's static web. The poem is certainly about life and art, as everyone says, but it remembers that art has different media with different technical problems. As far as movement in time goes, poetry can do what pictures may despair of.

The emphasis on movement in the lines of *The Lady of Shalott* is in strong contrast to *Mariana*. Both poems were taken as subjects by Pre-Raphaelite painters, not only for their nostalgic charm but also for the object-lessons they offered in problems of representation.[2] In *Mariana* (1830) there is no mirror; the poem itself is a kind of reflection of Mariana's unreflective mind. The pendant poem *Mariana in the South* is much less remarkable as it translates watery native fenlands into the arid South of France, because there is a mirror in which the woman contemplates both her melancholy and her perfect face, an image repeated in the Madonna to whom she prays. Such clearly defined repetition means that *Mariana in the South* (1832; 1842) can get within sight of an ending, when love and grief can both be lost in death. *Mariana* has no real ending, and many beginnings in its wealth of literary sources. One of these is a fragment by Sappho which Tennyson had already imitated twice: he said that the discovery he most hoped for was of more poems by this woman of the Greek heroic age, preferring her lyric metres to their Latin equivalents.[3] Several of Tennyson's earlier poems have sources in writing by women, *Dora* and *The Miller's Daughter* in works by Miss Mitford, *The Lady of Shalott* in an Italian novella by a woman, though he added the most significant elements, the curse, the mirror, the weaving. Other influences on *Mariana* were Keats's *Isabella* and Samuel Rogers' *Captivity*, which Tennyson knew by heart into his old age. In *Captivity* a young woman is guarded by an old nurse with a rusted key:

> And terraced walls their black reflection throw
> On the green-mantled moat that sleeps below.
>
> (Ricks, *Poems*, p. 187)

The epigraph of *Mariana* is from Shakespeare's *Measure for Measure*. 'Mariana in the moated grange' is enigmatic; as with the later monologues we do not know how much the context of the sources should affect response. Shakespeare's Mariana enjoyed intercourse with her reluctant lover by a trick of comedy arranged on her behalf, and was married to him by a Duke's decree. However Tennyson's addition of another melancholy pendant suggests that the frustrated woman is valuable to him as a type who would lose her emotional charge if she were arbitrarily rescued. Endless

Sapphic yearning offered a more perverse pleasure. 'I waste my heart in signs', says the Prince, as if he is deferring the marital duty of consummation for pleasure in words; we might have expected him to say 'sighs' but he has no longer any cause for sighing (*The Princess* VII, 338). Mariana and the Prince suggest why Tennyson's writing needed sometimes to secure happy sexuality in images of domesticity and procreation, with sturdy fathers, rosy mothers and graded offspring, as at the end of *The Two Voices*. Something ecstatically perverse, islanded like the lotos-eaters and longing for oblivion, has to be firmly denied.

The rhythmic and imagistic effect of *Mariana* is of something enclosed like the Lady of Shalott's island, and endless, denying time, narrative and movement. Stanzas with repeated rhyme schemes like those of this poem can be compared to elaborately jewelled caskets, in contrast to the linearity of ballads or the irregular movement of odes or free verse, which can seem to track free expression of argument and emotion; treasured containers which suggested female genitals to Freud. *Mariana*'s rhyme scheme is a b a b c d d c e f e f. The circling quatrain at the heart of each stanza, always expressively returning to its beginning as in the *In Memoriam* stanza, is held within more ordinary quatrains, the last of which always rhymes 'dreary / said / aweary / dead'; but it can never feel like the end because we get used to it always coming back. The rhythm of *Mariana* offers a sullenly pleasurable resistance to circumstance, an adolescent assertion of self-will saying at least, 'I'd rather be dead than put up with this.' This self-infolding is characteristic of Idyl ladies, Rose in *The Gardener's Daughter*, Flora in *The Day-Dream* and Ida at crucial moments in *The Princess*, of the soul in *The Palace of Art* and the poet in some lyrics of *In Memoriam*. It is a negation which involves the drawing-in of forces in order perhaps to assert the self differently. *Mariana* is the most powerful expression, very early, of such a moment, though its assertiveness exists only as strong gloom in image and rhythm, not as narrative possibility except in the desire for an end to it all preferred over patience.

Tennyson's early poetry presented female 'types' – types of yearning and frustration such as *Fatima* and *Oenone* were always printed together, while *Mariana* was always printed next to *Isabel*, an idealization of the mature woman. But neither *Mariana* nor *The Lady of Shalott* yield their full interest as protests against the condition of women. Women in the Idyls were used as objects for the exploration of desire, and *Mariana* and *The Lady of Shalott* are equally traditional. Their female subjects are used to project the problems of the artist. It might be that Emily Sellwood like Elizabeth Barrett and Mary Russell Mitford suspected that Tennyson's early poems showed a low estimate of women; and either external or internal criticism may have pushed him to represent a woman speaking in her own right, in Princess Ida.[4] For the moment, the Lady and Mariana are androgynes, 'typing all'.

The drive of Romantic poetry is to integrate the language of the self with its object (nature, the world), an attempt that repeatedly fails: 'Fled is that vision: do I wake or sleep?' (Keats, *Ode to a Nightingale*). *Mariana* calls into question even a momentary integrity between the Romantic vision and its signs. In Coleridge's *Dejection: an Ode* the natural world at the beginning is a projection of the poet's mental state, but nature's independent changes (a rising storm) affect his mood beneath his conscious will, by virtue of a mutual sympathy which contradicts the poem's assertion that mood and will, and especially joy, are primary. Everything in *Mariana* is a product of her inconsolable will; how she experiences her environment is the only thing, apparently, over which she has any control, and she holds on to her view of it relentlessly. A crust of moss, rust, dust, covers everything inside and out; the sunbeam in the last stanza is no ray of hope, but a way of showing up the dust, 'thick-moted', as it lies 'athwart the chambers'. There is hardly any movement, no flowing river to contrast her state: the black waters of the sluice sleep, and what creeps on them is only the infinitesimal growth of more mosses. Someone, the speaker of the poem, has a perspective on her, as in *The Lady of Shalott*, though there this unnamed presence is less puzzling because of the conventions of story-telling. Mariana herself neither says nor sees much, glancing out only at night and refusing to look at 'the sweet heaven' in any transitional state, morning or evening. That someone *can* say 'sweet heaven' is the only indication of a possible criticism of Mariana, whose sense is confounded, so that some other observer is needed to say what her state of mind is. Indications of time confuse her, the slow clock ticking and so on, and she loathes the afternoon sun most: time for her is something mouldering and rotten, a haunting by old faces, footsteps, voices: most movingly in the first stanza, with its signs of careful tending in the past. The present participle 'clinking' is a kind of mistake, negated in advance by knowledge that though once people did come, they don't now; the latch can't be clinking because it's unlifted:

>The rusted nails fell from the knots
>That held the pear to the gable wall.
>The broken sheds looked sad and strange:
>Unlifted was the clinking latch . . .   (3–6)

Because Mariana is not wrestling to either understand or transcend her condition the poem is strikingly different from Coleridge's *Dejection*, which turns on the double meaning of 'to move'. The problems of *Mariana* are not resolved in writing, the will to say 'I cannot be roused or moved' is not contradicted. In *Dejection* the winds do rouse the poet and simultaneously express his mood mounting into consciousness: it is a drama of psychological change. *Mariana*'s problems are ones for the interpreter: the central figure does not change, and there is no access to nature as anything more than a metaphor for her mental state, 'The level waste, the rounding gray'.[5] If *Mariana* were a Romantic poem the signs with which it is packed ought to offer access both to the subject and to her imaginative self-transcendence in identification with nature and the world. But speaker and subject are not one, not even one enough for us to say 'Here is a speaker in more than one mind' nor different enough for us to say 'Here is a critical view of this subject'. Similarly with the signs of the environment. They are not independent of Mariana since they are presented exclusively as expressions of her mood, but that mood is quite insistently indifferent to them: in the first eight lines of each stanza we read the natural signs, and in the last four Mariana's endless refrain which takes no notice of them. The signs assert absence ('He cometh not') and mean nothing but an emotional state which is imputed to everything and therefore cannot reach to anything outside itself. The nearest thing to something 'other' is the poplar tree of the fourth, fifth and seventh stanzas: the only tree around, it shakes but grows, 'silver-green' and not rotting in spite of its gnarled age. The two presentations of it in stanza five could have initiated some change – first it is a shadow swaying on the curtains, then when the winds are still it falls more definitely 'Upon her bed, across her brow'; something from outside making itself felt in the closed chamber. But it is forgotten in the next stanza, and in the last it is the sunbeam that crosses the room, while the poplar responds to the wooing of the wind, aloof. If the wind and the tree did invite a change of mood, Mariana did not respond.

The pleasure of *Mariana* and *The Lady of Shalott* is in the weaving of picture and rhythm. In the classical and dramatic monologues there is a different rhythm, the authoritative tread of the iambic pentameter. *Oenone* (1832; 1842) mingles its heroine's fixed mood of erotic frustration and desire for vengeance with the mythological narrative which explains it, and mixes the evocation of that mood and of female beauty in landscape with a moral which thoroughly disapproves of it, when the goddess of wisdom defines power as living by law in 'Self-reverence, self-knowledge, self-control'. The first fourteen lines were wonderfully revised to make the scene suggest both love-making and history, the exposure of Troy to Greece:

> There lies a vale in Ida, lovelier
> Than all the valleys of Ionian hills.
> The swimming vapour slopes athwart the glen,
> Puts forth an arm, and creeps from pine to pine,
> And loiters, slowly drawn. On either hand
> The lawns and meadow-ledges midway down
> Hang rich in flowers, and far below them roars
> The long brook falling through the cloven ravine
> In cataract after cataract to the sea.
> Behind the valley topmost Gargarus
> Stands up and takes the morning: but in front
> The gorges, opening wide apart, reveal
> Troas and Ilion's columned citadel,
> The crown of Troas.

Tennyson like Turner did not develop his work on classical subjects into a narrative continuity. In a story of the siege and fall of Troy *Oenone* would follow on from *The Hesperides*, though they are set worlds apart by the pentameters of the one and the rhythmic imagism of the other. In Turner's painting of 1806 the Goddess of Discord, a grey cowled figure, takes a golden apple from the Garden of the Hesperides; a whole branch of golden fruit bows down to the ground on the right, offering itself freely to the peaceful women around; to the left more happy figures are reflected in a pool, while the cloudy dragon slumbers on the heights above, echoing the dark Goddess in the otherwise unanxious scene. The future of Troy broods over the painting. In Oenone's story her lover Paris, prince of Troy, has been given the golden apple to award to one of three goddesses. He rejects the goddesses of power and wisdom, and gives it to the goddess of love, who rewards him with 'The fairest and most loving wife in Greece' – not the Trojan Oenone, but Helen, whose rape leads to the burning of Troy. When Tennyson wrote a pendant, *The*

Death of Oenone, in 1889–90, to show her final reconciliation to her 'husband', his comment that the new poem was 'even more strictly classical in form and language' than the old one, suggests that *Oenone* was an exercise in a form later used with more freedom and confidence (Ricks, *Poems*, p. 1427). With *Ulysses*, *Tithonus* and *Tiresias* he took up male subjects, as with the English Idyls he had moved from female objects of desire to masculine business.

Elizabeth Barrett Browning commented on the speaking subjects of Tennyson's poems:

Tennyson seldom uses the *ego* of poet-dom; and when he does you generally find that he does not refer to himself, but to some imaginary person. He permits the reader to behold the workings of his individuality, only by a reflex action . . . We know nothing of him, except that he is a poet; and this, though it is something to be sure, does not help us to pronounce distinctly upon what may be called the mental intention of his poetry.[6]

In dramatic monologues a speaker who is not the poet addresses a listener who is not the reader; a brief definition to which many modifications would have to be made to cover all examples. Many forerunners have been claimed for the form, including Ovid's *Heroides*, the laments of deserted heroines. The kind of poem that we think of as clearly dramatic monologue was developed by Tennyson and Robert Browning almost simultaneously, in the fourth decade of the nineteenth century. It was one way of imitating Shakespeare, which is one reason why monologues are often in blank verse, and this is fused with the realism of the novel, specific moments and environments being understood to determine action and character; the form can also shade off into lyric impersonation. As Elizabeth Barrett Browning suggested, we have no direct access to self-expression in Tennyson's poems generally, since even moods and attitudes with biographical parallels are being tried out as much as indulged, in ways which express and invite critical response.

Browning's monologues have greater realistic specification, accentuating the sense of speech from another time and place. Tennyson's are more classical in assuming an educated knowledge of the situation from which the character speaks, whether it's myth or the biblical story of Rizpah (2 Samuel XXI, 8–10) which he uses as an analogue to a newspaper story. As both Robert Langbaum and Alan Sinfield have suggested, the development and response to dramatic monologue in the early Victorian period was a reaction to Romantic self-expression.[7] Sinfield defines it as a feint between fiction and self-expression which escaped the burden of expressing feelings which would be expected to reveal some Truth about Reality to the Age. Browning's early attempts at self-revelation were attacked as too obscure and pretentious, and Tennyson would have come in for more of this sort of criticism had he persisted with and published poems like *Perdidi Diem*. The need for self-protection can be seen in the insistence on an adopted persona in the title of *Supposed Confessions* . . ., and in the containment of uncertainty within a little narrative in *The Two Voices*. Robert Langbaum in *The Poetry of Experience* considered dramatic monologues more from the point of view of the reader. One project of Romanticism was the familiarization of alien experience, made possible by increased awareness of historical and cultural difference, which was to be both acknowledged and overcome by imaginative sympathy. Compacted into a monologue, this produced what Langbaum calls tension between sympathy and judgement, embodying and dramatizing changes in attitude. Understanding the past or other cultures was not the only matter at issue: a historical sense intensified awareness of the present, the moment from which one wrote, as having its own peculiar character.

Emphasis on reader response draws attention to the effect of the silent interlocutor, the audience to which the monologue is supposed to be addressed in the first instance, although the speaker may essentially be a soliloquist rather than one intent on rhetorical persuasion. Nevertheless he/she is always being listened to, and it is this implied presence which makes the monologue dramatic rather than lyrical, and which writes into the poem the suspiciousness of judgement. This does not mean that every reader must identify with the listener, but that response is complicated. In *Rizpah* (1880) sympathy is clearly meant to be with the speaker, an old woman who has gathered up the bones of a son hanged for robbing the mail, to bury them in consecrated ground so that he might rise whole on the Day of Judgement. The interlocutor is a lady visitor who wants to save the dying old woman's soul, and it is she who is judged by the old woman's story or, rather, the institutions of the ruling class which she represents, which condemned the son before his crime and beyond death, are judged by the old woman's passion, rage, and final dignified readiness to acknowledge the lady's futile wish to be kind, after her fury:

And if *he* be lost – but to save my soul that is all your desire:
Do you think that I care for *my* soul if my boy be gone to the fire?
I have been with God in the dark – go, go, you may leave me alone . . .
                                                                    (77–9)

Tennyson may have associated the newspaper story with the biblical Rizpah because that theme had been treated by Turner. In Plate 46 of Turner's *Liber Studiorum* (1812), taken from an 1802 painting, Rizpah sits cowled in grey darkness by the corpses of her dead sons in the left foreground, while above a rising hill to the right a bird flies in the brightening sky over paradisal stooks of corn. The sense of ideal light springing from darkness and suffering was shared by Tennyson and Turner as a metaphysical concept and as a technical effect to be produced in their different media. In both, Toryish pessimism coexisted with radical opposition to state institutions and their judgements: Turner was nicknamed 'the Overturner', and *Rizpah* was one poem of Tennyson's which Swinburne passionately admired. Although the poem like the painting celebrates the power of mother-love, its expression is subversive; macabre also: 'the bones that sucked me . . . I kissed 'em' (53, 55) – Tennyson's own name for it was 'The Bones'. The implied criticism of the interlocutor invites readers to distance themselves from the operation of middle-class institutions of law, medicine and religion, and to doubt the charity of patronage.

Criticism of *Ulysses* has made quite a problem of whom he is addressing before he turns at line 45 to invite his fellow mariners (in the Homeric original they were all dead by then) to sail with him again. It's certainly not his wife, Penelope. The presence of an audience has not been much considered for *St Simeon Stylites* (1842), but it is equally significant. Both poems have something to do with fame, becoming a 'portion of that around me', in the words of Byron's traveller Childe Harold which Ulysses echoes. Leigh Hunt called *St Simeon Stylites* satirical, but W. E. Fredeman insists that it is not satirical but ironic.[8] The question turns on whether the poem is seen as an attack on 'the pseudo-aspirations of egotistical asceticism and superstition' (Hunt), or as a study in pride and isolation in which both poet and reader could be self-critically embroiled, as Fredeman says. Simeon is a type of the ascetic, a hermit who withdrew from other people by setting himself up on ever higher pillars, from which his epithet Stylites derives. He moves away vertically as Ulysses does horizontally. As a satirical figure Simeon would attack the enthusiasm of Evangelical preachers such as Charles Simeon, famous in Cambridge during Tennyson's time there, with their stress on personal salvation and experience of Christ. But since it could also be read as a Protestant attack on Roman Catholicism for fetishizing self-punishment, as a satire its aim would be oddly divided. Simeon's thighs are 'rotted with the dew', but he is still able to stand on two legs; in the source he has to stand on one leg for a year, and that Tennyson omitted this detail may be significant. His Simeon is not a joke, he is terrible.

However it is not quite convincing that 'we', poet and reader, can feel called into question by such a figure, as Hunt's response suggests. Simeon is too grotesque for identification. Like the speakers of several of Tennyson's early poems he suffers from remorse with no sufficient cause given (156). He believes that his self-imposed suffering will redeem him and, more than that, bring him sainthood, a complete cleansing from his foul body (210). He calls on his listeners below to model themselves on him, but he reserves to himself alone the heights from which he challenges all the saints, who may have suffered martyrdom once

> but I die here
> Today, and whole years long, a life of death.   (52–3)

His perverse self-assertion rivals Christ, a parody *in extremis* of the doctrine of salvation through suffering which Tennyson was often enough to take straight, for example in *Enoch Arden*. However even from this darkness light can be seen. From a Christian point of view, Simeon has denied all his Lord's gifts:

> men on earth
> House in the shade of comfortable roofs,
> Sit with their wives by fires, eat wholesome food,
> And wear warm clothes, and even beasts have stalls . . . (104–7)

Although he shows envy of God too as having both the comfort he denies himself and the power to look down with Lucretian superbity, Simeon actually prefers his own curious sublimity:

> I wake: the chill stars sparkle; I am wet
> With drenching dews, or stiff with crackling frost. (112–13)

He only mentions habitual comfort as a pretext for self-promotion and self-pity; what he really values, or the value he is there to express, is the sudden gift of really seeing and feeling existence, as very strange. His final prayer is that his audience may take

67

'Example, pattern', but he also prays 'lead them to thy light', which the Christian reader would see by now as very different from Simeon's. The reader's response is split between understanding Simeon, and judging otherwise, with that Anglican Broad Church tolerance which was Tennyson's most definite religious affiliation.

The psychology of the poem is complex, the pleasure it offers that of intelligent analysis; I have said little of the grim sense that Simeon may be learning at the last, and trying not to, that his whole life has been a mistake. He is not merely a butt of satire which leaves the reader untouched, but if we take the poem as an ironic study of pride in isolation, then the fact that Simeon has worked miracles, and apparently does so in the course of the poem (142–5) is anomalous. As Christopher Ricks has pointed out, the poem is called *St Simeon Stylites*; his desire for sainthood was not self-delusion. To have asked questions of the poem only in terms of the speaker's personality judged from a 'right' position was a mistake. The significant thing is that for all his grotesque struggling he has an audience who seem to worship him rather than jeer. The source of the poem was William Hone's *Every-Day Book: or Everlasting Calendar of Popular Amusements* (1825), and that subtitle is important as a tacit context for the poem. In Hone's book Simeon's abbot ruled that his mortifications should be more private: that was why he adopted the secret penance of twisting a rope so tightly round his loins that it ate into the flesh, as in the poem (60–9). His subsequent hermitage and mortifications attract visitors and are said to have worked miracles 'Whereof my fame is loud among mankind' (80), at which point he exclaims, to his credit:

> Thou, O God,
> Knowest alone whether this was or no.
> Have mercy, mercy! cover all my sin.   (81–3)

That this horribly deluded figure attracts credulity is as much the point of the poem as Simeon's character alone; his withdrawal in contempt from common human life captures the public imagination. It reworks very oddly the Idyls' concern with relations between imaginative retirement and public life, as if *Perdidi Diem* had become Tennyson's claim to fame. By taking it for his title Fredeman called attention to Simeon's sense of himself as 'A sign betwixt the meadow and the cloud' (14), between the ordinary life which is the site of the Idyls, and sublimity. His intense private vision, feeling through his body the wet and chill of the world, relates to the figure he makes, 'The watcher on the column to the end' (60). There is no one religious or psychological moral to the poem: as it provokes meditation on these things, it also offers an image of the writer's guilty but necessary distance from habitual unverbalizing life.

Ulysses knows himself as a sign: 'I am become a name' (11). Ordinary existence is impossible because he is a literary hero. It is not that he has absorbed all his experience as a hoard off which he can live, folded in himself, but that his self has become inseparable from the world of adventure, physical and intellectual, with which his fame has identified him: 'I am a part of all that I have met' (18), not 'it is all part of me'. He is a special case in terms of the lines in *The Golden Year* manuscript on rest and motion, where travelling onwards to gain more is seen as natural but as costing 'what he is'. What Ulysses is is coextensive with literature. For the poet, bearing in mind that this poem was a response to Hallam's death, writing is a heroic alternative both to mere existence and to death. Ulysses' identity cannot be at home in Ithaca as an idyllic refuge, but only in travelling towards a distant goal. Tennyson said of this poem that 'it gave my feeling of going forward and braving the struggle of life perhaps more simply than anything in *In Memoriam*' (Ricks, *Poems*, p. 560). In taking a central hero, not a marginal figure like Oenone or a grotesque like Simeon, he accepts a destiny as a major poet, following Homer and Dante, in the line in which Hallam had placed him.

In the *Odyssey* XI, 100–37, the seer Tiresias prophesies that after Ulysses's return he will go forth again, but will die possibly far from the sea (the interpretation is doubtful), 'a death so gentle, that shall lay thee low when thou art overcome with sleek old age, and thy people shall dwell in prosperity around thee'. Tennyson's Ulysses refuses that sleek and gentle death, leaving Ithaca's prosperity to the care of his son Telemachus. In Dante's *Inferno* XXVI, 90–124, Ulysses speaks from the circle of hell reserved for those who have given bad counsel. He had not returned at all to crown Penelope with joy, or to be a good father, but had gone right on 'T'explore the world, and search the ways of life, / Man's evil and his virtue.' Dante's Ulysses is the type of the intellectual as hero, who prefers masculine enterprise to the joys and duties of domesticity. With such sources it is easy to see why the kind of value signified by Tennyson's Ulysses has been in dispute: for example he has been read as an ironic study of the anti-social self-concern of any hero. Homer was not concerned with this sort of moral, and Dante's Ulysses is ambivalent, not worthless just because he is damned. Tennyson's own account gives his poem a simple message, 'that still life must be fought out to the end', which can cover a multitude of sins and free the poem from crude moralism one way or the other. To take Ulysses, or Simeon, as either spokesmen or targets is to mistake the nature of poems whose language presents a mode of existing. *The Lotos-Eaters* explored a will to quietude, *Ulysses* explores desire and loss. The name Ulysses is the sign of mobility, of refusing limits. The refuge is given to Telemachus, 'centred in the sphere / Of common duties' (39–40) – not here cathected, lit up by the language, because 'common duties' are not what *this* poem concerns itself with. Because the positions of father and son are disturbed from the pattern usual for adventure stories ('In the year 17—, in defiance of my father's wishes, I set out . . .') it is possible to entertain at least two contrasting patterns for a life, instead of assuming a single inevitable cycle from active youth to quiescent age ('My father was right all along'). Death is suggested throughout *Ulysses*, in its slow rhythms and the darkness on the sea, but the old man prefers to challenge it rather than let it encroach and eat him away:

> And this gray spirit yearning in desire
> To follow knowledge like a sinking star,
> Beyond the utmost bound of human thought.   (30–2)

'This gray spirit' does sound as though Ulysses were already in the underworld; but the poem's desire of oblivion only gains interest from its tension with the manifest will, like that of Milton's Satan, 'not to yield'. On one level the poem is rhetorical, conscious of its listeners. The king announces his intention to abdicate, then once more summons, or summons up, his mariners, in a ceremonial movement from court to harbour: 'This is my son . . . There lies the port.' The more inward soliloquy desires to regress, never to have been born of woman, to return to the inorganic, the unconscious. *Ulysses* dramatizes not the death drive but its repression, its conversion into curiosity, desire for travel and knowledge, for something more not less, as *The Two Voices* puts it. Desire for 'Something more' (*Ulysses*, 27) rejects hoarding, sleeping and feeding – measuring and doling out suggest the distribution of food as well as the administration of law (3, 4) – but takes its metaphors from such basic human needs:

'I will drink / Life to the lees' (6–7), 'always roaming with a hungry heart' (12). The most heroic images suggest the body taking the brunt of elemental forces:

> Through scudding drifts the rainy Hyades
> Vext the dim sea . . .
> And drunk delight of battle with my peers,
> Far on the ringing plains of windy Troy. (10–11, 16–17)

Desire is different from the satisfaction of needs, which bores Ulysses. Homer's *Odyssey* began with his detention on Calypso's island, longing for home, the first of many traps and lures like the sirens and the island of the lotos-eaters; the narrative suggests manhood as a moving-on from female refuges. In Tennyson's poem return to Ithaca, the ultimate refuge which made the moving-on necessary, is felt not as satisfaction but as starvation by an aged and barren woman (1–5). In the original story Ulysses' wife Penelope had been waiting for twenty years, weaving. She has said that she will choose one of her suitors once the weaving is finished; every night she undoes what she has woven during the day. The function of this is to validate her husband's will to return: her faithfulness ensures against the possibility imagined rather obsessively in Tennyson's work, in *In Memoriam* XC, in *Enoch Arden* and *The Lotos-Eaters*, that those returning would prove unwelcome, life's processes having continued easily without them. *Ulysses* reverses this: his return to what should have been the final haven is felt as a dull obligation, not as fulfilment. The emptying out of Penelope as a sign marking true value – she is not named – is as striking as the absence of the Lady of Shalott's face from her mirror. Desire cannot be fulfilled, but must always be displaced on to something else:

> I am a part of all that I have met;
> Yet all experience is an arch wherethrough
> Gleams that untravelled world, whose margin fades
> For ever and for ever when I move.
> How dull it is to pause, to make an end,
> To rust unburnished, not to shine in use!
> As though to breathe were life. Life piled on life
> Were all too little, and of one to me
> Little remains: but every hour is saved
> From that eternal silence, something more,
> A bringer of new things; and vile it were
> For some three suns to store and hoard myself,
> And this gray spirit yearning in desire
> To follow knowledge like a sinking star,
> Beyond the utmost bound of human thought. (18–32)

This imagination of a future is marked by ambivalence about the gathering of sustenance, retention, and letting go. Ulysses wants to be both an experiencing subject and an object, ''honour bright' from use, like a great piece of armour as a work of art. 'Honour bright' derives from Shakespeare's *Troilus and Cressida* III, iii, 150–3, and this whole speech of Shakespeare's Ulysses is resonant for Tennyson's poem with its theme of fame – the self-esteem of the Greek hero Achilles being hoarded sullenly in his tent, while the public which applauds the actions of Ajax 'like an arch reverb'rate / The voice again' (120–1). It also provides the image of Time as a greedy eater, which may have influenced the metaphor of hoarding which so curiously dominates Tennyson's poem; an image of anal retention by which Ulysses becomes for himself a consumed object to be held on to:

> Time hath, my lord, a wallet at his back,
> Wherein he puts alms for oblivion,
> A great-sized monster of ingratitudes.
> Those scraps are good deeds past, which are devoured
> As soon as they are made, forgot as soon
> As done.   (*Troilus and Cressida* III, iii, 45–50)

As an object Ulysses would not need to breathe even, since breathing means infantile dependence on the mother, feeding and sleeping. But at this point Ulysses has become in his imagination a feeder and a hoarder himself: with many lives stored up, he regrets this one that he has nearly consumed already, saving hours from the eternal silence and greedily thinking of each as a bringer of new things. This moment of greedy amassing, when consuming and being consumed by Time become one, is as much a part of the unconscious and 'dark reverse' of *Ulysses* as the more readily idealized desire of oblivion. It provokes right away a crisis and reversal in the poem: hoading is vile, and so Ulysses imagines himself as a bodiless spirit reaching beyond the bounds.

To the literary fathers that haunt *Ulysses* could be added Turner's *Ulysses Deriding Polyphemus*, exhibited in 1829, in which the red banner bearing the hero's name catches the eye rather more than his own tiny figure. The painting takes a moment when Ulysses is on his way to Ithaca once more, escaping the giant who has fed off his mariners and whom he has blinded. Like the dragon in *The Goddess of Discord* the giant's bulk is almost indistinguishable from rock and cloud mass, 'part of all', just as Ulysses is hardly to be distinguished from his ship. The painting suggests the escape of a son from patriarchal power. The eye is drawn towards a great sunburst on the right that suggests glorious freedom but also danger – its most intense light is barred by a streak of duller cloud. Turner used to attach lines of poetry, by himself and others, to his paintings, as if purely graphic means could never be enough: he might have accepted Tennyson's *In Memoriam* XLVII, 'Farewell! We lose ourselves in light' as an epigraph for his Ulysses. It is a painting which strains at the limits in representing movement pictorially: the ship appears to be heading straight for the viewer, but if it were to pull across and round towards the sun to which the viewer's eye is drawn as the only way out, its helmsman would see that gleaming untravelled world through two arches of rock.

For Tennyson's old hero the light of anticipation wanes, fades, sinks; the real seas 'gloom dark', moaning with many voices, Turner's along with Homer, Dante and Shakespeare. Finally he reaches a deeply moving balance between the drives for accumulated life and for extinction, and the death which will come whether desired or not:

> It may be that the gulfs will wash us down:
> It may be we shall touch the Happy Isles,
> And see the great Achilles, whom we knew.
> Though much is taken, much abides; and though
> We are not now that strength which in old days
> Moved earth and heaven; that which we are, we are . . . (62–7)

Ulysses is both an idealistic poem and a very physical one, in its language; to the last the heroes may be 'washed down' or 'touch' at least the place where the heroic Achilles, an old acquaintance, abides. Negotiating extremes, Ulysses asserts 'the will', while accepting those limits which are beyond control.

Mariana suggested that there was no necessary link between feeling and the natural world. *Tithonus* (1833; 1860) undoes Shelley's notion of an ideal, quasi-divine, endorsement for poetic language. Shelley's spirit of poetry, his Witch of Atlas, was said to be able to take a human being and mingle it with her own ideality:

> Alas! Aurora, what wouldst thou have given
> For such a charm when Tithon became gray?
>> (*The Witch of Atlas*, 57–8)

In the myth the goddess of the dawn, Aurora or Eos, had granted immortality to her human lover Tithon without thinking, being so far from human herself, to grant him also eternal youth; nor had he, enchanted with divinity, thought to ask it, and the spell once made can't be changed. In Tennyson's monologue, terribly old but unable to die, he cries: 'How can my nature longer mix with thine?'(65). He has attained the condition which both Tiresias and Lucretius desire, of looking back down on the world from an immense distance in space and time, separated from pleasure and pain. He exists in an impasse, a perpetual border state of which his desire, Aurora, is the encircling limit.

Tennyson called *Tithonus* a pendant to *Ulysses*. It counters the desire for more by suggesting that there is a position from which merely routine life, undistinguished almost from animal or vegetative or even inorganic being, is enviable:

> The woods decay, the woods decay and fall,
> The vapours weep their burthen to the ground,
> Man comes and tills the field and lies beneath,
> And after many a summer dies the swan.
> Me only cruel immortality
> Consumes: I wither slowly in thine arms,
> Here at the quiet limit of the world . . .   (1–7)

Tithonus's being and desire are consummated and consumed in endless aging, making manifest that which was latent in *Ulysses*, an entirely passive wish for oblivion, without the act of suicide which is Lucretius's chosen way out. All of these monologues with their aged male speakers assume a vantage point from which life is surveyed, as if in the hour before death. In their concern with desire and patience, time and limits, they re-engage the problems of the political poems and of *Mariana* and *The Lady of Shalott*. In the latter a cataclysmic change takes place, which could have positive results if it changed the consciousness of Sir Lancelot or the reader. *Mariana* excludes almost all change, but it is not quiescent, in its acute impatience with the tiny changes and recurrences of the routine. Its power is that of inertia, the weight of its mood resisting any distraction, any involuntary seduction into delight. In this respect Mariana is kin to Ulysses, in her inability to bear the slow-paced, the natural. Ulysses can will movement and action, however disastrous for himself and his companions: he is the sign of restless motion out, she of immurement and immobility. Time for Mariana is present – day, night, the clock ticking – but jumbled and meaningless. Her poem ends at, say, four in the afternoon, as long an hour as the one before dawn but with only night to come, yet again; an hour that suggests no beginning and no end.

74

'Gradualism' leads to despair in which time and meaningful process are consumed in intolerable consciousness of self. Simeon, in contrast, assumes control, calculating the hour of his death as precisely as he measured the height of his pillars, 'A quarter before twelve' (218).

Tithonus is not simply an alternative to *Ulysses*, liberal-mindedly putting the other side of the question; it is yet another version of a complex of anxieties, in which the patient working of existence now becomes the unattainable object of desire. As in *Ulysses* the object attained is shunned: 'Ah! keep me not for ever in the East' (*Tithon*, 54). Within the embrace of his beloved Tithonus looks back with envy to the dark world where he was born, to a state in which 'man' is composted like leaf-mould, to bear further fruit in a process beyond the conscious will. The emblematic swan sings – or rather its dying implies the famous music that celebrates life in the moment before it ends – and so do the vapours: the burden of work imposed on man in Genesis is displaced onto the mists to become a song, the 'burthen' or refrain of lyric. These first lines suggest Tithonus's personal hell of impotence along with the processes of natural life and death immensely extended in perspective. Not merely leaves fall, but whole woods, while Tithonus is forever 'decaying, never to be decayed', like the hellish woods of Wordsworth's *The Prelude* VI, 557 (a passage published in 1845, before Tennyson revised *Tithon*). Christopher Ricks's analysis of Tennyson's 'most assuredly successful poem', his 'subtlest and most beautiful exploration of the impulse to suicide', praises its 'exquisite chill', intensified by the urgent ordinariness of some few of its moments: 'Why wilt thou ever scare me with thy tears?' suggests how little, for all the poem's perfect finish, Tithonus has accepted that this is his condition for ever (Ricks, *Tennyson*, pp. 129–32). 'Scare', as Ricks says, is naked and unprotected, like Tithonus's wrinkled feet on the glimmering thresholds of the fair courts of dawn (67–8). *Tithonus* is very much a poem of the surface, without ambivalent depth: erotic desire and anger at being maimed by Aurora's horses, the Hours, are fully present and brought under the sign of aesthetic order, the intolerable converted into the beautiful.

Ulysses desired to pass beyond the bounds, Tithonus lies at the limits of the knowable world. In *Tithon* the description of lovemaking did suggest a breaking of boundaries, mingling mortal and immortal (41–53), but its revision in *Tithonus* stays with Aurora's essence as outlining a given cycle:

I used to watch – if I be he that watched –
The lucid outline forming round thee; saw
The dim curls kindle into sunny rings;
Changed with thy mystic change, and felt my blood
Glow with the glow that slowly crimsoned all
Thy presence and thy portals . . .   (52–7)

As listener Aurora, formally addressed even though she is absent for most of the poem, is as far as possible from the reader. The poem's dynamics reproduce her cyclic essence, her curls, her wheeling out from and back to Tithonus's fixed point within her courts. The end is with Tithonus's wish for an end, for a moment blissfully imagined as already far in the past, but answered by what is really about to happen as it always will, regardless: 'thee returning on thy silver wheels'. Because her movements are inevitable her response to him is enigmatic, loving but incapable of changing anything. The tears she leaves on his cheek are also a metaphor of her attribute, the dew, and would fall even if she felt nothing. Her image as a natural divinity controls the poem, and is as frustratingly unreachable as Tithonus's past mortal self.

Tiresias is another speaker caught 'betwixt the meadow and the cloud', and is deeply ill-tempered about it, unlike Tithonus and deserving far more than Ulysses the criticism which the latter has come in for, for his resentment at not being recognized in his time, and his callousness toward a younger generation. It is not clear that this ill-temper is displayed as an ironic intent of the monologue: the tension between speaker and interlocutor, story and soliloquy, is muddily handled. *Tiresias* was partly written in 1833 but not published until 1885. More than the other monologues it turns on a dramatic action, the suicide which Tiresias the blind seer urges on the young prince of Thebes, Menoeceus, predicting that it will save the city. It may be meant to prefigure the redemptive sacrifice of Christ, as *Demeter and Persephone* does, but since we know nothing of the young man's state of mind this doesn't work well, though like *Demeter and Persephone* it arises from a concern with the modern significance of inherited myth, and the ways in which 'divine purpose' is like human consciousness in its relation to history. Tiresias tells the young man how the founding myth of Thebes:

made me yearn
For larger glimpses of that more than man

Which rolls the heavens, and lifts, and lays the deep,
Yet loves and hates with mortal hates and loves,
And moves unseen among the ways of men.   (19–23)

This enquiry is mixed with political pessimism:

Who ever turned upon his heel to hear
My warning that the tyranny of one
Was prelude to the tyranny of all?
My counsel that the tyranny of all
Led backward to the tyranny of one?   (71–5)

The problem with Tiresias is that he is a spokesman for certain values, and asks for sympathy as a disregarded prophet as well. The poem is a dead end, depressively picking over elements that provide the motive force for exploration in other poems. The ignoring of some elements in the myth in order to superimpose Christian significance is puzzling, both in the light of Tennyson's interests in other poems and of modern interest in the myth. Tiresias remembers the Sphinx that has threatened Thebes, riddling, woman-breasted and destructive, so that the story of Oedipus who solved her riddle is implicit, though he is not named. But the story in Ovid's *Metamorphoses* III, of how Tiresias experienced life as both a man and a woman, which T. S. Eliot was to use in *The Waste Land*, is not used by Tennyson; androgyny is unwanted here. In Tennyson's poem Tiresias's punishment for seeing the goddess of wisdom naked is blindness and disbelief in his prophetic foresight. He is very much a father figure, addressing Menoeceus as a son who is 'wise enough, / Though young, to love thy wiser' (148–9), and therefore kill himself, becoming one of the martyrs whose famous names 'coerce' and 'conciliate' others to equal sacrifice for 'that sweet mother land which gave them birth' (116–19). The poem is apathetic to potential resonance in its material; Menoeceus is the reverse of Oedipus who defied Tiresias's advice in order to learn the truth of his origins, how he had killed his father and married his mother. Tiresias promises him that he will become a name 'graven on memorial columns', a signifying statue such as he himself has wished to be (78–83), and a hand reaching through the years – an image that clearly meant a good deal to Tennyson, since he had used it in *Hail Briton!* and was to use it again in *In Memoriam* LXXX. But here the kindling of 'generous purpose' by example is unpleasantly coercive:

and thou refusing this,
Unvenerable will thy memory be
While men shall move the lips.   (127–9)

There is little generosity in Tiresias's envy of the young man for
being able to die significantly, since he takes no cognizance of the
difference between their relations to life; Menoeceus never speaks,
nor is his exactly a famous name. This is a soliloquy requiring
sympathy for the speaker's nostalgia and desire, but it is of the
'son' that suicidal action is required. He just goes off to kill
himself, and it's hard not to dramatize this mentally without a
sullen shrug. Yet it is not clear that the monologue is meant to invite a blackly humorous judgement on Tiresias's talk. When Tennyson finally published it he said 'the world will receive lessons
thus when it discards them in modern garb', as if he were in
Tiresias's shoes, the Laureate sending young soldiers off to die for
the Empire (Ricks, *Poems*, p. 568). The closing concern is not with
the young man at all, but with the old man's desire to be above
the human:

> clouded with the grateful incense-fume
> Of those who mix all odour to the Gods
> On one far height in one far-shining fire.   (175–7)

Tennyson would boast of the whole conclusion, as a sample of
his best blank verse. Its inhuman air acquired an ironic coda, an
involuntary parallel to the biographical motive of *Ulysses*. To
introduce the *Tiresias* volume Tennyson had written a poem for
Edward FitzGerald's birthday (his 74th, though Tennyson thought
75th). Before the poem was sent to him FitzGerald died. Tennyson
then added a conclusion critical of his aestheticism in *Tiresias. To
E. FitzGerald*, its original 56 lines an unbroken sentence, is a fine
affectionate tribute to a friendship and the friend, that works with
differences, not within the poet's ideas and feelings as in *In
Memoriam*, but between the friends. One of its pleasures is the
awareness that it might not be received as quite conciliatory, but
as another sally in a perpetual bickering, in which Tennyson sadly
had the last word:

> 'One height and one far-shining fire'
> And while I fancied that my friend
> For this brief idyll would require
> A less diffuse and opulent end,
> And would defend his judgement well,
> If I should deem it over nice –
> The tolling of his funeral bell
> Broke on my Pagan Paradise . . .   (57–64)

This 32-line conclusion acknowledges also the long golden lives that Tennyson and FitzGerald had enjoyed, in spite of Tennyson's gloomy fascination with martyrdom and suicide, and is grateful for a peaceful close to a long life. Possibly within the 1885 edition this poem did stand as an answer to *Tiresias*. Although the publication of *Tiresias* is in keeping with Tennyson's late pessimism about democracy, one version for the ending of *To E. FitzGerald* suggests that the more fluid hopefulness of the 1830s survived intermittently, that 'cataclysm' could be one way of development, not just the gratuitously destructive and unprincipled behaviour of a younger generation and of unfamiliar interest groups:

> Ah if I
> Should play Tiresias to the times,
> I fear I might but prophesy
> Of faded faiths, and civic crimes,
> And fierce Transition's blood-red morn,
> And years with lawless voices loud,
> Old vessels from their moorings torn,
> And cataclysm and thundercloud,
> And one lean hope, that at the last
> Perchance – if this small world endures –
> Our heirs may find the stormy Past
> Has left their Present purer.　(Ricks, *Poems*, pp. 1319–20)

Lucretius, published in *Macmillan's Magazine* in May 1868, succeeds where *Tiresias* fails, in the ironic relation between speaker and listener, soliloquy and story. Human existence, routine for Ulysses and vegetative for Tithonus, is for Lucretius a stifling, jostling animal closeness; his desire is for patience and transcendence. The patience he wants is endorsed by his model of the Gods as immune to suffering. But he is content neither with the idea of the Gods as changeable, nor with their supposed indifference. The restless discontent of his thinking is deeply involved with questions about the humanity and sexuality of the divine as he imagines it. Among his grotesque visions one is of the breasts of Helen, before which a sword wavers and sinks down, unable to assault such beauty – a vision of the 'phallic mother' of Freudian theory, as if the power of the female image must be attacked if it is not to destroy masculinity. The fire that burned Troy shoots from the breasts, scorching the dreamer. Lucretius analyses this as the vengeance of Venus, the return of the sexuality he has too much repressed (60–9). He goes on to split his idea of Venus into the seductress whom Paris chose, and a grand maternal figure like the Venus Generatrix who had appeared as an androgyne in Spenser's *The Faerie Queene* IV, x:

> The all-generating powers and genial heat
> Of Nature, when she strikes through the thick blood
> Of cattle, and light is large, and lambs are glad
> Nosing the mother's udder . . .   (*Lucretius*, 97–100)

Tennyson here restores in an alarming manner the female figure which had been all but excluded in *Ulysses* and *Tiresias*, and in *Tithon* was a limit, of very limited power. Lucretius sees the powers of Venus as coextensive with Nature, and only apparently 'the work of mighty Gods' (102). He needs to imagine Gods as cool and distant, both from the human and from each other, haunting 'The lucid interspace of world and world' (105). This poem is very fully concerned with how the world is, how life is, in terms of the values of sexual relations, of science and religion, and of politics. Following on Hugh Munro's edition of Lucretius in 1864 and followed by John Tyndall's Belfast Address in 1874, it was part of a new interest in Lucretius's atomistic materialism which played a major role in polemics about science and religion. Tennyson may also have felt some parallel between the historical context of Lucretius's work, and contemporary politics. In the lifetime of Lucretius there were civil wars before and after the tyranny of Sulla; the revolt of Spartacus and the gladiators; an external war, and the conspiracy of Catiline – famous examples of civil disorder to the classically educated. When Tennyson was writing the poem in 1865 the second Reform Bill was being discussed, which was nearly to double the size of the electorate: agitation for it involved clashes between the Reform League, which argued for the enfranchisement of the working class on the grounds of its manhood, and the Reform Union, which wanted suffrage for householders only. Though this was hardly civil war, anxiety was intensified by the effects of cholera, bad harvests, and financial disasters.[9] In July came the violent demonstration in Hyde Park. Tennyson feared the premature enfranchisement of the uneducated; he never believed that the country was ready for democracy and though as a peer in 1884 he voted for the third Reform Bill, this was because Gladstone had persuaded him that to delay was more dangerous.

In the poem Lucretius's imagination is violent, and he fears violence, praying Venus to keep Mars 'from the lust of blood / That makes a steaming slaughter-house of Rome' (83–4). Or rather he would pray, on two conditions: if he believed her to be a God rather than a natural force, and if he believed that Gods could 'like ourselves / Touch, and be touched' (80–1). This is the other face of his desire for remoteness. It is the conflict in his ideas about the powers that determine life and thereby offer grounds for human values, that makes *Lucretius* significant for Tennyson's work generally: the chill intact distance commonly associated with masculinity, set against the warmth of accepting natural existence under the sign of the mother. But the conflict is not resolved by Lucretius's philosophic reason. The desirable remoteness of the Gods is felt as cruel parental indifference, and leads to despair; when Venus is prayed to again it is in her role as destroyer, like the Hindu Kali:

> Let her, that is the womb and tomb of all,
> Great Nature, take, and forcing far apart
> Those blind beginnings that have made me man,
> Dash them anew together at her will
> Through all her cycles . . .   (243–7)

Those who wanted rights for women in education, employment and politics could hardly feel grateful for such images of female power. Lucretius stabs himself, taking a woman as his model, Lucretia, who had been raped by the tyrant Tarquin, as he has been invaded by lust from his wife's potion. Her death led to the founding of the Republic, his marks its destruction: a contrast which suggests Tennyson's divided feelings between fear of democracy and allegiance to the old reforming tradition.

Lucretius's suicide takes us back from his soliloquy to its story-frame. In talking about the 'myriad nakedness' that tormented him, Lucretius never mentioned his wife. The frame (which prevents it from being quite strictly a dramatic monologue) does little to evoke sympathy for the wife, but clearly he has been as little capable of touching or being touched as the Gods he imagined. He is called her 'master' twice in the first seven lines, and when she runs to greet him with a kiss he takes 'small notice, or austerely' (8). All his agony has been heard by her as no more than a distant raging, and when she finally runs to him his last command is that she should not care. In his indifference to his relation to her he has been responsible for his own disaster – his wildly fragmented imaginations of female forms and powers begin to restore what his philosophy had left out. *Demeter and Persephone* (1889) completes the imaginative restoration of 'woman-power'. Although Demeter as the archaic energies of the earth is something other than the Gods, her daughter Persephone is both human pain under the fear of death and a prefiguration of Christ who will finally

> reap with me,
> Earth-mother, in the harvest hymns of Earth
> The worship which is Love . . .   (145–7)

The monologues are metaphors for states of mind, divided between rest and motion, soliloquy and narrative, metaphor and
metonymy. Metaphor is equivalent to condensation in Freudian
terminology, and makes one thing signify another in a way that
suggests that unity, the satisfaction of desire, is an attainable state
of being. Metonymy is equivalent to displacement, the substitution of one object for another in an endless chain of desire. *Ulysses*
as rewritten by Tennyson becomes a sign of desire's metonymic
character, of its always being for something else; in the end, for
death as an end to displacement.

When Simeon called himself a sign it was in the theological
sense: he wanted to be a manifestation of divine intervention. The
Idyls reached toward unities – with the beloved, with nature –
and found only echoes and reflections. *Mariana* was enclosed by
signs which produce the poem's mood but are not her perceptions:
'The blue fly sung in the pane' (63) is sheer noise, distracting. By
calling attention to the window itself (surely dusty) it suggests that
it is an obstruction, not something to see the world through: a sign
between. The scepticism in which Tennyson's Romantic idealism
ended anticipates the focus of post-modernist theory on signifying
and representation as problematic. Simeon's theological sense of
sign is ultimately no different, since it suggests the impossibility
of full significance; knowledge of the truth is endlessly deferred, in
spite of his attempts to fix it in time and space.

The Prince's lovely words about golden autumn reeling, which
I have already quoted, strike him with doubt immediately: 'I
waste my heart in signs.' *The Princess* turns from myths to explore,
though fantastically, the relation of sexual desire to the aspirations
of nineteenth-century woman.

3

The Princess: mimicry and metamorphosis

In every land I thought that, more or less,
   The stronger sterner nature overbore
The softer, uncontrolled by gentleness
   As selfish evermore:

And whether there were any means whereby,
   In some far aftertime, the gentler mind
Might reassume its just and full degree
   Of rule among mankind.
                    (*A Dream of Fair Women*, manuscript, 1832,
                                       Ricks, *Poems*, p. 442)

I dwell in Possibility –
A fairer House than Prose –   (Emily Dickinson, *c.* 1862)

The Princess is a hermaphrodite among poems, a thing that doesn't
easily fit into a category, and critics have been unhappy with it
from the beginning. Tennyson subtitled it 'A Medley'; it has been
accused of evasiveness about gender, poetry and power. It is de-
viant, challenging habits of reading and thinking; it is also
devious, and in more than one mind. Tennyson wanted it to
'enter in at all doors', and this implies commitment to what the
poem has to say, but what that might be is complicated by the way
it is addressed both to misogynists and to women wanting respect.
What persuades one set of readers still exacerbates the sensibilities
of others. It is difficult to fix a proper reading for a story whose
teller says

And I, betwixt them both, to please them both,
And yet to give the story as it rose,
I moved as in a strange diagonal,
And maybe neither pleased myself nor them.
                              (Conclusion, 25–8)

Both a will to please and a consciousness of inevitable dissatisfac-
tion are aspects of *The Princess* in the line it runs from male mocking to female 'realism', from burlesque to 'quite a solemn close'.
An important guide to its arguments comes in the Conclusion.

The Tory member's elder son, one of the story-telling party, blesses God for the channel that divides England from France, whose republics and revolutions he compares to Princess Ida's dream of developing women's powers: the 'narrow seas' keep foreign theory out. The poem's chief speaker disagrees:

> 'Have patience,' I replied, 'ourselves are full
> Of social wrong; and maybe wildest dreams
> Are but the needful prelude of the truth:
> For me, the genial day, the happy crowd,
> The sport half-science, fill me with a faith.'

(Conclusion, 72–6)

The story of Princess Ida is supposed to be told in turn by seven undergraduates during a public holiday. In the Conclusion the story we have read is about to be turned into the poem by the chief speaker: what we have read does not properly exist yet, everything is to be begun again, repeated with a difference. Although the story was not originally a single-voiced polemic, the final teller takes the part of the Prince throughout, so that his idealism about women's development has most authority. The argument of *The Princess* is related to debates in Parliament and outside about the status of women, especially married women; it displays the progressive attitudes which made radical women of the period quote *A Dream of Fair Women* (1832) in support of their case, but it also reveals anxiety about the consequences for male self-esteem and emotional dependency. It is a political poem and also, like the Idyls, a poem of love. The attempt to resolve these two motives in the final marriage produces some of the problems in interpreting the poem. The idealization of love – by Arthur Hallam, by Tennyson in poems of the 1830s and 40s – can appear in *The Princess* not as a liberation from social conventions and economic constraints, but as a limit placed on women.

Nevertheless *The Princess* is more concerned to open possibilities than to impose limits. 'It seems you love to cheat yourself with words' is Ida's comment on the Prince at his most idealistic, and he assents: 'I waste my heart in signs' (VII, 314, 358). This uncertainty about the world and its representations is everywhere in Tennyson's writing: a letter to Emily Sellwood from the late 1830s when he was beginning work on *The Princess* is instructive about its mood:

Annihilate within yourself these two dreams of Space and Time. To me often the far-off world seems nearer than the present, for in the present is always something unreal and indistinct, but the other seems a good solid planet, rolling round its green hills and paradises to the harmony of more steadfast laws. There steam up from about me mists of weakness, or sin, or despondency, and roll between me and the far planet, but it is there still.   (*Memoir* I, 171–2)

Mere day-dreaming or a 'needful prelude'? When Tennyson added the Prince's strange seizures that interrupt the narrative in the edition of 1851 it was not to complicate the character's psychology or to show him as defective, but to guide reading of the poem by a sense that present conditions are not fixed, but could be different: what is present to experience can feel more strange than the imaginary. If this view is accepted, these moments in the poem can work to link wild dreams with truth, with the possibility at least of changing perceptions.

A reading of this odd poem does need to know who its friends were – that is, from which nineteenth-century readers it was asking for acceptance, and to what kinds of writing it was related. Its noble characters, quest for the love of a lady and final tournament derive from Tennyson's interest in medieval romance. John Killham, in his pioneering and still very useful study of *The Princess*, showed how much this interest was a 'reflection of the age' – exemplified in the tournament staged at the Scottish baronial castle of Eglinton in 1839, where one of three daughters of the playwright Sheridan was 'Queen of Beauty'; her sister Caroline Norton played a significant role in struggles for legal change in the status of women. The 'frame' of *The Princess* and its wonderful prospects – stormscapes, starscapes, riverscapes, skyscapes and seascapes – relate it to the English Idyls, a form which opens up a pleasurable space in which possibilities can be entertained, possibilities of love, work and knowledge, the grounds of present and future value.

One source for the story is Shakespeare's *Love's Labour's Lost* (1598). Killham was sceptical about the need to find sources for the story, but this was the by-product of his honourable demonstration that it needed none beyond the contemporary concern with women's education and rights. I have no doubt that *Love's Labour's Lost* was on Tennyson's mind, and comparison of the play and the poem is interesting. In Shakespeare's early comedy the King of Navarre retires with some of his gentlemen to study for three years, refusing the company of women as a distraction from serious study. At once his refuge is intruded upon, and he is reminded of the problems it creates in the light of other duties: the Princess of France with her ladies arrives on a diplomatic mission for her father. The comedy ends with the father's death, and the ladies with whom the gentlemen have fallen in love themselves impose a year-long separation: the king is forbidden that which he had sought to exclude. In Tennyson's story Ida has set up a women's college on the border of her father's kingdom and barred men from entry, refusing to recognize her betrothal as an infant to the Prince of the neighbouring kingdom.

When the Canadian S. E. Dawson edited *The Princess* in 1882 Tennyson approved of his commentary and noted 'if women ever were to play such freaks, the burlesque and the tragic might go hand in hand' (Ricks, *Poems*, p. 743). This does not simply mean that Tennyson thought female separatism freakish; he may be remembering the end of the King of Navarre's 'freak' in loss and separation. The practice of segregating men for their education has a long history whose effects are still felt. One working title for the poem was 'The New University' but Tennyson did not work much at the newness: the curriculum and institutional practices of Ida's college remain close to those he had known at Cambridge. As Elizabeth Barrett commented to Mary Russell Mitford in May, 1848:

What woman will tell the great poet that Mary Wollstonecraft herself never dreamed of setting up collegiate states, proctordoms, and the rest, which is a worn-out plaything in the hands of one sex already, and need not be *transferred* in order to be proved ridiculous?[1]

But Tennyson respected women's claims to educational equality. He was to sign Emily Davies's memorial of 1865–7 on the need to provide for the higher education of women, and some elements in the frame of *The Princess* were borrowed from a novel, *Eustace Conway*, by another worker in that cause, F. D. Maurice – for example, the name Vivyan, the touchy aunt, the independent-minded daughter ready to change places with the undergraduate son.

Love's Labour's Lost was first performed as a Christmas entertainment at court, and although the frame of *The Princess* is set on a summer holiday its idea of telling a story from one speaker to another derives from a Christmas game (Prologue, 176–216). We are reminded of Shakespearean comedy again when the aunt, whose bid for a heroic and solemn story has been laughed at, tells the young people to do it 'As you will; / . . . or what you will'. *As You Like It* and *Twelfth Night: or What You Will* are remembered there: both involve women dressed as men, reversals of power and final reconciliations resulting from such reversals. The pleasure of turning the tables and imagining how things could be different derives both from the Idyls and from Shakespeare's comedies: Christopher Ricks seems surprised when he calls the style 'liberated, almost sportive' (*Tennyson*, p. 197), but it is the right one for this mood and not a refusal to take the issues seriously. The aunt asks 'Why not a summer's as a winter's tale?', and it has been suggested that when Ida falls in love (VII, 145–7) the final act of *A Winter's Tale* is recalled, when Queen Hermione, supposed a statue, comes to life again. Another late romance which meant much to Tennyson, *Cymbeline*, is also something of a medley, its questionable moral psychology and improbable events culminating in a last scene of reunion and rejoicing against the odds. The relation between *The Princess* and Shakespeare, however, is different from that between *The Princess* and Tennyson's own Idyls. The frame of *The Princess* is similar to the Idyls, with their scene-setting and prospects and their juxtapositions of different points of view, whereas the comedies are gestured toward allusively, their themes and spirit called to mind. One structural element which may have been encouraged by *Love's Labour's Lost* is the insertion of the songs between the parts of the poem in the third edition of 1850, though Tennyson said he had always meant to put them in. He said they were 'the best interpreters' of the poem because they linked all the parts by reminding the reader of the child. If we think of these songs in comparison to those in *Love's Labour's Lost* there is a striking difference: while Shakespeare's are all songs of seasonality and fertility, Tennyson's are mainly of loss and separation, reminders of familial anxiety not of satisfaction or community. Like the Prince's seizures they call the linear narrative in question, bringing in uncertainties.

Another influence, one which Killham did explore, was that of Eastern tales of women distinguished for wit, wisdom and beauty: Noureddin the Fair Persian, and Turandot, who warded off suitors by setting them riddles to solve. Ida with her attendant tamed leopards is very much the Eastern Queen of romance, dark against the Prince's fairness, even though her educational scheme is Western and classically based. Eastern here signifies warmer, more exaltedly erotic, like Mediterranean art: Tennyson might be remembering Titian's *Venus del Pardo*. This mild exoticism was developed during composition: the Northern name Eric for Ida's brother was changed to Arac, and their father's land was originally industrial, with smoke, pistons, cranes:

> Ringing of blocks and throb of hammers mixt
> With water split and split on groaning wheels.

(Manuscript, Ricks, Poems, p. 754)

The final orientation works with the idyllic, chivalric and Shakespearean elements to suggest that the story is not of something within experience, though something like it could be. As in historical or science fiction, an alien place and time is used to explore contemporary concerns freely, deferring commonsensical objections. To make Ida princess in a modern industrial state would have brought her closer to Victoria, and further from the aspirations of middle-class women.

An article by Leigh Hunt in 1839–40, which Killham quotes, comments on the new popularity of the *Arabian Nights* at a time of scientific and technological innovation: no contradiction in this, he says, not because fantasy is needed to compensate for mechanization, but because science is romantic. Scientists themselves expressed a sense of imaginative wonder, like that of the speaker in *Locksley Hall*, 'nourishing a youth sublime / With the fairy tales of science, and the long result of Time' (11–12). I have already noted how Tennyson's response to the tracts of time and space opened up by geology and astronomy was to view it all as if from a magic carpet. The presence of scientific experiment, observation and theory in both the frame and the story of *The Princess* 'reflects the age' in its looking backwards and forwards, and also says that wild dreams can become truth: science is an encouraging model for social and political change. Because of Tennyson's later fearfulness about such change it is important to note the broad reformism felt in his poetry of the 1830s and 40s: power should not fester in the hands of few but 'still should change and fleet' (*Hail Briton!*, 31); it is violence that he fears: 'How loathsome are the works of rage' (125). This is not restricted to fear of popular violence, but also can be seen in revisions relating to military action, as in the addition to Part VI of *The Princess* in 1850 of the line 'I trust that there is no one hurt to death'.[2] Tenderness about bodily harm was extended in old age to disapproval of blood sports; he did not actively participate in them in earlier life. The whole range of concerns connects back to Shelley's radicalism and forward to feminist campaigns, for example against vivisection at the end of the century. Like his Princess, Tennyson opposed vivisection, and on other issues too his poem shares common ground with the published views of feminists.

Radical arguments of the early nineteenth century compared the situation of women with that of slaves and of the working class. Tennyson had celebrated the abolition of slavery in an unpublished poem of 1832–4, *O mother Britain lift thou up*; women who had been active for abolition turned their organized energies to rights in education and employment, marriage and divorce. The whole question of women's status was under discussion, even though legal reform was very slow; struggles about property and divorce prepared the way for the suffrage campaign. In common law a married woman had no identity distinct from her husband's, and any money she earned was his property, regardless of his earnings or behaviour. The 1857 Divorce Act was the first recognition by Parliament that in certain cases married women should have control over their property. However the passing of this Act was one way of postponing the Married Women's Property Bill, which in its effective form, giving married women the same rights and responsibilities as the unmarried, was not passed for another twenty-five years. In 1857 arguments against this Bill were that it would place women in a 'strong-minded and independent position' and 'give a wife all the distinct rights of citizenship'.[3]

When Tennyson began work on *The Princess* in 1839 this would seem like a very early entry into such debates for someone of his class, with family connections to the established church, law and politics. Undoubtedly his sensitivity to his mother's experience influenced him. In *Isabel* (1830) he expressed the paradox of her saving strength in a marriage where she was officially subordinate:

> A clear stream flowing with a muddy one,
>   Till in its onward current it absorbs
>   With swifter movement and in purer light
>   The vexèd eddies of its wayward brother:
>   A leaning and upbearing parasite,
>   Clothing the stem, which else had fallen quite . . .(30–5)

But words he gives to Ida suggest that he had some knowledge of what radical journals had to say on the subject of women. In Part V Ida, faced with military force from the Prince's father and appealing to her brother for support, gives an impassioned panorama of women's subjection in many times and places, ending with the reform agitation of the 1830s:

> equal baseness lived in sleeker times
> With smoother men: the old leaven leavened all:
> Millions of throats would bawl for civil rights,
> No woman named: therefore I set my face
> Against all men, and lived but for mine own. (V, 375–9)

This kind of point was made against the internal power structure of the London Socialists in 1840, and by Owenite women in *The Crisis* in 1833, *The Pioneer* in 1834 and *The New Moral World* in 1843:

Have any of the self-named reforming parties, so vociferous now in England for their own rights, given a single thought to, or shown any desire for . . . change in this *Helot* condition of their country women?[4]

Ida ranks reformist Britons, proud of their freedom and liberalism, with their bugbears the Russian bully and the Oriental despot. As a figure in a fantasy she can speak words which Tennyson might have paused over had he represented her as a woman of the contemporary world throughout. This is not a matter of timidity, since the words are spoken and not undermined: the aim is to get people to read and consider what they dismiss out of hand in another, more easily placed, context. *The Princess* slides from a lighter tone, seductively confusing to fixed positions, to one that is more serious. It is a tactical move, rather than a shift in Tennyson's own position, as Killham suggested.

One element in the multiple readership imagined for *The Princess* can be represented by Edward Bull, the fat curate of *Edwin Morris*, whose views are echoed by the Prince's father. A living representative of such attitudes was J. M. Kemble, an Anglo-Saxon scholar and member of the famous theatrical family, who was both beloved and tolerated by Tennyson's circle of friends as an entertaining enthusiast. A radical traditionalist, like those who appealed to the days before the 'Norman yoke' as the source of English liberty, he insisted on native and original precedents for his beliefs. In 1838–9 he was working on questions of marriage and the family for *The Saxons in England* (1849), arguing that the rights of the father were traditionally paramount:

To the English principle I am bound to give my adhesion, inasmuch as the natural and original social law can recognise none but the father, either in the generation or in the subsequent rule, of the family: whatever the alleviation the practices of chivalry, the worship of the Virgin mother, and the Christian doctrine of the equality of man and woman before God, may have introduced, the original feeling is on the father's side, and the foundations of our law are based upon the all-sufficiency of his right. A woman is in the mund or keeping of a man; society exists for men only, that is, for women merely as far as they are represented by a man.[5]

Kemble was a bitter opponent of the Custody of Infants Act (1839), which offered separated or divorced women limited rights of access to their children. The moving spirit behind the Bill was Caroline Norton, the writer, whose estranged husband claimed her earnings and made access to their sons either distressing or impossible. The distress of Psyche in *The Princess* when Ida keeps her daughter from her may have been coloured by Caroline Norton's dramatization of a mother's feelings in her pamphlets and court appearances. Kemble persistently vilified Mrs Norton both in print and in correspondence with friends, regarding the Bill as a charter for libertine women; her public advocacy of her rights and her independent status in London's artistic society were both causes of his aversion. Tennyson shared some of these feelings; he shuddered to have her seated next to him at a dinner party given by Samuel Rogers in 1845, where she was the one woman among seven men, although after his marriage they were on visiting terms.

In one letter Kemble called Caroline Norton 'our would be Aspasia of modern times' – Aspasia had been hostess to literary and philosophical society in Athens, the mistress of Pericles, and Kemble uses the allusion to suggest that the Bill had only been heard because of 'favours' promised to those who promoted it. He deploys a whole range of images of 'woman-power', including Bradamante, Ariosto's woman warrior; Spenser's version of this type, Britomart, is mentioned with enthusiasm in the Prologue to *The Princess*. He refers to the St Simonian Female Messiah, and calls intellectual development the 'Anti-Christ of the Women of our day', 'the half education of the Understanding, which is preeminently the distinctive and characteristic of men'; souls as well as bodies are sexed, and the perfect humanity of the androgyne can only be reconstructed by the marriage of these utterly diverse sexes. I think that the early stages of *The Princess* were coloured by argument with Kemble, who was a great admirer of *The Gardener's Daughter* and wished that Tennyson might be circumcised for cutting it. He was not censorious about sexuality in writing: what enraged him was the intrusion of a woman into bachelor enclaves where men could happily engage in manly activities such as writing and politics, and fantasize about those so crucially different feminine beings. In contradiction, Tennyson's 'university of Women' promoted the intellectual development of women as a necessity. However one virtue of the all-women's college from a masculine-conservative point of view is that it rules out Aspasia, wheeling and dealing among men and using her sex to treacherous advantage. This role model is deliberately deprecated when Melissa, daughter of one of Ida's mentors, says she will not betray a trust 'for all Aspasia's cleverness' (II, 323). Though the narrative situation at this point makes the question of fidelity or treachery a ticklish one, the poem as a whole envisages women's development as taking place either in separatism or safely bonded into a marital situation. Although Ida begins by setting up a women-only college as if in defiance of Kemble's men-only society, in the end her aspirations for women are properly endorsed by her husband-to-be.

Before turning to the poem in more detail I want to note a particular masculine bias which has had considerable influence in distorting response to the poem. In 'The "High-born maiden" Symbol in Tennyson' Lionel Stevenson includes *The Princess* in a series of poems which he says project the artist's 'anima', the 'feminine principle' of Jungian psychoanalysis (and also in alchemy). In the first phase the melancholy maiden of Shelley's *To a Skylark* is used to explore psycho-aesthetic problems, as in *The Lady of Shalott*; in the second this figure is condemned for proud self-sufficiency, as in *The Palace of Art*; ultimately it is used as a mere narrative device, devoid of anxiety. Stevenson puts *The Princess* in the second phase: Ida's 'intellectual arrogance' must be 'broken down by love and all the demands of practical life'. Fitting *The Princess* into this pattern has just suited those who see Ida as 'warped' and 'obsessive', and her ambitions for women as an 'unnatural and humourless rebellion', laying claim to 'power grotesquely inappropriate to womanhood'.[6] However the poem does not present her enterprise as essentially negative: she gains the passionate advocacy of the Prince, as well as the rather spluttering support of her brother, a prototype of the 'very strong man Kwasind':

> And there's a downright honest meaning in her;
> She flies too high, she flies too high! and yet
> She asked but space and fairplay for her scheme . . .
> I thought her half-right talking of her wrongs;
> I say she flies too high, 'sdeath! what of that?
> I take her for the flower of womankind,

And so I often told her, right or wrong,
And, Prince, she can be sweet to those she loves . . .
                                   (V, 270–2, 275–9)

To accept Stevenson's symbolic pattern for *The Princess* is to
travesty it, and to ignore what Tennyson was attempting with the
woman as speaking subject as well as the object of desire. Ida is
not a projection of masculine 'anima' but an attempt to put the
point of view of a woman with a strong will directed to a noble
cause. Her justified satirical animus against men's treatment of
women builds to an admirable direct assertion of women's
autonomy, of the 'living will' which Tennyson, as in *In Memoriam*
CXXXI, so much desired:

> Would this same mock-love, and this
> Mock-Hymen were laid up like winter bats,
> Till all men grew to rate us at our worth,
> Not vassals to be beat, nor pretty babes
> To be dandled, no, but living wills, and sphered
> Whole in ourselves and owed to none.   (IV, 125–30)

In Part IV when the Prince rescues Ida from the river he holds in
his arms, he says 'The weight of all the hopes of half the world'
(166). She has said herself that she wants to work for 'our dear
sisters' liberties', that 'their welfare is a passion to us' (III, 271,
264). She may be seen as a monster but she accepts this as the consequence of the cramping and dwarfing of 'normal' women (III,
259–64). The Prince at the end pledges his support, taking up her
image but substituting 'godlike' for 'monstrous':

> Henceforth thou hast a helper, me, that know
> The woman's cause is man's: they rise or sink
> Together, dwarfed or godlike, bond or free . . .
> If she be small, slight-natured, miserable,
> How shall men grow? but work no more alone!
> Our place is much: as far as in us lies
> We two will serve them both in aiding her –
> Will clear away the parasitic forms
> That seem to hold her up but drag her down –
> Will leave her space to burgeon out of all
> Within her – let her make herself her own
> To give or keep . . .   (VII, 242–4, 249–57)

Lines 249–50 suggest the 1842 report on the employment of
women and children in mines, and the commentaries of Harriet
Martineau and Anna Jameson, which juxtaposed the notion of

woman's influence in the home to the facts of women's waged work in conditions likely to damage their health and that of growing and unborn generations: while identifying the interests of men with those of women, the Prince also acknowledges in lines 256–7 the force of Ida's desire not to be 'owed' to anyone (IV, 130), keeping a sense of possibilities for growth as yet unknown, and awareness of how frustrating some ways of 'elevating woman' could be. While he goes on to preserve some masculine/feminine oppositions, his speech is specifically thought through and open to what women may want – the poem's distancing and play has opened up a space for such thinking.

The Prince at first thought Ida in error to the extent that she did not recognize her superiority to other women (III, 92–6). Ida does not isolate herself as a wise woman in an ivory tower, or set riddles to show off her cleverness: she works with and for 'our dear sisters'. But that phrase has the superior unctuousness of a vicar carrying on about brotherhood: the intention is right, the situation is not. Sisterhood is not well represented. There is a gulf between Ida and her two lecturers, Blanche and Psyche, and the students, who have chosen to be there but are described by the Prince as distinctly passive, doves to Psyche's falcon, while the older ones mutter against their seclusion from men and domestic authority (II, 87–91, 438–42). The only student singled out is Melissa and she is almost immediately involved with Psyche in deceiving her mother, Blanche, and Ida, about the presence of the Prince and his friends disguised as students. This gulf is produced by Tennyson's way of thinking, characteristic of his generation, in terms of leadership by an intellectual elite, a responsible class to show the way, and this affects the frame also.

The festival in the Prologue to *The Princess* is based on a particular occasion, 6 July 1842, when Edmund Lushington threw open his grounds at Park House to the local Mechanics' Institute. In the poem Sir Walter Vivian, 'a great broad-shouldered genial Englishman', experimental farmer, magistrate and patron of 'some thirty charities' including the Mechanics' Institute, has opened his grounds to his tenants and beneficiaries. The whole day with its instructive pastimes is embraced and framed by his patronage (Prologue, 1–6; Conclusion, 80–105). Those enjoying it are as remote from the party of undergraduates, friends of the son of the house, as her students are from Ida. The disillusioning distance between the ideals of Ida and the Prince (or of Leonard in *The Golden Year*) and their realization, between the present

94

moment and the egalitarian future, is equivalent to the gap between patrons and beneficiaries, the teachers and the multitude. In *Love's Labour's Lost* much of the comedy came from the contrast of court and country characters, mutually mocking. *The Princess* in frame and story is essentially concerned with a single class, the educated middle class and gentry, although, as in folk tales, in the story they're called Kings and Princesses. There is no space for the old comedy of gentle and simple; the lectures and discussions are mostly straight-faced, not mockeries of learned fashions as in Shakespeare's play.

The Prologue presents us with a jumble: the crowd in the sun, above it the more secluded Abbey ruins where the tale is told, the Greek-styled house packed with the spoils of time and empire, relics of chivalry and prehistory. It is like a game with fragmentary clues, whose solution begins to be revealed in Psyche's lecture on development (II, 101–64). Some of the elements are pieced together again at the heart of the story, in the transition from Part III to IV. Ida and the Prince (still incognito) are on a geological expedition in the hills, hammering at 'shale and hornblende, rag and trap and tuff, / Amygdaloid and trachyte' (III, 344–5). They have just set up a silken pavilion which has embroidered on it the triumph of Corinna over Pindar in a poetry competition. Part III ends with a wonderfully cadenced personification of the sun, following all those stony names:

> till the Sun
> Grew broader toward his death, and fell, and all
> The rosy heights came out above the lawns.   (345–7)

Ida, who has just spoken rather poetically herself of 'soft white vapour' streaking towers built to the sun, begins Part IV in pedantic contrast:

> There sinks the nebulous star we call the Sun,
> If that hypothesis of theirs be sound.

Here she is rather like the academics of *Love's Labour's Lost*, and the effect is pertinent to the whole scene: her image is not so vulnerable that it can't carry humour as well as nobility. An idyllic poetical contest follows, in the shade of Corinna's pavilion, the note for which has been struck in that collision and fusion of scientific terminology and classically poetic language: a tour-de-force to show what can be done in poetry, where differences can work together. In Part III Ida and the Prince had been enjoying the pleasures of intellectual intercourse, discussing the exclusion of vivisection and therefore anatomy from her curriculum, and the problems of this for the study of medecine (III, 288–303), as well as metaphysics, where Ida's view that Time is an illusion produced by limited perception echoes Tennyson's letter to Emily Sellwood:

> But if the shadow will we work, and mould
> The woman to the fuller day.   (314–15)

The poem's concern with illusion and development persists within the contest of science and poetry, preparing for the Prince's final vision of Ida's dream, the free intellectual development of women, as the last and finest stage of human evolution (VII, 239–80).

At the end of Part III the poet is represented by a 'woman-conqueror', girt with florid maidens, while the geologists are pretty little things:

> Many a little hand
> Glanced like a touch of sunshine on the rocks,
> Many a light foot shone like a jewel set
> In the dark crag . . .   (338–41)

These images reverse expected associations, but the oppositions on which such reversals depend vanish in 'Tears, idle tears', the first contender in the singing-match of Part IV, as they do in the lyric set between the two Parts, 'The splendour falls on castle walls.' The latter is a moment of poise between the two versions of the sunset, of outgoing and receding, between retrospect and prospect: the theme of the child and development is tenuously maintained in the contrast between the echoes of the bugle dying but also 'thinner, clearer, farther going!', and the human echoes which 'roll from soul to soul, / And grow for ever and for ever.' 'Tears, idle tears', with its sensations of rising and sinking, waking and dying, is Tennyson's finest evocation of purely aesthetic emotion, which explores Hallam's idea in his essay 'On Sympathy', that it is to the pastness of what we remember that we owe the pleasure of remembering it.[7] It is challenged by Ida's heroic optimism as to the superiority of action over sensation, another of Tennyson's voices from the Idyls, and itself shadowed by acknowledgement of mortality:

> While down the streams that float us each and all
> To the issue, goes, like glittering bergs of ice,
> Throne after throne, and molten on the waste

Becomes a cloud: for all things serve their time
Toward that great year of equal mights and rights,
Nor would I fight with iron laws, in the end
Found golden: let the past be past . . .   (IV, 52–8)

As far as argument goes the contest is evenly matched; Ida is not
necessarily meant to have the worst of it, nor is she humourless:
her mood during this game is between amusement and 'shining
expectation'. At this moment, the happiest in the poem, her
peroration on women's 'living wills' is answered by Cyril's
'careless tavern-catch / Of Moll and Meg.' The Prince's shocked
and chivalrous reaction, 'Forebear, Sir', betrays how they have
been deceiving Ida, and leads to the final contest of arms.

I have plunged into the middle of the story to show how well the
famous 'bits of good poetry' in *The Princess* can work significantly
in the narrative. But there are undoubtedly problems with the
relation between narrative, lyric and discourse, between light-
hearted eclecticism and serious meaning. Ultimately the poem
does not simply assert or reverse conventional attitudes to gender,
it takes risks and explores both gender and genre, and this inevitably produces real embarrassments. In the return to the frame
between Parts IV and V Lilia rejects the 'raillery, or grotesque,
or false sublime' of the story so far (so that the poem contains its
own self-criticism), and calls for a change of tune from the next
teller: 'make us all we would be, great and good'. We have to
assume, then, that one of the original story-tellers was responsible
for the mock-respect paid to Ida's laws by the local inn-keeper: at
least his attitude makes sure that one perennial response to
changes in role for women is not suppressed:

> He always made a point to post with mares;
> His daughter and his housemaid were the boys:
> The land, he understood, for miles about
> Was tilled by women; all the swine were sows,
> And all the dogs –   (I, 187–91)

We are kept reminded that the heroes are 'unmanned' by women's
dress, and this makes Cyril's insistence on his sex, as he falls for
Psyche, feel very peculiar:

> With me, Sir, entered in the bigger boy,
> The Head of all the golden-shafted firm,
> The long-limbed lad that had a Psyche too;
> He cleft me through the stomacher . . .
>   (II, 382–5)

He means Cupid, of course, but his brazenly phallic language exposes the awkwardness of the poem's romance form: young man seeks beloved, overcoming an obstacle (in this case herself) to win her. The Prince is flanked by two companions to make up a composite figure of manhood – the trio of dreamer, man of action and joker so often found in adventure stories (here, Florian is colourless while Cyril grabs both the roles of manly man and joker). The Prince as dreamer of the poem's ideals is also the artist lover of an Idyl. This is signified by his springtime amorousness and the 'feminine' tenderness of his appearance, blue-eyed 'with lengths of yellow ringlet like a girl' (I, 1–3), just like the sunny rings of girlish curls of the lover in the manuscript of *The Gardener's Daughter*. His sensitive respect for women is in strong contrast to his bullish father. He deceives Ida, however, and critics such as John Killham and D. S. Hair have been quick to call his entry into her grounds a symbolic rape, penetrating the forbidden place.

Ida also has two companions. Blanche is a crude stereotype, an aging woman with dyed hair, jealous and fretful after an unhappy marriage (III, 63–8). She is treated as if she were a villain (like the Queen in *Cymbeline*) but since she has no crucial role in the plot she obviously functions as a warning negative image of intellectual ambition in women. It could be argued that she balances Cyril's crude manliness, but though he really does do harm he is exculpated as she is not (IV, 224–38). Psyche, also a widow and Florian's sister, is an able lecturer but goes to pieces in the face of the masculine invasion. That Ida is flanked by this pair tends to suggest that her quality is exceptional, no guide to other women, and this is what the Prince had argued about her (III, 92–6). He is much better served: his friends give him a base in masculinity, while intimating that this does not exclude gentleness and flexibility. Florian joins with Melissa in nursing and love, Cyril admires Psyche's intelligence as well as her fortune, and shows feeling for her child. Ida may sing of 'living wills' but both Psyche and the Prince fear her own 'iron will' (II, 185–7; VI, 102). In this respect *The Princess* has a clear masculine bias. It is common in anti-feminist arguments to say that the exceptional case cannot be a model for the majority of women. Writers like George Eliot and Elizabeth Barrett Browning were very conscious of being exceptional. Tennyson makes the Prince more advanced and egalitarian in his closing speech on the subject (VII, 239–79), but opposed to this discourse are the more habitual assumptions which dictate the pattern of how Ida is related to other women in the poem.

In the Prologue, which mediates between these romance figures and the nineteenth-century readership, two women are singled out: Lilia the daughter of the house, 'wild with sport / Half child half woman', and the unmarried aunt to whom she looks for guidance; there is no mother, nor is there any Blanche. The aunt hopes for great things from the tale and from the day: 'An universal culture for the crowd, / And all things great.' It is Lilia who catches up the narrator's enthusiasm for the woman warrior, who chafes at conventions and wishes for a college education to match her brother's. There is much that is bantering, of the 'little hands' and 'light feet' variety, but the narrator is sensitive to the feelings of the aunt in the undergraduates' company, and of Lilia as she shakes aside 'The hand that played the patron with her curls.' The songs between the Parts are supposed to be sung by all the women there, 'Like linnets in the pauses of the wind.' This division of labour has been taken as reproducing traditional conventions of the feminine and the masculine; some French feminist theory also defines the feminine as rhythmic, and located in the gaps of masculine narrative or discourse. *The Princess* is not single-minded about this. It is Ida who rejects the siren voice of lyricism, 'So sweet a voice and vague, fatal to men', for 'A trumpet in the distance pealing news' (IV, 46, 63). Two lines of the Prince's final vision of men growing more like women and women growing more like men can be read as meaning that 'woman' would remain essentially musical, 'man' verbal, but this is not absolutely clear:

> Till at the last she set herself to man,
> Like perfect music unto noble words.   (VII, 269–70)

The syntax suggests that she is 'perfect music' and man 'noble words', but semantically it is words which are set to music rather than the other way round, so that there is half a chance of keeping words for women; even syntactically it is 'she' who is the active subject of the sentence. The lack of authoritative clarity in these lines suggests the Prince's liberal pluralism, which can equally be read as evasiveness. Later in his speech his ideal memory of his mother has her girdled with the music of male minds; and in the Conclusion, 13–21, the women's singing is said to have changed the tone of the narrative; it is they who are called 'realists', meaning those who believe ideas can be made real.

Ida is a projection of Lilia's desires, and the support she wins from her brother alters the attitude of the brother in the frame, Walter, who had thought it funny to imagine his little sister as

'some great Princess, six feet high, / Grand, epic, homicidal'
(218–19) but who in the Conclusion says 'I wish she had not
yielded' (5). Her father Gama is all contradiction, both 'dry' and
'oily', and 'not like a king' (I, 116–17, 162). His fiercest critic as
he dodges responsibility is the Prince's father, and as the nature
of Ida and Arac is credited to their dead mother, Gama lacks all
paternal authority: the way he is presented tends to suggest that
Ida has been spoiled, although readers need not accept the other
king's view that men are to blame if wives and daughters get out
of hand. Gama's evasiveness, neither supporting nor diplo-
matically managing the consequences of Ida's enterprise, leads
directly to the Prince's fraud and the other king's use of force. The
Prince, at odds with his father from first to last, makes his saintly
mother the authority for his ideals: she was typically feminine as
the father is typically masculine:

> Not learned save in gracious household ways,
> Not perfect, nay, but full of tender wants,
> No Angel, but a dearer being, all dipt
> In Angel instincts, breathing Paradise,
> Interpreter between the gods and men,
> Who looked all native to her place, and yet
> On tiptoe seemed to touch upon a sphere
> Too gross to tread . . .   (VII, 299–306)

Tennyson here reverses the hierarchy of Milton's *Paradise Lost*,
where Adam was the mediator between God and Eve. It would be
improper to ignore the tribute paid to Tennyson's mother and to
the historical role of women in mothering and domestic work. But
Ida, however broken-down and sorrowful at this point, is rather
quick to dissociate herself from the Prince's emblem of Woman's
influence. And indeed most women want to tread on the ground
if they can.

Gama as a type of evasiveness presents the damaging other face
of open-mindedness. Though the poem promotes the development
of women's powers, its concern with sexuality and 'childward
care' sets limits to such development. I do not want to evade the
implications of how the poem comes to its conclusion. A draft for
the Prince's speech in Part VII sets to one side the lonely ideal of
the androgyne, as a celibate; the omission of these lines from the
published poem suggests that they were getting Tennyson into
deep waters as to the relation between the ideal human being and
sexuality:

And if aught be compromising in itself
The man, the woman, let it sit [apart]
Godlike, alone, or only rapt on heaven –
What need for such to wed? or if there be
Men–women, let them wed with women–men
And make a proper marriage . . .   (Ricks, *Poems*, p. 838)

When Ida kissed the Prince 'Her falser self slipt from her like a
robe, / And left her woman' (VII, 146–7): all heroic models strip-
ped from the naked truth of the body. The poem itself is not quite
truthful: it wants the image of undressing at the bedside but does
not fully admit this, meaning instead that Ida's essence is contained in her being a woman, physically and emotionally. What
of the Prince? After the kiss he lapses back into a passive trance,
observing Ida.

Ida and the Prince have been presented as opposites rather than
as variably different: she the sterner, he the gentler. She speaks for
science, he for poetry; within poetry she has the heroic voice, he
the lyric; she stands for social purpose and the work of the world,
he for love. His feminine values triumph over her masculine victory in battle: her sanctuary is violated not by force but by the
need to nurse the wounded men. His voice takes over to argue her
cause: he becomes masculine like her, as she becomes 'woman'.

The odd heroine or woman of power has never been a cultural
problem, and female figures have regularly been used to represent
human ideals. Like Tennyson in *A Dream of Fair Women*, Ida could
summon up many biblical and classical models, although the
philosopher Hypatia, the poet Sappho and modern examples such
as Mary Wollstonecraft are absent: the physical assertion of
defiance and power dominates her roll-call. The Prince's
transvestism remains a problem; that the poem risks its hero looking silly is as much a virtue, though an embarrassing one, as its
noble representation of Ida and her arguments. The disrobing of
Ida to naked woman, however, is not equally matched; the Prince
changes his dress for armour, cased in triple-manliness like Tennyson's image of the androgynous poet in those unpublished 1839
lines which are my opening epigraph. It is worth tracing just how
this is represented, because cross-dressing, and by extension
change of dress as a metamorphosis of the self, can be read as
simply ridiculous, whereas for this poem a sense of difficulties
encountered is more productive. The same potential for misreading through insistence on already existing categories is present in
Tennyson's re-visions of inherited myths. The back gates of Ida's

college bear the image of Actaeon, the hunter of game, who was metamorphosed into his prey the stag when he saw Diana the goddess of chastity bathing. Here he becomes part of the enclosing ironwork, his antlers spiking the top (IV, 182–8). 'Man is the hunter; woman is his game' (V, 147), the Prince's father's cliché, is reversed in the myth. In *Tennyson and Tradition* Robert Pattison comments that it is as well the Prince is escaping Ida's college, 'for Actaeon's fate awaits him if he remains' (p. 97). But at this point the Prince is not escaping but deliberately returning to explain himself; like Actaeon he regrets 'His rash intrusion, manlike' (IV, 186). However worthy this may be he is still dressed as a woman and still finds it all fun, dodging Ida's guards among roses and fountains to the bubbling of nightingales: 'secret laughter tickled all my soul' (IV, 241–51). He is a schoolboy, ready to own up. When he returns to his father's camp he is suddenly seen from a manly point of view, 'a draggled mawkin' (V, 25).

Ida's brothers share this view of the Prince's father, seeing his reluctance to fight as of a piece with his having worn women's dress. But although he puts on armour his real bravery is in arguing against his father and resisting the battle which he thinks can only increase Ida's revulsion. Aren't women 'truer to the life within? / Severer in the logic of a life?' (V, 181–2) –

> Not like the piebald miscellany, man,
> Bursts of great heart and slips in sensual mire,
> But whole and one: and take them all-in-all,
> Were we ourselves but half as good, as kind,
> As truthful, much that Ida claims as right
> Had ne'er been mooted, but as frankly theirs
> As dues of nature. To our point: not war:
> Lest I lose all.   (V, 190–7)

That image of men as dirty and mixed in nature, to be redeemed by putting a proper value on women, has been almost literally represented by the Prince in the poem so far; bedraggled because he was drenched in saving Ida from the river, he slipped and fell on his face when Ida's guards caught him. His 'femininity' is a matter of his poetic and loving sensibility, and his idealism; he is not asexual like the androgyne in the manuscript. The idealization of women, the equation of sensuality with filthiness, and unease about the aggressiveness of taking the initiative, made the issue of love-making terribly problematic for poets like Tennyson and Patmore, as Carol Christ has noted.[8] When the Prince wakes from his trance to kiss Ida it is like a dream beyond the conscious will;

like his seizures, sexual desire is a lapsing out of the real conditions of life. As Ida finally comes close to him

> In that fine air I tremble, all the past
> Melts mist-like into this bright hour, and this
> Is morn to more, and all the rich to-come
> Reels, as the golden Autumn reels
> Athwart the smoke of burning weeds . . .   (VII, 333–7)

It is the perfect Idyllic moment, the six lines drawing in the past to their centre, the bright morning, and unfolding toward a future all the more ecstatic for the haze through which it is seen, a future which includes the golden year, the far-off planet of harmony, with sexual love. Knowledge of mortality is part of the ecstasy, and the swooning, the satisfied murmuring of the 'm's and 'r's, coexists with a wondering energy in the rhythm, the startling emphasis thrown on 'Reels'; the line recovers balance again with the reiteration, 'reels'.

This consummation in language is the Prince's. What about Ida? Her last words are ones of doubt. It is worth comparing her mood at the close of *The Princess* with the one Idyl which takes account of a woman's response to poetry in which she is the object of desire. *The Day-Dream* (1842) is a version of the Sleeping Beauty story, rich in luxuriant images 'Like long-tailed birds of Paradise / That float through Heaven, and cannot light'. In its Envoi the poet is reproved by the lady whom he has been wooing with so much pleasure: like Lilia and Ida she is frustrated, wants something more serious. The poet, who can't wake her to love with the luxuries Kemble and Hallam so admired, describes her as 'all too dearly self-involved', and this is a good word for Ida in Parts VI and VII. The term is not necessarily a negative one, because it has the connotations of depth and potential energy which characterize Tennyson's idyllic imagery. Cyril calls Ida 'Fixed in yourself' (VI, 161) but like all the men who at this point are urging Ida to show more feeling, to restore the child to Psyche and be reconciled to her friend, he has little idea of what she is feeling. As they criticize her she barely listens, sinking into herself:

> drained of her force
> By many a varying influence and so long.
> Down through her limbs a drooping languor wept:
> Her head a little bent; and on her mouth
> A doubtful smile dwelt like a clouded moon
> In a still water . . .   (VI, 249–54)

This withdrawal into depths which for now seem lifeless (but 'still waters run deep') is continued in the stormscape which Ida watches from the roof in her isolation and melancholy:

> void was her use,
> And she as one that climbs a peak to gaze
> O'er land and main, and sees a great black cloud
> Drag inward from the deeps, a wall of night,
> Blot out the slope of sea from verge to shore,
> And suck the blinding splendour from the sand,
> And quenching lake by lake and tarn by tarn
> Expunge the world: so fared she gazing there;
> So blackened all her world in secret, blank
> And waste it seemed and vain; till down she came,
> And found fair peace once more among the sick.
>
> (VII, 19–29)

Such a conversion of depression into an epic simile of gloomy magnificence, starting from the most ordinary phrase ('a great black cloud' can be compared to the transformed familiarity of 'still water'), is far from trivializing Ida's aspirations or her despair at their wrecking. The analytic presentation of this prolonged mood of loss and self-criticism is what makes the close of the poem more solemn, not the battle.

As the Prince was compelled into 'masculine' behaviour which by no means came naturally to him, so Ida is moved by events to more 'womanly' feelings; changes which draw them together since they do not cancel their original dispositions. Ida had wished that children grew 'like field-flowers everywhere', wanting to change the world rather than be limited by motherhood (III, 234–50). Taking Psyche's child into her care, into her bed, had soothed her anger, in spite of its element of vindictiveness. A pun on the phrase 'losing the child' runs through the poem. Ida had used it to mean that women must think of themselves as fully adult human beings (I, 134–40); the Prince while accepting this was anxious that development should not mean failure in 'childward care' or losing 'the childlike in the larger mind' (VII, 267–8). The Prince himself is always presented as very youthful. When he suggested that her work might lose her 'what every woman counts her due, / Love, children, happiness' (III, 228–9) she responds more maturely that these are hardly one and the same thing:

> Children – that men may pluck them from our hearts,
> Kill us with pity, break us with ourselves –   (III, 240–1)

The victory of Ida's brothers in the tournament results in her loss both of the child and of her college. It is in nursing the Prince that the feelings of mutual dependency aroused by the child find a new object. What wins finally is need, especially men's need both to be nursed by women and to think of themselves as chivalrous towards women: it is in this light that women are beautified and angelized (VII, 5–13), though this passage is at once matched by Ida's blank and stormy mood. Her neediness is produced as a complement to the Prince's; but a residue of doubt and musing remains for both Ida and Lilia at the end (VII, 312–18; Conclusion, 29–35). There is no final delight for Ida, to match her victory song (VI, 17–42).

Three things need to be said about the resolution of the story. It can be read as reducing women back to the 'naked truth' of the body, making heterosexuality and reproduction limits on what women may be. Against such a reading should be set the whole representation of Ida, the serious treatment accorded her arguments and her feelings. The next thing to be said is that the definition of women in terms of men's needs is an old and oppressive one. Although this view controls the resolution of the narrative, so that masculine vulnerability succeeds where a triumph of force would have been unacceptable, the poem does give memorable voice to other attitudes ('Whole in ourselves and owed to none') and keeps open a space for something else in the residue of pensiveness in Lilia and Ida: they are not made to utterly accede. The poem remains attentive to different voices. The third thing is to do justice to Tennyson's sensitive intelligence in making care for children, and the complex emotional dependency adults derive from that care, part of a consideration both of sexuality and of the conditions of women's lives. To say this is not necessarily restrictive either about women's choices or about sexuality. Celibacy has always been an option, and in the twentieth century the choice of sexual pleasure can leave reproduction to the side; yet all human adults need a responsible view of the relations between 'childward care' and emotional need; it is not a matter of sentimentality, beneath intellectual attention.

Because *The Princess* is not a restrictive poem it raises problems about open-mindedness and evasion, about ambivalence as indecision or as negotiating real difficulties. The opposition of gentle Prince and stern Princess is overcome in a poetry of metamorphosis intensely charged with sexual feeling: moving seas, rich colour and light, large prospects; swelling and furrowing; anticipation:

> half in doze I seemed
> To float about a glimmering night, and watch
> A full sea glazed with muffled moonlight, swell
> On some dark shore just seen that it was rich.   (I, 242–5)

The poem is suffused with 'the rich to-come', open with possibilities 'just seen', not already known but not feared. The sense of fullness, of being pregnant with latent meanings, comes in part from the gathering up and repetition of images: of moisture on flowers, for example. Love grows in Ida with 'tenderness touch by touch' beside her despair, 'an Alpine harebell hung with tears / By some cold morning glacier' (VII, 99, 100–1). The Prince is 'like a flower that cannot all unfold, / So drenched it is with tempest, to the sun' (VII, 126–7). These images recall Melissa and Florian:

> when two dewdrops on the petal shake
> To the same sweet air, and tremble deeper down,
> And slip at once all-fragrant into one.   (VII, 53–5)

This wet and tremulous prettiness, whose attributes are shared equally between the sexes (even Cyril is compared to a water-lily), prepares the way for the finest lyric of sexual love, as does 'Ask me no more', the lyric between Parts VI and VII, which offers access to Ida's not yet conscious feelings, trembling between negation and invitation. When the refrain is finally repeated it means there is no more need to ask. So the negatives of 'Now sleeps the crimson petal' are only a fraction away from immediate fulfilment, now:

> Now sleeps the crimson petal, now the white;
> Nor waves the cypress in the palace walk;
> Nor winks the gold fin in the porphyry font:
> The fire-fly wakens: waken thou with me.
>
> Now droops the milkwhite peacock like a ghost,
> And like a ghost she glimmers on to me.
>
> Now lies the Earth all Danaë to the stars,
> And all thy heart lies open unto me.
>
> Now slides the silent meteor on, and leaves
> A shining furrow, as thy thoughts in me.

> Now folds the lily all her sweetness up,
> And slips into the bosom of the lake:
> So fold thyself, my dearest, thou, and slip
> Into my bosom and be lost in me. (VII, 161–74)

The pleasures of this lyric are those of difference, crimson against white, sleeping and waking; the metaphors of sexual difference are boldly obvious, with the masculine cypress, fin and flying insect (like Blake's invisible worm in 'O rose thou art sick') and the feminine flower, crimson like Blake's for sensuality and shame, white for chastity and seductive frailty, vague like the peacock, chill like the font. It is a very simple and a very sophisticated lyric, both traditional and highly personal in its intimate urging, 'to me', 'unto me' and so on, acting as a rhyme – 'Come down, O maid' repeats this conjuring by repetition, 'come thou down', 'So waste not thou; but come.' The use of repeated words as rhyme, the number of couplets, and the images, derive from a form of Persian poetry, the *ghazal*, though much of the imagery is familiar from earlier lines in *The Princess*, for example the beginning of Part III. Each stanza, the three inner couplets embraced by quatrains, evokes a picture, but the stillness of the pictorial is countered because the second element in almost every line is a verb suggesting movement, except for the initial 'sleeps' and the central pause, 'lies . . . lies open'. The pause is one of consummation and metamorphosis. 'Heart' and then 'thoughts', lying open and furrowing, inevitably suggest parts of the body, but in pleasure there is no opposition between body and consciousness. In the myth of Danaë Zeus was metamorphosed into a shower of golden rain, perhaps already suggested in the flickering foreplay of gold fin and fire-fly. Tennyson's version is not of a rape but of an exchange between heaven and earth, the meteor becoming a plough, the earthly body air. The speaker of the poem is male, but both lovers change as he is furrowed by her thoughts and becomes the lake into which she slips. Genital pleasure, passivity and activity, penetration and infolding, are mixed and doubled.

Some reviewers of Tennyson's early poetry compared it to metaphysical lyrics of the seventeenth century. One of his modern biographers, Robert Bernard Martin, has argued almost obsessively for a low level of sexual feeling in him and his work. On the contrary, he wrote the best erotic verse since that of the seventeenth century, which at its best, as here, can acknowledge equally active sexual feeling in a woman, while allowing also the pleasure of passivity. The speaker of both 'Now sleeps the crimson petal' and 'Come down, O maid' is male, but both are read by Ida. The Prince is thus spared the aggression of sexual invitation, while Ida finally accepts the lyric voice. Nevertheless, these are not her own words, but containers for feeling, already available. After the kiss she was still musing, a little separate. So was Tennyson. In the 1848 Lincoln proofs of *The Princess* he wrote in four lines between lines 402 and 403 of Part II; unpublished, they were meant to be spoken by Cyril as he prays to maintain his female disguise:

> Shot-silken elf, buoy'd on a veering air,
> Sphered in an ever-breaking bubble, one
> That ever blows itself again, descend(,)
> Transex me; soul of mincing mimicry . . .

The illusions of metamorphosis here appear as mimicry, transvestism, a boy's joke depending on irreducible difference; though the iridescent bubble of unity, impermanent, is seen as something that can come again and again, momentarily. The 'elf' could be Cupid, already invoked by Cyril as 'the bigger boy / The Head of all the golden-shafted firm' (II, 382–3), but it could also be poetry, whose unfixed meanings Tennyson was later to compare to shot-silk. In the writing of poetry perhaps the sexual androgyne could survive. Cyril is not an authoritative voice in *The Princess* but he is important because he will not let go of the embarrassments of sexual difference. His name suggests the patriarchal capitals of the Cyrillic alphabet; on the other hand, it can be rewritten as 'lyric'. *In Memoriam*, though it finally became something of a monument to the dead friend, with its Roman numerals and Latin title, keeps the changefulness, feminine and human, of lyric poetry.

4

In Memoriam: 'some wild Poet'

My own dim life should teach me this,
  That life shall live for evermore,
  Else earth is darkness at the core,
And dust and ashes all that is;

This round of green, this orb of flame,
  Fantastic beauty; such as lurks
  In some wild Poet, when he works
Without a conscience or an aim.   (XXXIV, 1–8)

In Memoriam, begun tentatively in 1833 and published in 1850, is
made up of 131 lyrics of between three and thirty stanzas, with the
rhyme scheme a b b a. It is framed by a Prologue and Epilogue
(so called by A. C. Bradley in his Commentary); eight other sections and some fragments also survive, and two sections were
added after publication: LIX in 1851 as a pendant to III and
XXXIX in 1869 as a pendant to II. 'A restless congeries of
feminine lyrics', the Marxist critic Terry Eagleton called it,[1] taking the word *congeries* from Christopher Ricks, who thinks that *In
Memoriam* evades the 'proper responsibilities of the long poem',
and remains 'weaving, not growing or building'. Its most important analogue for him is Shakespeare's sonnet series. This problem of *In Memoriam*'s unity links its lack of monumental organiza-
tion to the use of heterosexual analogies for a friendship between
men; at least, Ricks's discussion moves, by way of comparison to
the Sonnets, from the question of unity to that of the poet's possible homosexuality, as if the two questions were connected. Yet
mid-nineteenth-century England took the poem to its heart.

    Though experiences of reading *In Memoriam* differ, critical
discussion has to engage with this question of the relation between
its local qualities and the whole. There are obvious cross-
connections, but Ricks rules these out, as not structurally crucial.
T. S. Eliot, who preferred *In Memoriam*'s doubts to its faith, saw
it as a diary: one had to read the whole in order to appreciate the
good bits. Timothy Peltason's recent *Reading In Memoriam* converts
the poem's indeterminacy into a strength, seeing the problem of
the structure as its subject: the relation of moments to the

processes of time, of parts to whole.[2] In those years of composition Tennyson was re-reading himself as he wrote so that the poem continually builds in self-criticism, and particular groupings of sections, within the three-year structure marked out by the Christmas and other anniversary poems, are often overridden. A run of poems may work around one set of ideas – whether the dead may appear to the living, whether benefit can come from suffering and evil – but individual lyrics within such groups may call back across the whole poem's distances, as when CVII rewrites LXXXVI for a different season, or XCV recalls the concern of XLV with how individuals are 'framed' through language and the body. Linear sequence is always there but not necessarily of much importance: the visionary confidence which XCV attains is hardly noticed by the following sections.

In Memoriam is a poem which tracks the experience of memory in time, not one which grows or builds to a single climax or conclusion. It entertains speculations and fantasies, asking itself over and over 'What would it feel like if that were true?' In section XIV, for example, the poet says he would not feel it to be strange if Arthur Hallam stepped off the ship bringing home his body. Return, the persistence of life, is what we're used to; the strangeness is in the reality of 'thy dark freight, a vanished life' (X) – the abstraction syntactically equivalent to the weight of a mere burden transported. Both those sections try to find words for the strange difference to habitual living of death. Meaning in language is produced by differences between its elements. In diction, rhythm and syntax *In Memoriam* uses a limited range; few vowels and consonants are used in any one section so that their repetition produces horizontal and vertical patterns, as Alan Sinfield has shown; parallel phrases and clauses are frequent, or clauses with the same general function in the sentence.[3] This syntax matches the characteristic arguments by analogy, and the aptness of feeling to stanza form which Christopher Ricks described:

a b b a, which can 'circle moaning in the air', returning to its setting out, and with fertile circularity staving off its deepest terror of arrival at desolation and indifference.　　　　　　　　　　　　(Ricks, *Tennyson*, p. 228)

Language, its recurrences and differences, weaves over the gap made by consciousness of death. The whole of *In Memoriam* in its structure and argument is made by gradually produced relationships. The knitting together of an idea of Hallam and of his death is accompanied by thoughts about how the new-born infant is knit together by the experiences of the body and by language into a human individual in a community. Holding and touching are important: the hand which writes and weaves together becomes a metonymy (the part for the whole) for *In Memoriam*'s major concern, relatedness.

Elements of an unpublished section, 'Are these the far-famed Victor Hours' (Ricks, *Poems*, p. 1776), are dispersed like other parts of rejected lyrics through the published poem, for example in the 'Wild Hours' of CXXVIII, which concludes a sequence that takes the place 'Victor Hours' had held in the Trinity manuscript. A vision of absolute security in CXXVI is maintained through to CXXVIII in spite of revolutions (like those which took place across Europe in 1848, though Tennyson said he wrote these poems before then) and in spite of tremendous changes to the earth, on which the spirit of Hallam is imagined smiling with superhuman confidence. Hallam had encouraged Tennyson in belief in general laws by which God worked through nature, so that apparently destructive change could be taken as part of a benign and progressive purpose, a view which CXXVIII in the end tentatively affirms:

> I see in part
> That all, as in some piece of art,
> Is toil co-operant to an end.

The acceptance of a purposive view, however, remains hypothetical, and what the end may be matters less than that there should be one. In a much earlier section, XXXIV, it had been claimed that without the conviction of immortality there could be no purpose either for the individual conscience or in poetry. A possible identity for the 'wild Poet' here is suggested by the allusions in this and the following poem to Shelley, especially the analogy between the soul's warmth and the earth's central fires, from *Prometheus Unbound*.[4] This is used elsewhere in *In Memoriam* as well (for example in CXXIV), but so is the idea of streams deriving from a central ocean (CXXXI), long discredited as science. The truth of such theories does not matter compared to their power of affirming origins from which individuals may derive their nature and purpose, in harmony with larger processes: the attitude makes use of scientific theories but subordinates them to the values they can be made to sustain. Since theories of the material world are appealed to as evidence but given no absolute status, the grounds of idealism are, 'in part', shaky.

In XXXIV 'some wild Poet' who works without purpose is compared to an earth which is 'darkness at the core', producing only an illusion of 'Fantastic beauty', greenness where there is really only dust and ashes. In the poem Tennyson rejected (but cannibalized) an ideal love triumphs over time, both that of an individual life and the longer reaches revealed by astronomy and geology:

> Are these the far-famed Victor Hours
>   That ride to death the griefs of men?
>   I fear not; if I feared them, then
> Is this blind flight the winged Powers.
>
> Behold, ye cannot bring but good,
>   And see, ye dare not touch the truth,
>   Nor Sorrow beauteous in her youth,
> Nor love that holds a constant mood.
>
> You must be wiser than your looks,
>   Or wise yourselves, or wisdom-led,
>   Else this wild whisper round my head
> Were idler than a flight of rooks.
>
> Go forward! crumble down a throne,
>   Dissolve a world, condense a star,
>   Unsocket all the joints of war,
> And fuse a people into one.   (Ricks, *Poems*, p. 1776)

The language of the poem is powerfully chaotic, assimilating the baroque or neo-classical hours-as-horses to the naturalistic flight of rooks, seizing scientific observation for visionary conviction ('behold and *see!*'). Simultaneously the claim that the Hours cannot touch emotional truth is belied by the way they dominate the poem, environing the mind, trampling down, unsocketing joints – a startling metaphor of dispersal for a poem about death, and gruesomely contradictory since it is meant to favour pacificism. The imaginative drive of their language, though it is denied by the surface intention, associates these apocalyptic Hours with the wild poets of revolutionary purpose, Tennyson's predecessors Byron and Shelley. The last stanza re-fuses them all, Byron, Shelley and Tennyson, idealism and the processes of time, in the radical projects of destroying monarchs, ending war, and uniting the world in dynamic harmony with geological and astronomical destruction and creation.

112

Some of the unsocketed parts of 'Victor Hours' were dispersed in the rest of *In Memoriam*; its Romantic violence and exhilaration remain possibilities even into the Epilogue. Conflict between wild feeling and serenity (based on classicism or on enlightened reason) was the first move in putting *In Memoriam* together. In the struggle between the poet and time relations shift: in section I wildness of feeling is felt not as flight but as depth and intensity, rooted to one spot in opposition to reasonable acceptance of change in time:

> Let Love clasp Grief lest both be drown'd,
>   Let darkness keep her raven gloss:
>   Ah, sweeter to be drunk with loss,
> To dance with death, to beat the ground,
>
> Than that the victor Hours should scorn
>   The long result of love, and boast,
>   'Behold the man that loved and lost,
> But all he was is overworn.'

The very first lines, which stand as a kind of epigraph in both the major manuscripts, the Lincoln and the Trinity, recall two predecessors and call on them for a position to take about death, its aftermath and possible profits. One is Byron; the one specifically referred to is Goethe, whose work fused natural philosophy and poetry, science and imagination. Tennyson called him the foremost of modern lyric poets for his unity in variety, 'consummate in so many different styles', and believed some of his last words to have been 'from changes to higher changes' (Ricks, *Poems*, p. 864):

> I held it truth, with him who sings
>   To one clear harp in divers tones,
>   That men may rise on stepping-stones
> Of their dead selves to higher things.

The idea of rising in development is Goethean, but the metaphor of stepping-stones probably derives from Byron's *The Siege of Corinth*, 239–41:

> Or pave the path with many a corpse,
> O'er which the following brave may rise,
> Their stepping-stone – the last who dies!

In Memoriam turns on the question of how death and the idea of the self are related. Goethe's self survived and rose on dead selves. But suppose the superseded self is the one who loved? The serene rational idea is darkened by memory of Byron's lines, confusing the dead self with the corpse of the friend. To rise on this self would be like welcoming the Victor Hours that ride memory to death, would be like trampling the corpse. *In Memoriam*'s first choice about death's aftermath is to fuse the idea of self with that of the dead friend, to preserve both.

In the third stanza of section I which I quoted first, it is the ground which is to be trampled, not in Byron's forward march but still in triumph over time. The image of the drunken dance echoes Milton's *Comus*, 143–4:

> Come, knit hands, and beat the ground
> In a light fantastic round.

The 'raven gloss' of darkness had already recalled this third predecessor:

> At every fall smoothing the raven doune
> Of darkness till it smil'd.   (*Comus*, 251–2)

As Alan Sinfield comments, the *In Memoriam* poet here knits hands with Milton's libertine, refusing the consolations of Christian virtue and of reason. In retrospect it can be seen that this position is only placed first so that it can be answered – but not too quickly, or easily, or entirely. Three very different poets are honoured in the memory and changed; a use of allusion more typical of *In Memoriam*'s processes than a conflict of opposites would be.

Ideas and images from section I are called on throughout *In Memoriam*: fusion of the self and the dead friend, rising and change, the beating of the ground in dance or the beating of a clock – dance and chronometry are both periodic and rhythmic, like poems in metre (see II and CXVII). 'Ground' can mean both the earth and grounds of belief, which the poem sometimes seeks in theories of the material world. This physical-philosophical pun is not apparent in section I considered in isolation, but the similar one on 'hold' is visible in the shift from 'hold' as past belief ('I held it truth') to physical embrace, albeit between abstract personifications ('Let Love clasp Grief'). Holding as a defence against loss persists into the succeeding sections – in III there is the question whether Sorrow (blind and, like Nature, hollow) should be embraced or crushed before it enters the mind, and clasping or grasping is the whole motive force of II:

> Old Yew, which graspest at the stones
> That name the under-lying dead,
> Thy fibres net the dreamless head,
> Thy roots are wrapt about the bones.

The branches like stiff fingers grasping the headstone evoke as in a mirror reflection the roots beneath that hold the nameless skull and bones, deprived of individuality. 'Wrapt' suggests a tranced embrace, but 'thy fibres net' has a finer penetrating power, a Jacobean ghastliness. Given the strong idealism present in *In Memoriam* it is as well to acknowledge also that it faces, and right away, the rival fusions brought about by physical decay, and the skull beneath the face:

> I wage not any feud with Death
>   For changes wrought on form and face;
>   No lower life that earth's embrace
> May breed with him, can fright my faith.   (LXXXII)

Harold Nicolson said that Tennyson should be read carelessly or not at all[5]: much dwelling on II can bring the thought that the 'dreamless head' could conceivably be conscious of its awful hairnet, since that which is denied is always brought to mind. *In Memoriam* is perversely rich in negative qualifiers – nameless, helmless, fruitless, countless, sightless – that serve its obsession with 'absence, darkness, death; things which are not' (John Donne, *A Nocturnal upon St Lucy's Day*, 18). As in Henry James's ghost stories, the mind that imagines is more terrifying than its phantoms. So in XII the living poet becomes 'A weight of nerves without a mind', and in VII the revenant haunting the dark house is the survivor not the dead man, and not the night but the blank day and the noise of life are 'ghastly'.

The second stanza of II seems at first to offer a traditional pastoral consolation, seasons and births coming round again:

> The seasons bring the flower again,
>   And bring the firstling to the flock;
>   And in the dusk of thee, the clock
> Beats out the little lives of men.

The first two lines are treacherously seductive: the final item in the list is a dour stroke whose secondary sense of 'batters' has support from 'beat' in I and the 'branding' summer suns of the next stanza. In the fourth and final stanza the longing to be held so as to calm the horror of negation takes its strongest and strangest form as the poet imagines himself 'to fail from out my blood', growing one with the yew tree's strangling embrace.

Morbidity rapt about the bones offered a way in to sympathy with *In Memoriam* for those early twentieth-century poets and critics who were so anxious to reject its Victorian ruminative moralizing: Eliot, Auden, Nicolson. At the same time they deprecated the poem's artfulness as excessive. But its literariness, its self-references and transformations of earlier poets, hold the poem together and are the condition for its moments of intensity. Its recent editors, Susan Shatto and Marion Shaw, have shown what an armature of authority it has from those Roman elegiac poets, in whom Tennyson had his first education from his father. Like Shakespeare's Sonnets and *In Memoriam*, Roman elegies were linked by a common metre, and in its larger framework *In Memoriam* is compared by Shatto and Shaw to the funeral lament derived from Alexandrian poetry.[6] Where such an origin is most explicit, as in the dependence of XXI–XXVII and XXXVII–XXXVIII on the pastoral elegy (a particular form of the lament), it has been generally disliked by English critics. Nevertheless, the flexibility with which the poem finds analogies for the relation to Hallam in other relations, particularly those of women to men, always had an alibi available in these classical models, where the one mourned or reproached or welcomed might be female or male. Nervousness about 'feminine' emotion could always have been soothed by the assurance that there was a classical (therefore authoritative and manly) model being imitated.

Roman elegies were not necessarily poems of grief – they were analyses of emotion, of love. *In Memoriam*'s claims about constancy and immortality have precedents in them, and so do a number of 'occasions' for writing – the night-time lament at being excluded from the beloved's house, the farewell hope for a traveller's safe journey, the speech of welcome to a new arrival, the birthday ode and all kinds of celebration such as the *epithalamion*, the marriage song. Books of elegies grouped poems together for similarities in theme, style or occasion, so that the reader's experience as with *In Memoriam* is of both variety and relatedness. As a model the elegies combine formal sense of occasion with intimacy. 'Wild' Romantic emotion had classical roots for Byron and Shelley, and for Tennyson; it was a tradition that offered 'containers' for expression – the ship as moving coffin, the locked house, the wedding ceremony. These classical precedents may have been used self-protectively in the composition of *In Memoriam*, as a 'set mechanic exercise' (the original reading of V in the Lincoln manuscript, Ricks, *Poems*, p. 868) to control and focus the 'unquiet heart and brain', the inertia or chaos of despair; but they do not restrict and close it off.

Meaning and pleasure in individual sections depend on their relation to the whole, and to the conventions of style and model which make difference possible. Questions about reassuring unity and the shocking sense of division, about recurrent cycles and circling, are elements of the whole as a process of relation maintained by recurrent ideas and images. The first words are 'I held', the last 'the whole creation moves'. The pun on 'hold' as belief and embrace persists in the image of the hand. I have reserved until now the second stanza of section I, which opposes to the reasonable idea of intending to benefit by the past the conviction that this is too calculating in the light of bereavement; grief is not a commodity on which one earns interest:

> But who shall so forecast the years
> And find in loss a gain to match?
> Or reach a hand thro' time to catch
> The far-off interest of tears?

This question is answered in LXXX, where Hallam is imagined in the poet's situation, an example to him of the survivor who is capable of gaining from loss. 'Credit' here means both belief in Hallam and his emotional resourcefulness which is the ground of that belief:

> He bears the burden of the weeks
> But turns the burden into gain.

> His credit thus shall set me free;
> And, influence-rich to soothe and save,
> Unused example from the grave
> Reach out dead hands to comfort me.

An unused account, on which no interest has yet been drawn, is also a metaphor hitherto unused because it is so boldly modern, with its base in capitalist finance. Financial credit indeed depends on creditability, the belief that a guarantor has sufficient funds to pay off a loan. Like the comfort to be had from dead hands, however, the metaphor remains questionable in the sphere of emotion: the poet appears too much of a passive beneficiary to follow the example he sets up. Belief drawing on such funds is linked to the image of hands reaching out through time and space, through that Vastness which haunted the poet as wiping out values based on human relations.

Hands also appear as an assurance of friendship and domestic relations – 'clasping brother-hands' (LXXXV), 'in a circle

117

hand-in-hand' (XXX). Particular friendships, sister and brother relations, and the giving of hands in marriage are closely linked: in LXXIX the phrase 'More than my brothers are to me' is justified in an affectionate tribute to Charles Tennyson Turner, whose marriage to Lousia Sellwood is the subject of XCVIII, while the Epilogue celebrates the marriage of Cecilia Tennyson to Edmund Lushington, the new friend clasped as a brother and more in LXXXV. The poem has one base in this intimate family network to which Hallam is connected; and this base also defines his difference. In XCVIII Charles and Louisa are to visit 'That City', Vienna, where Hallam died, and which the poet will never visit in spite of Hallam's praise of the fireworks. In XL he had rejected widowing as an analogy for Hallam's departure for Vienna and from life, and tried instead to compare him to a bride leaving her parents' home, a separation that could become

> A link among the days, to knit
> The generations each with each.

But finally this kind of linking is contrasted to the purely manly leave-taking of himself and Hallam for a longer journey than either foresaw:

> But thou and I have shaken hands,
> Till growing winters lay me low;
> My paths are in the fields I know,
> And thine in undiscover'd lands.

In some lines written late in 1833, which Hallam Tennyson called 'the germ of *In Memoriam*' (Ricks, *Poems*, p. 555), desire for 'A hand that can be clasp'd no more' (VII) is set against Vastness:

> Time bears my soul into the waste.
> I seek the voice I loved – ah where
> Is that dear hand that I should press,
> Those honoured brows that I would kiss?
> Lo! the broad Heavens cold and bare,
> The stars that know not my distress.

(Ricks, *Poems*, p. 555)

This hand that reaches out to touch and draw into an embrace is also associated with impotence, and with guilt. In LV 'lame hands' that fail like Nature and Sorrow to hold anything 'grope' and crawl

> Upon the great world's altar-stairs
> That slope through darkness up to God.

118

These lines affirm the God which they fail to believe in securely, but in LXXII, which records the anniversary of Hallam's death, a hand does reach out through space and time, cruelly:

> Day, mark'd as with some hideous crime,
> When the dark hand struck down thro' time,
> And cancell'd nature's best . . .

It is easy there to remember the Lincoln and Trinity manuscripts, long narrow ledgers like 'butchers' account books' (Martin, p. 324) in which Tennyson put together the sequences of poems, and to think of Hallam as an item cancelled from an account. In LXXXV the hand's action is gentler:

> in Vienna's fatal walls
> God's finger touch'd him, and he slept.

There is no direct development between these two images, no irony or explication of the change in feeling, so that the particular reassurance of Hallam's hands in LXXX and CXIX is easily fused with the general assurance of divine creativity in CXXIV:

> And out of darkness came the hands
> That reach through nature, moulding men.

Of long poems, and his own hope of surviving in writing, Tennyson said:

All the big things had been done. To get the workmanship as nearly perfect as possible is the best chance for going down the stream of time. A small vessel on fine lines is likely to float further than a great raft.

(Ricks, *Poems*, p. 1460)

In Memoriam has evidently been experienced as something of a raft, or a convoy in which some vessels are more wieldy than others. Its unity is what can be sensed at particular moments, and this differs on different readings. For Tennyson himself the connections of a poem when it was first written were likely to be different from those it could have in working it into a sequence. Changing relations were built into the process of composition and that of reading, which Tennyson shared with other readers. Of the short poem he said that it 'should have a definite shape, like the curve . . . assumed by a severed tress or the rind of an apple when flung on the floor'.[7] The crafting of such 'spontaneous' shapes has always been valued in *In Memoriam*, six of whose sections are single sentences: XI, XIV, LXIV, LXXXVI, CXXIX and CXXXI.

Of these XI and LXXXVI are peculiarly perfect examples, in different ways. Both are prospect poems, looking out over a landscape and relating its smallest to its largest effects. Alan Sinfield, who writes well on both poems, notes that XI has unusually few transitive verbs, and relates this to the stillness which is the poem's theme, and the disconnection between nature, the poet's mood and the state of death. But each moment of intransitiveness is at once altered by a preposition – 'pattering to', 'twinkle into', 'sweeps with . . . To mingle with', 'redden to', 'sway themselves in', 'heaves with'. The repetition of 'calm' stanza by stanza makes a rocking movement like that of the sea, forwards and back, within which tiny precise sounds and sights, the chestnut pattering, gossamer threads twinkling, are contrasted to the broad sweep of land, air and sea. The poem's gaze and its pulse contract to expand:

> Calm and deep peace on this high wold,
>   And on these dews that drench the furze,
>   And all the silvery gossamers
> That twinkle into green and gold:
>
> Calm and still light on yon great plain
>   That sweeps with all its autumn bowers,
>   And crowded farms and lessening towers,
> To mingle with the bounding main:
>
> Calm and deep peace in this wide air . . .

That rocking also suggests the poet's disquiet, a more disturbed breathing, when it is condensed into two lines:

> And in my heart, if calm at all,
>   If any calm, a calm despair . . .

The cause of that despair, his friend's dead calm, is finally revealed:

> Calm on the seas, and silver sleep,
>   And waves that sway themselves in rest,
>   And dead calm in that noble breast
> Which heaves but with the heaving deep.

The human attributes, breathing, sleeping, power to move at will, are displaced onto the sea, which produces an illusion of the corpse breathing. The poem is a great example of Tennysonian beauty, which is also psychologically very acute and disturbing. The macabre transference harbours what is to become a consolation,

since the same pulse heaving rhythmically through landscape, sea
and corpse prefigures the visionary experience of XCV:

> So word by word, and line by line,
>> The dead man touch'd me from the past,
>> And all at once it seem'd at last
> The living soul was flash'd on mine,
>
> And mine in this was wound, and whirl'd
>> About empyreal heights of thought,
>> And came on that which is, and caught
> The deep pulsations of the world.

Breathing and emotion are also linked in the prospect of
LXXXVI. In contrast to XI where the stanzas are isolated from
each other by colons, Tennyson indicated that its first four and a
half lines must be spoken in a single breath; each stanza overruns
into the next. What pauses there are come within the lines, except
for three brief intakes, most significantly after 'Doubt and Death'
(11). For Christians the breath is a symbol of the Holy Ghost, and
the physical assurance needed to read LXXXVI aloud prepares
the way for the mysticism of XCV.[8] The metaphysical claim that
body and world are interinanimated is made first by the spoken
language, the sustaining of a deep breath:

> Sweet after showers, ambrosial air,
>> That rollest from the gorgeous gloom
>> Of evening over brake and bloom
> And meadow, slowly breathing bare
>
> The round of space, and rapt below
>> Thro' all the dewy-tassell'd wood,
>> And shadowing down the horned flood
> In ripples, fan my brows and blow
>
> The fever from my cheek, and sigh
>> The full new life that feeds thy breath
>> Throughout my frame, till Doubt and Death,
> Ill brethren, let the fancy fly
>
> From belt to belt of crimson seas
>> On leagues of odour streaming far,
>> To where in yonder orient star
> A hundred spirits whisper 'Peace'.

The new life does not let go of old associations, for example
Dante's *Vita Nuova* which Hallam had translated. For all the single
drive of its articulation the lyric is too rich for an interpretation

that could still capture its effect of wholeness. 'Dewy-tassell'd', an effect that is just there in the scene, also suggests a metamorphosis of the far-off interest of tears ('after showers') into delicate beauty. The air, the medium for seeing and drinking in the larger shapes and the minutiae of the prospect, feeds itself before nourishing the poet, maternally. The robed and perfumed sunset (ambrosial gorgeousness gives an effect of ritual which returns in the odours and crimson belts of the last stanza) rapturously unwraps, bares, consciousness of the world in space, the largest prospect possible. Within the movement of the air and mood which is the poem's medium and its theme, rhyme beats the divisions which are also links. The inner rhymes of the first three stanzas are solidly consonantal, while the outer rhymes connecting the stanzas are open-vowelled, releasing the breath. The inner rhyme of the last stanza is open-vowelled, but the outer pair of rhymes is slightly false, because the sibilant of 'Peace' is not so heavy as that of 'seas'. Its truer rhyme would be the assonantal one with the poem's first word, so bringing, it all full circle to 'Sweet . . . Peace'. Like Tennyson's analogies for the short poem it is natural, rich and simple.

That orient star at the end of LXXXVI recalls the end of XLVI and anticipates the end of LXXXIX. It is Venus, the planet of Love and closest to the earth, appearing on both horizons as the morning and evening star, the Hesper/Phosphor of IX and CXXI. This fusing of classical allusion and astronomy consummates several images that present the self and its experience as a possible whole, rounded into an orb, and the world as a similar whole within the universe: 'the perfect star / We saw not, when we moved therein' (XXIV). The assurance which *In Memoriam* does reach about the whole story of the earth, from pre-history to 'one far-off divine event' (Epilogue), is a response to anxiety, and awareness that what it would like to assert on the grounds of momentary experiences cannot be constantly and certainly known is written into the poem. Its desire for solid gound, a world on which a stand can be taken, was produced by a real shock of separation. Its particular items of knowledge about the geological and astronomical, and to a lesser extent the biological, history and pre-history of the earth and human life, are fused toward a sense of benevolent purpose. That metaphor of fusion, so frequent in *In Memoriam*, had one ground in Hallam's praise in his 1831 review of Tennyson's 'vivid, picturesque delineation of objects, and the peculiar skill with which he holds them all *fused*, to borrow a metaphor from science, in a medium of strong emotion'.

In Memoriam works by metaphysical analogies between the human, the divine and the natural – analogies which it does not trust except as a way of working, of keeping going. Metaphysical imaginations of what an individual's state might be after death are matched by a material psychological account of how an individual self is acquired through language. The very fine lyric on infancy, XLV, is not unrelated to the constellation of images of moving rounds and orbs, which is carried on in XLVI and XLVII:

> The baby new to earth and sky,
>> What time his tender palm is prest
>> Against the circle of the breast,
> Has ever thought that 'this is I':
>
> But as he grows he gathers much,
>> And learns the use of 'I', and 'me',
>> And finds 'I am not what I see,
> And other than the things I touch'.
>
> So rounds he to a separate mind
>> From whence clear memory may begin,
>> As thro' the frame that binds him in
> His isolation grows defined . . .

The new-born's first relationship is with the mother, the curve of her breast one with the inner curve of his hand. But as 'he' rounds out physically he is gathering things intellectually, poor baby, through language which gives him an ego identity, shutting him in as himself, separate from his mother and what he touches. Here the separation from the mother's body is felt as painful loss, but the loss of such an achieved identity is feared in XLVII, since that would make an individual reunion with Hallam impossible. The argument remains in two minds about separate identity and fusion, in a way characteristic of *In Memoriam*'s division between rational argument and intuition. In the whole poem's emotional drive intuitive idealism triumphs, but locally it can reject its own analogies, and see all notions of evolution and reunion after death as merely imputed by desire:

> What find I in the highest place,
>> But mine own phantom chanting hymns?
>> And in the depth of death there swims
> The reflex of a human face.   (CVIII)

In XLV the punctuation marks both the reassurance and the threat that there is in being separately enclosed, rounded off. A conscious identity is acquired when learned language replaces the touching of mother and infant, teaching difference. In LIV Tennyson uses 'infant' to mean 'with no language but a cry', invoking the Latin root *infans*, unable to speak; he commented on the multiple resources of English, saying that 'baby' would have been ridiculous there. In XLV he used the tenderer word 'baby': the contrast between the bodies touching and the quotation marks enforces the strangeness of this first experience of loss and separation, as if the baby could be required not only to speak but to write. In the third stanza 'frame' means both the growing body and the system of language, losing the distinction between the baby and the socially shared language of self-and-other. The final stanza which I have not quoted tacks XLV on to the discussion about life after death, for which individuation is seen as a preparation, but the most moving and interesting connection between XLV and the whole poem is in its imagining of the entry into language, and how that relates to the body, relationship and loss. Like breathing, touch is part of the base of *In Memoriam*'s imaginative language in the body, especially its earliest experiences with the mother.

In Memoriam is haunted by the notion of something outside of language and resistant to it (see V, XIX, XX), a lack which it converts into power, as the child in Freudian theory finds substitutes in words and objects for its lost closeness to the mother. The poet's vision in XCV, produced by reading Hallam's letters in solitude after a sociable evening, relates the spiritual experience of fusion with the living soul to the wordlessness of the infant's imaginary unity:

> Vague words! but ah, how hard to frame
> In matter-moulded forms of speech,
> Or ev'n for intellect to reach
> Thro' memory that which I became . . .

Nonetheless it was the written letters that brought on this vision. As in XLV conscious memory with its frame of language cuts off the undifferentiated unity as it struggles to find words for it. In XCV desire is projected into verbal and natural signs of its lost object, first in the repetition of stanza 4 so that a dark natural embrace, maternal and deathly, makes a frame for the vision:

> The white kine glimmer'd, and the trees
> Laid their dark arms about the field. (stanzas 4 and 13)

With feeling so embraced, the energy of desire can be caught up again in the breeze, nature's breath figured in the disturbed and emphatic rhythm. The initial stress thrown on 'Rock'd' (58) makes the more usual stress on the inner rhymes 'swung' and 'flung' feel more reckless. Though in meaning 'Rock'd' and 'swung' take up the notion of cradling suggested by the trees' embrace, this is secondary to the rhythmic exhilaration (echoed in the Epilogue, 60–4):

> But suck'd from out the distant gloom
>   A breeze began to tremble o'er
>   The large leaves of the sycamore,
> And fluctuate all the still perfume,
>
> And gathering freshlier overhead,
>   Rock'd the full-foliaged elms, and swung
>   The heavy-folded rose, and flung
> The lilies to and fro, and said
>
> 'The dawn, the dawn' . . .   (XCV, 53–61)

'Suck'd' also suggests infancy – the air as in LXXXVI feeds itself before it rocks the poet and the natural world together, to animate as much as soothe. As in LXXXVI the articulation of breath in speaking the lines affirms the emotion as the breast and mouth move. The closing image unites opposites in 'boundless day'.

Being separated off is one theme of XL–XLVII, involved with the corresponding idea of being knit together in a body and knit together in a community by language. Another humbly basic image which organizes various associations is the door, a metonymy for bounds and limits, that which can be closed off or opened. The notion of the mind as a room or house was there in III ('upon the threshold of the mind'), and the idea of language as a prison in XLV may have been suggested by the baby in XLIV who 'forgets the days before / God shut the doorways of his head'. Tennyson's note to these lines excluded the meaning of pre-existence, which Wordsworth's *Immortality Ode* had entertained:

The dead after this life may have no remembrance of life, like the living babe who forgets the time before the sutures of the skull are closed, yet the living babe grows in knowledge, and though the remembrance of his earliest days has vanished, yet with his increasing knowledge there comes a dreamy vision of what has been.   (Ricks, *Poems*, p. 902)

This was a persistent fascination – he had argued from it in *The Two Voices*, 368–9, and later he speculated on a grandchild seeing a Christmas tree that he would remember 'all these lights and this splendour in future days as if it were a memory of another life'.[9] His interest in visionary experience included a rationalizing psychological curiosity, whose conclusions could then be used as analogies for his conviction of immortality.

Closed doors in *In Memoriam* are an image of identity that is in the world but isolated, and repeat the shock of separation from Hallam, and Hallam's separation from life. In the first Christmas poem the voice of the church bells from different villages which ring out the same message of peace and goodwill:

> Swell out and fail, as if a door
> Were shut between me and the sound . . .   (XXVIII)

Not hearing the bells is equated with moments in the previous year when the poet wished 'my hold on life would break'. An attempt is made in CVIII to resolve the guilt of shutting himself away from living society:

> I will not shut me from my kind,
> And, lest I stiffen into stone,
> I will not eat my heart alone,
> Nor feed with sighs a passing wind.

This is the section that rationalizes away the idealization of Hallam, as a set of projections by the 'barren' and 'vacant' poet; but the decision to live socially is coloured by the depressive quality of the self-images that attend it. The stony image reappears in the Epilogue, 15–16, 'like a statue solid-set, / And moulded in colossal calm', but in spite of persisting so far it belongs with a group of images which the poem seeks to move beyond, of rooted or frozen fixity, of clinging to a void. In CVIII the poet means to refuse stiffening and being shut in; in CVII a powerful rewriting of LXXXVI for a freezing climate finally has the snow melt as it meets the salt sea, and invites a contrasting interior world of social life, to replace the ethereal vision of reunion:

> fiercely flies
> The blast of North and East, and ice
> Makes daggers at the sharpen'd eaves,
>
> And bristles all the brakes and thorns
> To yon hard crescent, as she hangs
> Above the wood which grides and clangs
> Its leafless ribs and iron horns

> Together, in the drifts that pass
>   To darken on the rolling brine
>   That breaks the coast. But fetch the wine,
> Arrange the board and brim the glass;
>
> Bring in great logs and let them lie,
>   To make a solid core of heat;
>   Be cheerful-minded, talk and treat
> Of all things ev'n as he were by . . .

The melting and exchange of cold for heat answer across *In Memoriam* to those lines in IV which were derived from Goethe, but turned his image of a constructive response to bereavement into a negative one. Goethe wrote in *Poetry and Truth* that he had formed the plan of his novel *The Sorrows of Young Werther* on hearing of the death of a young friend:

The elements of that composition seemed now to amalgamate, to form a whole, just as water, on the point of freezing in a vase, receives from the slightest concussion the form of a compact piece of ice.

Tennyson's unacknowledged and possibly unconscious memory of this uses the natural observation as an image not for poetic composition but for the shock to the chilled mind which leads to the breaking of the container:

Water can be brought below freezing-point and not turn into ice – if it be kept still; but if it be moved suddenly it turns into ice and may break the vase

> Break, thou deep vase of chilling tears,
> That grief hath shaken into frost![10]

These changes in corresponding images in *In Memoriam* are a more subtle form of elegiac variation than the overt correspondences of the anniversary poems and the pendants, such as VII and CXIX (addressed to Hallam's house) or II and XXXIX (to the yew tree). At times the structuring is 'monodramatic', as in *Maud*: different moods of poems in a sequence confront one another. Before the serene consolation of IX ('Fair ship') is set one of the bleakest expressions of grief, VII ('Dark house'), which is not found in any of the manuscript sequences or in the trial edition published in March 1850 (Ricks, *Poems*, p. 856). It is set between two much weaker poems, which like some other sections recall domestic anecdotal paintings and give some substance to Tennyson's claim for the impersonality of *In Memoriam* ('It is rather the cry of the whole human race than mine', Ricks, *Poems*, p. 859).

ALFRED TENNYSON

VI musters a whole gallery of little pictures of sudden loss,
including as one of the many Tennyson himself writing to Hallam
in the hour of his death. There's the father drinking to the gallant
son at the moment of his death in battle, the mother praying for
her sailor son's safety as his corpse is buried at sea. The allusions
here can be compared to the vogue for attaching Shakespearean
quotations to paintings: 'vast and wandering grave' (16) recalls
the dream of drowning in *Richard III* I, iv, 39, while the first lines
echo Gertrude's reproach to Hamlet, 'Thou know'st 'tis common,
all that live must die' (I, ii, 72). The last portrait, the 'meek, unconscious dove' arranging her hair as her fiancé dies, has the loving detail and the *contrapposto*, the skill displayed in the turning of
a body engaged in some simple action, which Victorian artists
imitated so assiduously from the Renaissance. It is a theatrical
effect, like a pose on stage frozen to recall a painting:

> And, having left the glass, she turns
> Once more to set a ringlet right:

> And, even when she turn'd, the curse
> Had fallen, and her future Lord
> Was drown'd in passing thro' the ford
> Or killed in falling from his horse.

That 'Or' betrays a shrug of indifference – choose which accident
you prefer, it doesn't seriously matter. This is not definitely ironic
(Tennyson enjoyed the pathos and melodrama of popular theatre
and fiction), but it can be read either sentimentally or wearily.
The whole of VI is a poignant catalogue of commonplaces, so sad,
so apt; it is about how commonplace bereavement is:

> That loss is common would not make
> My own less bitter, rather more:
> Too common! . . .

The full potential of this section is not within its own boundaries
but in juxtaposition to the Hamlet-like solitude of VII; and its
most troubled images, the 'heavy-shotted hammock-shroud' and
wandering grave of the sea (15–16) suggest why 'Fair ship' (IX)
needs to be so serene.

'Dark house, has been depreciated by Dwight Culler and, in
comparison to Thomas Hardy's elegies, by Douglas Brown; they
suggest that grief is here presented as a luxury to be enjoyed. That
does rightly raise the question of what is going on when we enjoy
and appraise any poem of bereavement, but it is a short-sighted

response to VII, which is placed here to do what it can about this problem. It is difficult to find ground on which disagreements about sincerity in intimate poems of intense feeling can be decided; silence or tough-mindedness are not the only or the best responses. That Tennyson in deciding so belatedly to publish VII put it between VI and the Valentine-cum-mourning card VIII, suggests something more sensitively intelligent than indulgence or display. I find it very moving, but its placing deliberately provokes a critical view of the luxuries of grief; at the same time the house image, together with the ship in IX and the grave in XVIII, reminds the reader of the need for ritual and containment as something generic, shared in common:

> Dark house, by which once more I stand
>   Here in the long unlovely street,
>   Doors, where my heart was used to beat
> So quickly, waiting for a hand,
>
> A hand that can be clasp'd no more –
>   Behold me, for I cannot sleep,
>   And like a guilty thing I creep
> At earliest morning to the door.
>
> He is not here; but far away
>   The noise of life begins again,
>   And ghastly through the drizzling rain
> On the bald street breaks the blank day.

The house is a metaphor for the dead body; the poet 'like a guilty thing' recalls Wordsworth's *Immortality Ode*, 148–51 ('. . . our mortal Nature / Did tremble like a guilty Thing surprised') and the ghost of Hamlet's father at dawn (I, i, 153). But the poem is about the impossibility of substitution. The doors which could open for a welcome quickly stand in metonymically for the whole house, and their being closed frames the first two stanzas, in which the hand stands for the whole person. The rhythm of these first two stanzas runs on restlessly, the hand reaching impotently between them, a link only in words, closed off at the end of stanza two. The weaving, pleading rhythm is stopped by negation on the threshold of the final stanza: 'He is not here.' This may recall the words of the angel on Christ being risen from the tomb; a typological parallel is drawn between Hallam and Christ throughout *In Memoriam*, though Christianity as the base on which Tennyson drew needed as much support from feeling for Hallam as the other way round. Even bolder is the connection made between Christ and the secular loves of the classical elegies. As in Wordsworth's Ode the guilty thing is not a ghost but alive, and as in *Hamlet* the guilt is about the rival claims of the dead and the living. But these biblical and literary allusions within VII's bleak naturalism only reinforce the futility of substitution, the absence of the one whole living person desired.

The alliterativeness of VII has less to say about the street than about the obligations of writing verse, 'The sad mechanic exercise, / Like dull narcotics, numbing pain' (V), which is all that can be done about grief at this point. Alliteration makes the metre seem plodding even though it is halting and uneven, the walk of an injured man. The last line begins with a tripping anapaestic foot, but it has one stress missing at the end, while the second foot has two possible stresses; meanwhile the alliteration bitterly pretends that all is normal and regular, long and unlovely: 'On the bald / street breaks / the blank day.' This haunted hopelessness set between two mainly banal and pretty poems exposes all three to question – Hamlet against the 'shapes of grief', 'the trappings and the suits of woe' (*Hamlet* I, ii, 83, 85). VI had as its theme the impossibility of substitution (its last line is 'And unto me no second friend'), while that of VIII is the 'poor flower of poesy' as the substitute which may grow in a life left desolate. But it is in VII that these feelings are worked into the means of writing. The local quality of the writing gains from the secondary work of placing it, which also lifts VI and VIII beyond their intrinsic value. This is why readers need to be wary of splitting *In Memoriam* back into its units, and, contrarily, why thematic continuity is not the best way of understanding its difficult sense of relations and differences.

In *The Dialogic Imagination* the Russian critic Bakhtin contrasted the many voices of the novel with lyric poetry which, he claimed, was single-voiced and authoritative even when it spoke of doubt. There is some truth in this: formally and in its reception *In Memoriam* did become a monument to Hallam and to the art of Tennyson which he had so encouraged. But the writing experienced in the reading is not so single-voiced. The reader's position is normally one of overhearing enquiries addressed to the self or the dead, or to objects and abstractions which substitute for them. Occasionally an answer is made to a friend or critic, and this intensifies the effect of a monodrama taking place in real time, under changing influences and interventions. As a poem of relationships *In Memoriam* does not have a centre. But at the half-way mark there is a conflict between Christian tradition and scientific thinking, which does not fit in with the threefold division noted by A. C. Bradley in his *Commentary*, from Despair to Regret to Hope. This technically central break corresponds to one phase in the poem's composition; it is not a climax or a centripetal gathering-in, but a break in argument marked by drama. The Trinity manuscript seems to have closed originally with LVII; Tennyson commented, 'I thought this too sad for an ending.'[11]

Up to this point *In Memoriam* plays with speculations about immortality. LIV–LVI confront Christian belief with the evidences of natural science. The speaker in LIV diminishes from the generic plural ('Oh yet we trust that somehow good / Will be the final goal of ill') to the singular ('I can but trust that good shall fall / At last – far off – at last, to all') to the infant, 'with no language but a cry'. LV offers the hope that although Nature is careless of the single life she is careful of the type. Nature's immense prodigality was one premise for the theory of natural selection: 'choice' of the fittest to survive depends on a very wide range of candidates being available, though 'choice' belies the unpurposive nature of the process, which Darwin tried to express in the paradoxical term 'natural selection'. This was at odds with the Gospel promise that not a sparrow should fall without God's protective care. Even the hope of care for the type is eroded in LVI, which faces the evidence offered by Charles Lyell for the extinction of past species, so destroying the notion of species as ideal types in an ideal plan:

'The inhabitants of the globe, like all the other parts of it, are subject to change. It is not only the individual that perishes, but whole species.'

(Ricks, *Poems*, p. 911)

In the mental dialogue of LVI the poet responds to the evidence of extinction and Nature's materialism ('The spirit does but mean the breath') with deliberately dramatized hysteria:

> And he, shall he,
>
> Man, her last work, who seem'd so fair,
> Such splendid purpose in his eyes,
> Who roll'd the psalm to wintry skies,
> Who built him fanes of fruitless prayer,
>
> Who trusted God was love indeed
> And love Creation's final law –
> Tho' Nature, red in tooth and claw
> With ravine, shriek'd against his creed –

Who loved, who suffer'd countless ills,
　　Who battled for the True, the Just,
　　Be blown about the desert dust,
Or seal'd within the iron hills?

No more?

This question, whose syntax fossilizes and seals in the cumulative valuation of humanity, is answered by the quiet and quieting character of the following poem, whose first two stanzas counter the wildly sustained momentum of LVI with at least eleven brief statements and injunctions, before building again in the third stanza to the sustaining of one man's memory at least for an individual lifetime:

Peace; come away: the song of woe
　　Is after all an earthly song:
　　Peace; come away: we do him wrong
To sing so wildly: let us go.

Come; let us go: your cheeks are pale;
　　But half my life I leave behind:
　　Methinks my friend is richly shrined;
But I shall pass; my work will fail.

Yet in these ears, till hearing dies,
　　One set slow bell will seem to toll
　　The passing of the sweetest soul
That ever look'd with human eyes.

I hear it now, and o'er and o'er,
　　Eternal greetings to the dead;
　　And 'Ave, Ave, Ave', said,
'Adieu, adieu' for evermore.

The acceptance of modern scientific evidence for extinction is supported by classical authority in that last stanza of LVII. Tennyson himself compared it to the Roman elegist Catullus, and his 'atque in perpetuum, frater, ave atque vale' ('and for ever, brother, hail and farewell'), commenting 'Nor can any modern elegy so long as men retain the least hope in the after-life of those whom they loved, equal in pathos the desolation of that everlasting farewell' (Ricks, *Poems*, p. 913). Yet that was the note on which he momentarily ended. As *In Memoriam* continues from this point, personal immortality and reunion after death are no longer subjects of speculation, but are taken for granted as justified by feeling.

The idea of development, disjoined from the evolutionary mechanism of prodigality and selection, becomes a benign imagination of Hallam's progress after death, which is used as an analogy for the development of humanity; even in life he had been a type of such future perfection. In the Epilogue 'type' has a theological significance, only scientific in terms of the old natural philosophy. After the break *In Memoriam* does become more of the memoir Tennyson had been unable to write initially. LXVII–LXXI imagine ways in which Hallam could appear to the poet in visions of the night, but the bitter anniversary of his death, LXXII, comes in like a punishment for these wild fantasies, which are both unwilled and willed. They have a constructive result when the poet imagines how Hallam would have behaved in his place (LXXX), an example which makes possible the stronger visions of LXXXVI and XCV, which have their source in the whole conscious body, rather than in superstitions of seeing. Mingled with these visions and with the New Year and Spring poems (LXXXIII and LXXXVIII) come poems which honour Hallam's life and imagine what a lived future would have been for him (LXXXIV–CXIII). These are ways of accepting the difference, his death, as CVI does with a new kind of wildness, which fuses exhilaration with the social piety of a hymn, though its prayers for an end to inequality and war are Shelleyan. That the poet can now say 'Ring out, wild bells, and let him die' is a bold and necessary moment for a poem of bereavement.

The important thing about these memorial poems is that they do remember, put together again, Hallam as a friend who lived and could have lived on: they mime a process of reality-testing, rather than etherealizing Hallam into a sunset or whatever. This can now be done because Hallam's own ideas of human love as divine and of spiritual promptings as fully human have been accepted as ground to stand on, something to hold on to. Enthusiastic as these retrospective assessments of Hallam are, a section like CX presents the poet as having the right to pass judgement, not as a different sort of being. A comparable section slightly earlier, LXIV, fantasized the poet as a simple ploughman while comparing Hallam to 'some divinely gifted man / Whose life in low estate began', rather than the privileged person he was. An excessive aggregation of metaphoric verbs communicates some discomfort with this fancy: how could such a lively brute as this grasping social and intellectual wrestler, who is also described as a pillar and a centre, mould and shape whispers? The mystique of power and secretive statecraft associated with Hallam in LXIV had been opposed by middle-class reformers and radicals since the eighteenth century:

> Who breaks his birth's invidious bar,
>   And grasps the skirts of happy chance,
>   And breasts the blows of circumstance,
> And grapples with his evil star;
>
> Who makes by force his merit known
>   And lives to clutch the golden keys,
>   To mould a mighty state's decrees,
> And shape the whisper of a throne . . .

The language and the political thinking here are the worst in *In Memoriam*, mixing bourgeois mobility and access to power with the harsh violence that tended to accompany Tennyson's 'reverence' both for monarchy and for Carlylean Men of Destiny, possibly in defence against violent moods of despair. This sort of valuation of Hallam is attended by a politics of force and nationalism, aggressive against England's enemies and rebels, the 'blind hysterics' and 'red fool-fury' projected onto Celts and Frenchmen (CIX, CXXVII). Such attitudes, though they are far less frequent than Shelleyan idealism, are not explicitly subjected to doubt and question.

The sections which find analogies for the relation between the poet and his dead friend in class or gender inequality are in fact quite strictly localized. LX–LXII compare the mourner to a girl who has loved a man of higher rank; LXIII imagines a sympathy from the dead Hallam like that felt for a dog or a horse; LXIV has the ploughman musing on his socially mboile friend. Only XCVII revives this phase, comparing the poet to the neglected wife of a great scientist. I would be happy to think, without much conviction as to Tennyson's conscious intentions, that these hierarchies monodramatically enact a moment of self-abjection. Freud's study, 'Mourning and Melancholia', attributes such self-depreciations to the internalization of unconscious criticism of the beloved: the melancholic or bereaved person feels neglected and slighted, but claims to deserve this rather than blame the loved one. In *In Memoriam* this neurotic phase goes hand-in-hand with the ideology of superiority and inferiority in class, gender and race.

As a whole *In Memoriam* is not neurotic, because it is able to express and work through morbid feelings. It meets shock and endures by means of poetry, which both resists and accepts change. Its composition needed grounding in its classical models, but in responding to the immensely long time spans which the nineteenth century had newly to imagine, its form also mimics contemporary consciousness of evolution. It has its fossils, earlier lines embedded in its continual restructuring, as well as rifts and erosions, where the solid ground gives way and contact is lost. Equally contemporary is its argument for feeling as the ground of whatever values can be held: 'Thought drifting like the hills of sand' (an early manuscript line, Ricks, *Poems*, p. 866) is stabilized by the 'living will' arising in the 'spiritual rock' of CXXXI. In its composition over seventeen years and in its fictional span of three years, *In Memoriam* traces the action of memory in time and the effort of the will to secure the value of past affection and admiration, in the face of recurring despair. It broods and regresses, juxtaposing intense immediate feeling with the slackness of commonplaces, dramatizing moods of hysteria and terror, and of calm resignation and resolution. It is a remarkable process of self-therapy through writing, in which the fixed images of clinging to something not there are exorcized, by turning to the living social world in its intimate and domestic forms, and by exhilaration in natural description. Humphry House said of these natural descriptions that 'they stabilized his mind in the contemplation of unending processes', but they are not merely stable.[12] From the frozen container that could only change by breaking apart, and from the rootedness of the yew tree's embrace of the bones, *In Memoriam* breaks again and again, more and more towards the close, into celebrations of blossoming, of the flight and song of birds, of bells ringing and moon and stars rising – movements of the breath and spirit, of the air and in the air, which enact release:

> Wild bird, whose warble, liquid sweet,
>   Rings Eden through the budded quicks . . .
>   (LXXXVIII)

> Ring out, wild bells, to the wild sky . . .
> Ring out, wild bells, and let him die.   (CVI)

>   and overhead

> Begins the clash and clang that tells
>   The joy to every wandering breeze;
>   The blind wall rocks, and on the trees
> The dead leaf trembles to the bells . . .

Dumb is that tower which spake so loud,
And high in heaven the streaming cloud,
And on the downs a rising fire:

And rise, O moon, from yonder down . . .

(Epilogue, 60–4, 106–9)

The role of Merlin, the wizard of words who can make the moon
rise, is rightly assumed here. A diction that animates stones, a
movement rocking with surprising wayward force, to rise with
almost ominous excitement, command the reader to feel.

To ground belief in moments of emotion and the desire to
believe is ultimately sceptical. In *In Memoriam* neither scepticism
nor idealism based on a Christian education and mental set
prevails: both are threads in the poem's weave, in which intuition
and argument persist. The propagandist of scientific thinking,
John Tyndall, recorded Tennyson as saying: 'I should consider
that a liberty had been taken with me if I were made simply a
means of ushering in something higher than myself.' He also
groaned at the idea of ' "Something outside us that makes for
righteousness" – ugh!'[13] These apparent contradictions of *In
Memoriam*'s Prologue and Epilogue have to be understood in the
light of the poem's way of being written, and the sense of difference and relation emerging from that process. One of Hallam's
letters to Tennyson answered a question of the poet's which was
anxious about keeping things distinct: 'With respect to prayer,
how am I to distinguish the operations of God in me "from
motions in my own heart?" ' Hallam answered with two questions: 'Why should you distinguish them? or how do you know
there is any distinction?'[14] To collapse any difference between the
self and God – or the self and any other – is to open the way
to supreme arrogance, and close off any argument. In XCV, when
the poet was touched by a reading of Hallam's letters, difference
between human desire and whatever is the ground of everything
was lost. But that point can only be made through language and
its sense of difference, on which relations between one and another
depend. The idea of a self is based in the body and in language
which can frame the concepts 'I' and 'you'. The language of *In
Memoriam* keeps before the reader the ground of beliefs in bodily
knowledge and desire – breathing, being nourished, touching
and holding, within a larger world and universe.

The size and scope of *In Memoriam*, its reach through time, allow
us to live sympathetically, as we read, the experience of bereavement, which is both intimate and common, and whose power as

a subject comes from consciousness of what lies beyond experience and language. The privacy of experience is criticized within the poem, but it is not dismissed or reduced. It makes the choice which William Faulkner in *The Wild Palms* may have learned from Tennyson: 'Between grief and nothing I will choose grief', and makes it productive. The end has to be with another not the same, a birth not a funeral; not finally the mystic personal fusion of soul and soul but 'the whole creation moves'.

5

Maud, or the madness

We might discuss the Northern sin
Which made a selfish war begin;
   Dispute the claims, arrange the chances;
Emperor, Ottoman, which shall win:

Or whether war's avenging rod
Shall lash all Europe into blood;
   Till you should turn to dearer matters,
Dear to the man that is dear to God;

How best to help the slender store,
How mend the dwellings, of the poor;
   How gain in life, as life advances,
Valour and charity more and more . . .
                (To the Rev. F. D. Maurice, 29–40)

Tennyson wrote this in the year he wrote *Maud*, 1854, to his son's godfather who had just lost a professorship because of his moral courage in refusing to pretend to a belief in eternal punishment for sin. Some reviewers took it for granted that *Maud* supported the popular belief that the Crimean War was just what England needed, to transcend its social problems through a sense of national destiny. At a time when that war was barely a memory Blanche Warre-Cornish records Tennyson constantly interrupting a reading of the poem at lines about war as purifying or unifying, to defend himself:

When had he been the champion of war? The poem was a dramatic monologue. The sentiments were in the mouth of a madman. He wished he had called the poem as first planned, *Maud or the Madness*. Anyone can see that the words about war represent a mood. But the critics are nothing.[1]

This is not quite convincing. Though Tennyson may well have felt sceptical in retrospect, the madness of the speaker in *Maud* represents a national malaise, and the last Part implies a joint recovery of both the speaker and the nation:

My mood is changed . . .
It is better to fight for the good than to rail at the ill;
I have felt with my native land, I am one with my kind,
I embrace the purpose of God, and the doom assigned.

                                        (III, vi, 4, 57–9)

Like *The Princess*, *Maud* addressed a matter of urgent public concern, and it was inevitably read as a contribution to debate about the Crimean War. It deserved the comments of Goldwin Smith, for example, that external action could not substitute for reform, that suffering and financial corruption were increased not cured by war, and that to think of such conflict as therapeutic was hypocrisy:

We do not . . . literally *go* to war. We send our hired soldiers to attack a nation which may not be in need of the same regimen as ourselves. To most of us, the self-sacrifice involved in war with an enemy who cannot get at us consists in paying rather more taxes.

The Crimean War did increase taxation, and doubled the national debt. Goldwin Smith was equally acute about the instrumental use of 'Maud':

Women seem to have no function but that of casting out the demon of hypochondria from the breast of the solitary and relieving him of the melancholy which flows to him from all around him . . . They are the 'countercharm of space and hollow sky', without active life or interests of their own . . .[2]

Yet *Maud* is Tennyson's most adventurous poem, in its exploration of masculinity and aggression. It attracted the most bitter denunciation he had ever met, but it was more widely reviewed than earlier works, and not only with disapproval; nor were attitudes to the war the only cause of contention. Charles Kingsley, who himself wrote *Brave Words for Brave Soldiers and Sailors* of this war, thought *Maud* 'a sad falling off', an attempt at 'Spasmodic' poetry. The Spasmodic poets, Alexander Smith and Sydney Dobell, for example, attempted a very immediate expression of emotion, whose causes had to be retrospectively worked out. Both Brownings were influenced by their work and Tennyson, who knew Dobell, thought well of his long poem, *Balder* (1853). Its hero, like that of *Maud*, was identified by critics with the author, and damned for his 'repulsive egoism'.

Of all Tennyson's poems *Maud* was the one he was most eager to read aloud, and given its extreme emotion it would be easy to see this as akin to Dickens's notorious readings of the murder of

ALFRED TENNYSON

Nancy by Bill Sykes, in *Oliver Twist*. But a better understanding of these readings (private, not public like those of Dickens) also offers a guide to the nature of the poem. It had been denounced because it had been misread: Tennyson needed only to give voice to it and then understanding would come. It is a poem which depends on irrational feelings getting spoken: the confusion of an initial response to it can only be organized by empathy, by alertness to bodily sensations moulding and being moulded by thought. Many who heard Tennyson read it did revise an earlier hostility, Gladstone for one, though others remained merely irritated by Tennyson's nursing of the poem, and his sensitivity to criticism of it.

Another guide is Tennyson's response to the problems of what to call the lover and hero, who has no name. He wrote appreciatively to George Brimley, who had written a sympathetic review, but objected to the expression 'the writer of the fragments': 'surely the speaker or the thinker rather than the writer'.[3] What went into that objection? 'The writer of the fragments' quite properly distinguishes the character in the poem from its author. To call him 'the hero' is to make him too much of a definite figure in a narrative or drama, standing free from moment-to-moment empathy: as in Dwight Culler's fantasy of staging *Maud* as a theatrical monodrama, with a finale of banners and moving battleships, martial music, and Lieutenant Nameless saluting.[4] But to call him 'the writer' would imply too much premeditation, a retrospective view of his experience, and consciousness of an audience to be persuaded. Tennyson's response to Brimley suggests that he does not want the poem to be experienced as rhetorical in this way: almost he seems to be hankering after the experience of thought without the mediation of language, or, since that is impossible, an effect of spontaneous speech to the self. *Maud* is a psychic monodrama, in which 'different phases of passion in one person take the place of different characters'. A sensuous and emotional response is required, prior to an intellectual distance.

> I said to the lily, 'There is but one
>   With whom she has heart to be gay.
> When will the dancers leave her alone?
>   She is weary of dance and play'.
> Now half to the setting moon are gone,
>   And half to the rising day;

140

> Low on the sand and loud on the stone
> The last wheel echoes away.   (I, xxii, 868–75)

'Low on the sand and loud on the stone': such contrasting sounds matter in this section, where the speaker listens from outside to the formal tunes of woodwind, string and brass, until the waking bird makes the new silence audible; then the different noises of the carriages going give a feeling of wide wastes (stone, sand) beyond the garden where the poem has its heart. The silence of nature opposed to the clash and babble of social life becomes preternatural in the alertness of the speaker/listener, hearing his own feelings in the voices of flowers – a convention of Persian love poetry which Tennyson frequently raids in *Maud*, not least in this section. It's a magical and tense whispering, summoning up what he desires:

> Come into the garden, Maud,
> For the black bat, night, has flown,
> Come into the garden, Maud . . .   (I, xxii, 850–2)

Bold to quote it, though not so bold as to try and speak it aloud, since the orotundity of parlour singing haunts the lines, as well as a modern shyness, envious of such expressivity. The syncopated rhythm of these lines provides a continuo to the other sensations of this section: quiet dawn against noisy night, impressions of colour, black, then swooning pastel with Venus

> Beginning to faint in the light that she loves
> On a bed of daffodil sky . . .   (858–9)

After this, the more obvious contrast of red rose and white lily, red rose and white rose, disturbed by the intermediate blue of larkspurs and violets. The colours have a contrasting rhythm, together with something more subtle – syncope requires a beat and an offbeat, as asymmetry needs the notion of symmetry to work. Syncope means a swoon, a lapsing from regularity and continuity, which can be induced by regular alternations of sense impressions. Not only colour but light is imagined, especially in the image of Maud herself in 'gloss of satin and glimmer of pearls', the formal dress that would have glimmered in the night transformed into a rising sun in the pale dawn.

Mobility (and flight and falling) is another sensation of this poem, 'for the breeze of the morning moves', more freely than 'the dancers dancing in tune', and this catches up other sensations – of temperature (the chill of the outside suggested by tears and falling water, in contrast to the warmth of desire) and scent:

> And the woodbine spices are wafted abroad,
> And the musk of the rose is blown.

These perfumes inducing reverie are passively moved and passing, since 'blown' when used of flowers suggests their withering. The tense of the poem is mobile: it reviews the past and looks to the future, although the past and the future are confined to this night, imagined from a solitary present. These contrasts, movements, sensations, intensify in the last stanza, which imagines and summons Maud, sweet and mobile, an airy tread on the earth to whose beat the heart responds, or would respond, for the moment is still that of desire, and the future tense has passed into the conditional 'if only':

> She is coming, my own, my sweet;
> Were it ever so airy a tread,
> My heart would hear her and beat,
> Were it earth in an earthy bed;
> My dust would hear her and beat,
> Had I lain for a century dead;
> Would start and tremble under her feet,
> And blossom in purple and red.

Even in the swoon of imaginative death the heart is still preternaturally alert – 'my dust' is contradicted by the vivid sense of the pulsing organ full of blood. This conjunction of blossoms and blood, sexual love and violence, dominates *Maud*. As with the talking and listening flowers, the Persian convention of passion so intense that it will persist even after death and burial carries its original charge of erotic hyperbole, and adds to it a specific psychological realism, the dangerousness of the speaker's emotions.

Maud is a poem of aggressive desire, of the will to possess, as the pronouns here insist:

> I said to the rose, 'The brief night goes
> In babble and revel and wine.
> O young lord-lover, what sighs are those,
> For one that will never be thine?
> But mine, but mine', so I sware to the rose,
> 'For ever and ever, mine'.
>
> And the soul of the rose went into my blood,
> As the music clashed in the hall;

And long by the garden lake I stood,
  For I heard your rivulet fall
From the lake to the meadow and on to the wood,
  Our wood that is dearer than all . . .   (I, xxii, 876–87)

'But mine, but mine' is part of the threatening aspect of the
poem, latently dangerous even to Maud. This grasping is followed
by sharing: it is her rivulet (that is, the rivulet from the
hall owned by her father) but the wood it leads to is 'ours'.
The effect of this depends on moments earlier in the poem which
have stressed separate possession – 'my own dark garden
ground' (I, iii) where the speaker broods on the wealth of Maud's
family which he believes to depend on the ruin of his own father;
'our wood' (I, xii) means his family's wood into which Maud
has entered; then again Maud's 'garden of roses' and 'own little
oak-room' and 'own garden gate' which the speaker watches in
the dawn by the rivulet running down to 'my own dark wood'
(I, xiv).

The narrative, never separable as plot from the speaker's emotions, depends on this separateness of possession – the contrast
between those who have property and economic power like
Maud's family, and those who have not. Consequently houses and
their attached land are important, from the first sequence where
the houses and streets of the poor, 'hovelled and hustled together,
each sex, like swine', are set against 'the broad estate and the
Hall' now to 'be gilt by the touch of a millionaire' as Maud's
family return from abroad. These are economic facts about living
space – the spaces in which life is experienced – so that the
speaker's house becomes an image of his mind, like Mariana's
moated grange:

    Living alone in an empty house,
    Here half-hid in the gleaming wood,
    Where I hear the dead at midday moan,
    And the shrieking rush of the wainscot mouse,
    And my own sad name in corners cried,
    When the shiver of dancing leaves is thrown
    About its echoing chambers wide,
    Till a morbid-hate and a horror have grown
    Of a world in which I have hardly mixt,
    And a morbid eating lichen fixt
    On a heart half-turned to stone.   (I, vi, 257–67)

Half-wilfully Gothicizing, the speaker is imprisoned in his own
stoniness, but also in danger of being broken into – by Maud,

by economic aggression, by aspects of himself he wants to deny
but which are already eating him away:

> For a raven ever croaks, at my side,
> Keep watch and ward, keep watch and ward,
> Or thou wilt prove their tool.
> Yea, too, myself from myself I guard,
> For often a man's own angry pride
> Is cap and bells for a fool.   (I, vi, 246–51)

The image of breaking and entering moves invasively between
metaphor, fear of the self being entered by dangerous emotions,
and a realistic sense, from the value placed on property ('centre-
bits' being tools used by burglars):

> And Sleep must lie down armed, for the villainous centre-bits
> Grind on the wakeful ear in the hush of the moonless nights . . .
>   (I, i, 41–2)

This nightmare wakefulness, which the speaker presents as part of
his account of society, has its psychological origin for him in his
mother's scream as her husband's corpse was brought into the
house after his suicide: 'And my pulses closed their gates with a
shock on my heart' (I, i, 14).

When the speaker has killed Maud's brother and fled to Brittany,
in this exile and loneliness he notices a shell on the beach:

> See what a lovely shell,
> Small and pure as a pearl,
> Lying close to my foot,
> Frail, but a work divine,
> Made so fairly well
> With delicate spire and whorl,
> How exquisitely minute,
> A miracle of design!
>
> What is it? a learned man
> Could give it a clumsy name.
> Let him name it who can,
> The beauty would be the same.
>
> The tiny cell is forlorn,
> Void of the little living will
> That made it stir on the shore.
> Did he stand at the diamond door
> Of his house in a rainbow frill?
> Did he push, when he was uncurled,

A golden foot or a fairy horn
Through his dim water world?

Slight, to be crushed with a tap
Of my finger-nail on the sand,
Small, but a work divine,
Frail, but of force to withstand,
Year upon year, the shock
Of cataract seas that snap
The three decker's oaken spine
Athwart the ledges of rock,
Here on the Breton strand!   (II, ii, 49–77)

This lyric is itself a fossil, originally written in the 1830s, but it is placed here with psychological plausibility; the speaker himself comments as critics have done, that under emotional shock perception may focus on some apparently irrelevant thing. The Gothic fantasy of being enclosed and at risk in his own house showed a 'feminine' sensibility; here the lyric delicacy is feminine too (the fanciful prettiness of stanza three, imagining the tenderly vulnerable occupant), and dramatically appropriate to the moment – grace notes on the edge of hysteria, like Ophelia turning all to favour and to prettiness. The shell is a house whose occupant is gone, but because, though frail, it can withstand the seas better than the heroic three-decker, it becomes a metaphor for the 'living will', as in section CXXXI of *In Memoriam*, enduring when 'all that seems shall suffer shock' (Ricks, *Poems*, p. 1079). This lyric comes before the speaker's total breakdown into insanity, ending with a hope for Maud being comforted, before he knows of her death; it holds out the possibility of recovery. Tennyson noted: 'The shell undestroyed amid the storm perhaps symbolizes to him his own first and highest nature preserved amid the storms of passion.'

As an imaginative home the shell is not so empty as the speaker's house, which was desolate but desperately held on to as a form to hold him together. Beautiful in itself and strong, reviving for the moment a hint of natural theology ('a miracle of design'), it offers an image of a self which cannot be burgled, or fractured except by self-will. It is an ideal emblem of that which the speaker lacks for most of *Maud*: a self self-possessed. The lyric's short lines and the self-enclosed perfection of its first four stanzas contrast as a form for the speaker's consciousness to the strange long lines of I, i–iv, with their ranging and contradictory emotions, moved here and there by commonplace current scandal and prejudice, adopted with varying degrees of conviction as a protective armour of anger. These long lines are halted at the beginning of I, v by the lyric about Maud's song: the beginning of a desire for a more coherent self. In his original chaotic mood of angry impotence, wide open to paranoia because of his rage for self-protection –

> I keep but a man and a maid, ever ready to slander and steal;
> I know it, and smile a hard-set smile, like a stoic   (I, iv, 4)

– the speaker needed to hold on to 'my own dark garden ground', 'my own dark wood'. When he first sees Maud on her return she is enclosed in a carriage, behind glass (in contrast to his memory of her as a child, freely tumbling out of doors), and before he gains confidence in her love his awareness of her is very much as someone in her own space, under the guardianship of father and brother: 'Maud has a garden of roses' (I, xiv), her very own part of the 'high Hall garden'.

But the images of possession in I, xiv have a disturbing undercurrent, the 'dark undercurrent woe' that persists even into the magnificent love poem of I, xviii, from which the phrase comes. The roses, the lilies, the ramping lion at her gate clasped by the passion flower, help eroticize a space that is all the more vulnerable for being felt as so protected:

> Ah Maud, you milkwhite fawn, you are all unmeet for a wife.
> Your mother is mute in her grave as her image in marble above;
> Your father is ever in London, you wander about at your will;
> You have but fed on the roses and lain in the lilies of life.
>
> (I, iv, 158–61)

In I, xiv Maud is defined in and by her space, which the speaker seems to presume upon too far. Standing outside in the dawn, looking merely at 'the death-white curtain drawn', he imagines the interior, her private life:

> Maud's own little oak-room
> (Which Maud, like a precious stone
> Set in the heart of the carven gloom,
> Lights with herself, when alone
> She sits by her music and books
> And her brother lingers late
> With a roystering company) looks
> Upon Maud's own garden-gate:
> And I thought as I stood, if a hand, as white
> As ocean-foam in the moon, were laid

> On the hasp of the window, and my Delight
> Had a sudden desire, like a glorious ghost, to glide,
> Like a beam of the seventh Heaven, down to my side,
> There were but a step to be made.   (I, xiv, 497–510)

Maud as a jewel in a case, a Freudian object of desire, is inset in those brackets; but there is also sympathy for her enclosed there – the speaker attributes to her an affinity with his own solitude. Since the window's eye is closed by the curtains, it is really the speaker who 'looks', with some intensity. The lyric does not end in a benign ecstasy of spiritualized passion, but with the 'dark wood' again and the 'death-white curtain': the sudden fantasy that Maud is dead recalls his insomniac obsession with her image in I, iii:

> Luminous, gemlike, ghostlike, deathlike, half the night long
> Growing and fading and growing, till I could bear it no more,
> But arose, and all by myself in my own dark garden ground,
> Listening now to the tide in its broad-flung shipwrecking roar,
> Now to the scream of a maddened beach dragged down by the wave,
> Walked in a wintry wind by a ghastly glimmer, and found
> The shining daffodil dead, and Orion low in his grave.   (95–101)

Sexual passion leads to horror in I, xiv, and to the release of pent-up violence in I, iii, as the speaker projects his own feelings on to the wrecking sea, and into the strange corpses it leaves, the daffodil and the constellation Orion. This irrational horror lurks in *Maud*'s first image, 'the dreadful hollow behind the little wood' whose 'lips' are bloody. The name Maud can suggest 'maw', a gaping mouth, from the French *mordre*, to bite; one etymology gives its meaning as 'warrior maiden'; its sound suggests murder in German, *der Mord*. Ruby or Lily-Rose or Stella, names that could be associated with the delicate images of femininity in the poem, would not have this disturbing effect. The site of the father's suicide has superimposed on it an image of a woman's body bleeding from its nether mouth, the bloody blossom without fruit which haunts the whole poem. Once the association is made it cannot be warded off, but it means reading the poem below anything we can assume as conscious intention. One aim of 'spasmodic' poetry was to lower conscious controls. The dangerous undercurrent in the speaker's feelings about Maud is still there in the poem which follows 'Maud has a garden of roses', sustained by suspicion as to whether he really is dear to her:

So dark a mind within me dwells,
    And I make myself such evil cheer,
That if *I* be dear to some one else,
    Then some one else may have much to fear;
But if I be dear to some one else,
    Then I should be to myself more dear.
Shall I not take care of all that I think,
Yea even of wretched meat and drink,
    If I be dear,
    If I be dear to some one else.   (I, xv)

The obsessional repetition undermines the reasonable will to self-reform: it is the tense rhythm to which the sensual imagination moves that is important in *Maud*, and the feeling may prevail that there is one mind within the speaker, another inmate of the self, which is a threat to Maud – a morose husband, a Peeping Tom, or Jack the Ripper? Certainly some aspects of the speaker's sensibility breed extravagant fears and fantasies. In his concern with 'I', Maud fades to a vague victim of his intensity, 'some one else'.

From this point the speaker lays claim to Maud as he had done to his own dark spaces:

Think that I may hold dominion sweet,
Lord of the pulse that is lord of her breast . . . (I, xvi, 548–9)

The focus on his possessiveness is there in I, xxii, 5, and in I, xviii – that is, in his most passionate and generously loving lyrics:

My bride to be, my evermore delight,
My own heart's heart, my ownest own, farewell . . .
                                                    (I, xviii, 671–2)

If the degree of Tennyson's own distance from or engagement with the speaker's emotions is an issue in judging *Maud* – and I think it is a major one – then the insistence on the possessive is crucial, suggesting that the author is critical of the speaker but is deeply in tune with such feelings. The speaker makes a claim on Maud which, if true, would compromise the value for him of her free choice of him: that they were destined for each other by their fathers (I, vii). Quite surprisingly, given the negative character of both fathers, Tennyson added some lines in 1856 which make Maud endorse his dream from her memory:

Sealed her mine from her first sweet breath.
Mine, mine by a right, from birth till death.
Mine, mine – our fathers have been sworn.
                                                    (I, xix, 724–6)

Tennyson described the speaker as an egotist, raised above egoism and insanity 'through the unselfishness born of a great passion' (Ricks, *Poems*, p. 1039). Something of this is figured in the move from an insistent 'my own' to the shared tracts of love, 'Our wood, that is dearer than all', where their meeting-places are printed with her image (I, xxii, 887). But although a space of sharing is reached, inequality is built into the structure, and without it *Maud* could not be itself nor achieve the insights which it does. The speaker can never be 'placed' from an objective viewpoint. Maud does have a name by which she can be handled: the title of the poem is the name of the speaker's emotions about this woman, but she has no self, no consciousness to which the reader has access, in strong contrast to the free speech and brooding sensibility of Ida in *The Princess*. The ways in which she is imaged are split along the lines of the speaker's consciousness, which is protective towards her as his own, and aggressive towards her as owned by others; he sees her as both passive and as a provoker of violent feeling, almost at times as a sadistic dominatrix, trampling his heart under her feet. She is a fawn in King Solomon's garden, a perfect flower (but growing 'a little too ripe, too full'), a cold jewel or remote star. These images flicker in the phantasmagoria of his obsession:

> Cold and clear-cut face, why come you so cruelly meek,
> Breaking a slumber in which all spleenful folly was drowned,
> Pale with the golden beam of an eyelash dead on the cheek,
> Passionless, pale, cold face, star-sweet on a gloom profound;
> Womanlike, taking revenge too deep for a transient wrong
> Done but in thought to your beauty, and ever as pale as before
> Growing and fading and growing upon me without a sound,
> Luminous, gemlike, ghostlike, deathlike, half the night long
> Growing and fading and growing . . .   (I, iii)

Such images say more of the speaker than of Maud; no sooner does he think of her than he thinks of her dead, 'Dead perfection, no more' (I, ii). The conjunction of the daffodil ('narcissus', its species name, in the trial edition) with the hunter's constellation Orion, at the end of the section just quoted, is echoed in the contrast of black night and the star of love swooning in a daffodil sky, in I, xxii, 2, and finally in III, vi, 1. The echo suggests perhaps the doomed nature of their relationship, star-crossed like Romeo and Juliet, and the narcissism of the ideal passion that the speaker has summoned up for himself, as that which he needs or deserves as a reflection of himself. As in the English Idyls, ideal love is in danger of becoming a form of suicide, like that of Narcissus. Impossible to say how deliberate such a suggestion may be, but the nymph Echo, the someone else for whom Narcissus did not care, presides in the first stanza of *Maud*, though rhyming imperfectly:

> I hate the dreadful hollow behind the little wood,
> Its lips in the field above are dabbled with blood-red heath,
> The red-ribbed ledges drip with a silent horror of blood,
> And Echo there, whatever is asked her, answers 'Death'.

Maud's feminine images define by opposition the masculinity which the speaker desires for himself. Heir only to his father's failure, unmanned by the economic power which his society values, he seeks more archaic roles as a lover and a fighter. As the shell emblem offers a finer hope than enlistment, so the love relationship can find a third term between the bleeding body and the cut-glass lady:

> I have led her home, my love, my only friend.
> There is none like her, none . . .   (I, xviii, 599–600)

Maud here is neither a stereotype nor a vague 'some one else'. The 'clamorous heart' that so dominates the whole poem is at this moment no longer unbearably overcharged in its beating, and the dark undercurrent is transformed to a warm and sweet surface running:

> on and on
> Calming itself to the long-wished-for end,
> Full to the banks, close to the promised good.   (602–4)

Maud's light step is assimilated to the natural detail of the garden, the 'dry-tongued laurels' pattering talk'; the real gates that close do not close on his heart, liberated by love. 'There is none like her, none' – the refrain comes back a third time, but repetition here is assured delight, not being locked in suspicious obsession. The imagination travels East, as the precise stimuli of the Victorian novel in verse – the tremor at the hand just emerging from the glove, as in I, vi, 268–75 – give way to biblical epic, the garden of the Song of Solomon and of Adam and Eve before the fall:

> There is none like her, none
> Nor will be when our summers have deceased.
> O, art thou sighing for Lebanon
> In the long breeze that streams to thy delicious East,
> Sighing for Lebanon,
> Dark cedar, though thy limbs have here increased,

Upon a pastoral slope as fair,
And looking to the South, and fed
With honeyed rain and delicate air,
And haunted by the starry head
Of her whose gentle will has changed my fate,
And made my life a perfumed altar-flame;
And over whom thy darkness must have spread
With such delight as theirs of old, thy great
Forefathers of the thornless garden, there
Shadowing the snow-limbed Eve from whom she came.
(I, xviii, 611–26)

Still moving beyond, the poem imagines stars and space, at first alien, 'a stormy gulf . . . and hollow sky' in which the image of Maud as a pearl (like the shell) needs to be held as a reassuring 'countercharm', but finally expanding freely:

And ye meanwhile far over moor and fell
Beat to the noiseless music of the night!
Has our whole earth gone nearer to the glow
Of your soft splendours that you look so bright?
I have climbed nearer out of lonely Hell.
Beat, happy stars, timing with things below,
Beat with my heart more blest than heart can tell . . .
(I, xviii, 674–80)

Even the stars have become soft, happy and near, like Maud. Ominously, with the beating of the heart only in a momentary trance at one with 'the deep pulsations of the world', the undercurrent woe returns; resisted, but returning:

Blest, but for some dark undercurrent woe
That seems to draw – but it shall not be so:
Let all be well, be well.   (I, xviii, 681–3)

Much of *Maud*'s effect comes from its bodily sense of emotion, like Keats's image of the shocked heart, 'too small to hold its blood' (*The Fall of Hyperion*, 254). There are recurrent images of the body's weight, and of its lifting or dissolution. The poem begins with the heavy body of the father falling, to become 'a dead weight trailed'. This primal scene of horror in the house with its 'shuffled step', whispering, and heart-stopping shriek, is followed by an image of Maud's father as a vampire gorged with blood; and the speaker's heart turned to stone; in I, viii Maud sitting in church beneath a stone angel blushes, and his heart beats 'stronger / And thicker.' The relation of the speaker and Maud's brother is one

151

of stone against stone (I, xiii, 780); the weight first associated with the father's corpse is displaced onto feelings about the brother. Between the love poems, I, xviii and xxii, comes an attempt to bury the memory of the first scene, 'All this dead body of hate', accompanied by fear of becoming 'light-headed . . . Fantastically merry' (I, xix, 783–4), while still dreading the return of the brother whose absence has left the Hall 'the lighter by the loss of his weight' (I, xvi, 538). The sense of his over-heavy masculine body is reinforced by the comparison of him to an Assyrian bull, like the statue Layard had recently brought to England; he becomes the second corpse. In contrast to the weight of the corpse and of the passionate heart into which the whole life of the body seems at times to be condensed, is the fantastic nervous mobility of I, xxii, with its light stepping. These effects are brought together in the mad scene, II, vi, as the dust and bones of heart and body are still disturbed by continual noise and movement, wheels, horses, footsteps, and beg to be buried 'ever so little deeper', so that nervous consciousness may end. *Maud* is burdened with heavy corpses of men, one replacing another.

Maud dies too, though since this brief section (II, iii) preludes the speaker's furthest descent into insanity, readers who do not notice it can be excused: it could be a fantasy like that of his own death; he has always thought of her as ghostlike. Essentially Maud's death or survival is of little weight in her poem. One thread which we can pick out from the speaker's hectic reaction to his murder of her brother is that it has settled accounts. Personal vengeance is a crime of blood, unlike just war; but at least it gives a rational cause for guilt, in which the speaker includes himself with all those he has railed against (II, i, 45–8; II, v, 327–33). The animosity directed against the brother bulks large and masks deeper animosity, too deep almost for expression, against that always shadowy 'gray old wolf' the father. Vindictiveness against him is expressed in II, v, 291–4, but gives place to tears of pity:

> For what will the old man say
> When he comes to the second corpse in the pit?
>
> (II, v, 525–6)

In the death of his son Maud's father is imagined as forced to confront the original crime, his own, as if he might see it as retribution; guilt is shared. Since the corpses are doubled, one substituting for the other, we could also see the fathers doubled, the speaker's scores against both settled, so that he can at last feel pity and, as he emerges from neurosis, lay down the law about the distinction between war and private violence (II, v, 327–33). In the underlying psychology I have supposed, the speaker now feels himself to be a man, identified with other men. The resolution of animosity to fathers and rival sons has mattered more than the relation to Maud which has mediated it.

In *Victorian People* Asa Briggs noted that leading statesmen were unable to give any clear idea of why the Crimean War had broken out, or what purposes England's intervention was meant to secure. Nevertheless it was a highly popular war, whose propagandists saw Britain as a liberal policeman enforcing justice and freedom in the world. Later, as new technology made possible the most effective war reporting yet, and brought home the incompetence of its administration and the squalid reality of its suffering, what survived was popular idealization of the soldier, as the only solace for national pride.

The immediate cause of the war had been the Tsar's claim to exercise protective authority over all Christians under the rule of the Turkish Empire, which roused European fears about Russian encroachment on the Mediterranean. France and Britain became allies to support Turkey. This involved some curious shifts of sympathy for the national poet, Tennyson. Byron, whom he admired, had been the great poet of liberalism, supporting emergent nation states in their struggles to free themselves from imperial rule; he had died while contributing to the struggle of the Christian Greeks against the Turks. In his original mood of rancour and apathy the *Maud* speaker rejects this kind of Byronic role:

> The passionate heart of the poet is whirled into folly and vice.
> I would not marvel at either, but keep a temperate brain;
> For not to desire or admire, if a man could learn it, were more
> Than to walk all day like the sultan of old in a garden of spice . . .
> (I, iv, 140–3)

> Shall I weep if a Poland fall? shall I shriek if a Hungary fail?
> Or an infant civilisation be ruled with rod or with knout?
> *I* have not made the world, and He that made it will guide.
> (147–9)

He wants to see his apathy as a kind of Oriental detachment (such as Edward FitzGerald espoused); but when he is finally roused to participation in a shared cause it is for an alliance with the Turkish sultan. Eastern 'barbaric despotism' had to be identified with Russia alone, in the newspaper representation of the Crimean War as one between civilization and barbarism. The East, however, also represented a set of alternatives to the 'Mammon-worship' of industrialized civilization in Britain. Translations such as FitzGerald's of Omar Khayyám (1859) and travel books like *Eothen* (1844), by Tennyson's friend A. W. Kinglake, suggest the East as a place where domesticity, commerce and 'the British Goddess, Sleek Respectability' could be escaped, at least for a time.[5] The speaker in his apathy and the brother in his arrogance are both compared to sultans; but the speaker also yearns for a Great Man to rule, to simplify confused values. This was also a notion popular in newspapers at the time, part of the national mood that the speaker represents:

> Ah God, for a man with heart, head, hand,
> Like some of the simple great ones gone
> For ever and ever by,
> One still strong man in a blatant land,
> Whatever they call him, what care I,
> Aristocrat, democrat, autocrat – one
> Who can rule and dare not lie. (I, x, 5)

The French alliance also threw up contradictions. Many of the sentiments in *Maud* I, i and iv derive from a dialogue, 'Peace and War', in *Blackwood's Magazine* for November 1854. The article which followed this dialogue blamed the British for Russia's aggression: the animosity against the French aroused by Louis Napoleon's coup d'état in December 1851 had led Russia to suppose that Britain would not ally with France in support of Turkey. The word 'imperialism' was first used of Louis Napoleon's regime, which became the Second Empire: cutting across liberal bourgeois opinion, its appeal was populist, the tyranny of all through one so feared by Tennyson, who also shared fears that under this new Napoleon the French would invade Britain. He sent a bit of money to a Volunteer Rifle Corps raised by friends, though with a humorous sense of his sedentary and pacific situation:

The more noise we make in that way the better, and the more we practise the less likely are we to be called upon to perform . . . I think I could hit a Frenchman at 100 yards, if he did not frighten me.[6]

He made a good deal of noise in several poems of 1852, such as *Britons, Guard Your Own*, *Rifle Clubs!!!* and *Hands All Round!*, attacking the government for failure to manage and finance the army adequately. *Suggested by Reading an Article in a Newspaper*, published under the Arthurian pseudonym Taliessin, disingenuously praised two of these poems which had been published under the name of Merlin; its penultimate stanza criticizes modern youth in terms which prefigure the *Maud* speaker, but also rallies to the standard of manhood as he was to do:

> Better wild Mahmoud's war-cry once again!
> O fools, we want a manlike God and Godlike men.

The *Maud* speaker maintains this patriot's attack on government, in the description of the brother seeking a seat in Parliament and of the suitor he finds for Maud:

> a lord, a captain, a padded shape,
> A bought commission, a waxen face,
> A rabbit mouth that is ever agape –
> Bought? what is it he cannot buy?   (I, x, 358–61)

The spirit of the militarist poems, not fully integrated into the Laureate's public role, goes into *Maud*; so does the uncontrollable weeping of *Oh! that 'twere possible*, an earlier lyric on Tennyson's grief for Arthur Hallam which provided the nucleus around which *Maud* was written. The 'Peace and War' dialogue in *Blackwood's Magazine* offered one model for fusing such emotion with national identity and manly self-esteem. Hardly a dialogue, since the man of peace is only present to be patronized, it attacks Peace Societies, the Quakers (who had sent a delegation to the Tsar to promote peace) and northern manufacturers, as woman-dominated and womanish themselves, depending on 'a strong man armed' to defend their property while deploring aggression. The peace of commerce is 'a gigantic system of thieving and adulteration', 'a hollow and hating peace'. War offers a new chivalry – duelling like that of Scott's King Richard and Saladin (in *The Talisman*) promotes love between men, and self-love: 'he shows him his own manhood'. The dialogue ends by envisaging a blood brotherhood between Britain and France, sealed by war and maintained in peace, with Britain's 'masculine' moral strength married to the 'feminine' art of France to produce the perfect European, misquoting *The Princess*: 'Perfect music exalts noble words'.

If we see the *Maud* speaker as originally 'unmanned' because all his father had bequeathed him was commercial failure, the bleeding body of the first lines can now be read as an image of castration: the most literally dangerous face of becoming more like a woman. The speaker's expressed emotions about his father show more revulsion than compassion; there is barely an attempt to find alternative reasons for respecting him. His neurosis can be attributed to Oedipal guilt – as if he had inflicted on his father the wound, castration, which the son in Freudian theory is supposed to fear that the father could inflict on him. The inheritance of failure (the more rational cause of guilty resentment) depended on the values of modern European capitalism. As the poem yearns Eastward, like its cedar of Lebanon, the old manly roles of lover and fighter rear up. The hopefully androgynous ideals of *The Princess* and *In Memoriam* are lost in an aggressive masculinity, as the woman becomes a cipher, merely inspiring towards the cannons. The sanity of self-possession and the tenderness of relationship with another separate person, which are great moments in *Maud*, are overwhelmed in the final drive toward 'The blood-red blossom of war with a heart of fire' (III, vi, 53).

Nathaniel Hawthorne said that the Crimean War gave 'a vast impulse towards democracy' because it exposed the incompetence of Britain's established rulers. The scandal which the war became would have increased Tennyson's wish to disown the implications of *Maud*'s ending, so that he could claim to have been objectively and critically representing a national madness. In part, he had; but the poem's expressive power depends on the poet's involvement in the troubled feelings it evokes and explores. It cannot be said that in *Maud* Tennyson is 'typing all mankind': as in the word 'mankind' the woman as a subject in her own right is set aside, to serve masculine anxiety and assertion. It was the last long poem in which Tennyson took a chance with his readers' sympathies, and the only one in which he so deeply and openly explored the dangers of feeling.

Idylls of the King

The Mount was the most beautiful in the world, sometimes green and fresh in the beam of morning, sometimes all one splendour, folded in the golden mists of the West. But all underneath it was hollow, and the mountain trembled, when the seas rushed bellowing through the porphyry caves; and there ran a prophecy that the mountain and the city on some wild morning would topple into the abyss and be no more.

(Prose sketch, *c.* 1833, Ricks, *Poems*, p. 1461)

The *Idylls of the King* were in production for half a century, 1833–85, with major periods of work in 1855–9 and 1868–74. The 'matter of Britain', the stories of Arthur and his knights, had been considered and rejected by Milton and by Wordsworth as a subject for a national epic. In the early nineteenth century, when Scott's sense of history was popular, there were three new editions of Malory's *Morte d'Arthur*, a late fifteenth-century work which had used the old stories to promote the Tudor monarchy. In the nineteenth century research into and publication of early texts was part of the simultaneous recovery and invention of tradition. The Prince Consort had suggested that the Arthurian cycle was the equivalent of Germany's national cycle, the *Niebelungenslied*, and this led to the inclusion of Arthurian themes in William Dyce's new decorations of the Houses of Parliament. Public schools and the Oxford Union were similarly adorned; Tennyson's early lyrics on Galahad, Lancelot and Guinevere helped inspire the enthusiasm of William Morris, Burne-Jones and the Pre-Raphaelite painters. The material attracted both Tories and radicals such as Morris and F. J. Furnivall, the founder of the Early English Texts Society; there may have been a link with Freemasonry. Arthurian figures were frequently used to represent spiritual types; Prince Albert was painted in armour to symbolize his chivalry as a modern gentleman, as Tennyson described him in the *Dedication* to the 1862 edition of the *Idylls*, the year after his death.

However, Tennyson's work on the *Idylls* was always attended with doubt and hesitation. The prose draft, from about 1833, says of Camelot: 'But all underneath it was hollow.' The frame written for *Morte d'Arthur* (1842) says that an attempt to bring back 'the style of those heroic times' would be like trying to bring back the Mastodon, and *Morte d'Arthur* itself has more to do with enduring loss than with recovering an old order. The *Idylls* necessarily participated in the national craze, and both the *Dedication* and *To the Queen* (1873) indicate that Tennyson appreciated such a role for his long series, perhaps as mitigating its pessimism. He disliked readings that were too precisely allegorical, preferring to speak of a more general 'parabolic drift' permitting many meanings:

Poetry is like shot silk with many glancing colours. Every reader must find his own interpretation according to his ability and according to his sympathy with the poet. (Ricks, *Poems*, p. 1463)

The first four Idylls were published in 1859, as *Enid*, *Vivien*, *Elaine* and *Guinevere*, studies in 'The True and the False'. Existing originally as a unit in this way they represent 'woman's influence' on 'the dream of man coming into practical life and ruined by one sin'. Each was later worked into the whole series: for example, *The Coming of Arthur*, *Gareth and Lynette* and *Balin and Balan* all finally prepare the way for the revised *Merlin and Vivien*. Vivien is a Temptress, luridly presented and trivially conceived. She uses no magical powers but parades 'feminine' wiles: pouting or spiteful, she is disliked too much to be seductive, and it is a real puzzle why her nagging and her slander of Arthur's court should result in Merlin telling her the charm which gives her total power over him, so that he is imprisoned for ever. Merlin's submission to her deprives Arthur of magical assistance as Lancelot's betrayal will finally deprive him of half his physical forces. Since Merlin submits to a woman he sees as a kitten or a harlot – and malicious – the value of his supernatural forethought looks dubious. His opinions of women are crude clichés: Vivien's curiosity is 'this vice in you which ruined man / Through woman the first hour', and her imputation of her own baseness to others so as 'not to feel lowest' moves him to say that men 'at most differ as Heaven and Earth' while women, 'worst and best, as Heaven and Hell'. This leaves little ground for women to stand on.

In spite of its unconvincing psychology and moral that even the wisest man can be made a fool of by sex, *Merlin and Vivien* has some interest in relation to the *Idylls* as a whole. The most significant thing about Vivien is her triviality. She confirms Merlin in his melancholy at 'The meanest having power upon the highest' (188–94, added in 1873). Like Tristram in *The Last Tournament* (1871) she signifies 'the lustfulness of the flesh' which 'could not believe in anything good or great' (Ricks, *Poems*, p. 1593). Her imprisonment of Merlin in a hollow oak by means of his own learning represents the condition of knowledge in the nineteenth century – with no book of revealed truth and no direct access by magic (or visionary poetry) the understanding of things is locked up in the things themselves, accessible only by accumulated observation, experiment and speculative theory. *Merlin and Vivien* is a parable of this state of things coming about: orphaned of the supernatural music that had set the building of Camelot in motion, Arthur's kingdom is like nineteenth-century Britain. The 'laws' of science could offer no grounds for altruism and love. In fact, because Tennyson deliberately tried to avoid the marvellous except in writing of Arthur's coming and passing, *Merlin and Vivien* has a less than dramatic effect in the series.

Merlin prefigures an unhappy modern consciousness; his observation of the Orion nebula foreshadows the terrible science of astronomy, terrible to Tennyson because it dwarfed human time-spans and values:

> I never gazed upon it but I dreamt
> Of some vast charm concluded in that star
> To make fame nothing . . .   (*Merlin and Vivien*, 509–11)

Tennyson's own fascination with Orion was part of contemporary interest in 'the vastest object in the Universe – a firmament of stars too far away to be resolved into stars by the telescope, and yet so huge as to be seen by the naked eye' (Ricks, *Poems*, p. 1609): a visible sign of the limitations even of science. Merlin tells a story of the origin of his knowledge in a 'little glassy-headed hairless man', who is in every way an anti-type to the patriarchally hairy Merlin:

> And since he kept his mind on one sole aim,
> Nor ever touched fierce wine, nor tasted flesh,
> Nor owned a sensual wish, to him the wall
> That sunders ghosts and shadow-casting men
> Became a crystal, and he saw them through it,
> And heard their voices talk behind the wall,
> And learnt their elemental secrets, powers
> And forces . . .   (618–31)

Unlike any scientist, he had direct vision of the secrets of nature which he wrote down in a tiny book, its square of text like a blot, its script like the limbs of fleas, an irritant (665–77). Merlin's charm is an interpretation of the marginal comments on this unreadable text, 'And none can read the comments but myself' – a wry small myth of the transmission of knowledge. The problem of using old texts and beliefs is germane to the whole of the *Idylls*, especially to *The Holy Grail*.

Without the clear knowledge of his old original, Merlin is prey to melancholy; it is this which is really responsible for his failure of commitment to Arthur, as Tennyson presents it. He half-believes in Vivien's love; his disdain and indignation at her are also half-feelings. The one specific content of his prophetic melancholy is of Vivien's power to debase and paralyse ideals (300–3), and it serves only to debase and paralyse him. His desire for mastery in knowledge is subject to the uncertain moods of his body: the poem's strongest images are of emptiness, blindness, vastness, distracted by surface effects such as Vivien's robe 'In colour like the satin-shining palm / On sallows in the windy gleams of March' (222–3). The best of the poetry foreshadows his imprisonment, when what Keats called 'the feel of not to feel it' will lack even language:

> he was mute:
> So dark a forethought rolled about his brain,
> As on a dull day in an Ocean cave
> The blind wave feeling round his long sea-hall
> In silence . . .   (227–31)

The theme of Vivien's love song is 'the little rift within the lute' that stops the music, an image for mistrust as a kind of petty damage which destroys totally, like rot in stored fruit. Her refrain, 'trust me not at all or all in all', could work two ways, to warn of her treachery or to defend Arthur's idealism that would not see his friend's adultery with his wife. Vivien's love is of a material kind, like that of Guinevere and Lancelot, Tristram and Iseult, that 'carves / A portion from the present, eats / And uses, careless of the rest' (459–61), which she opposes to Merlin's concern for 'Fame' and 'use'. Like the text of science, her song is emblematic: an old one, its verses 'live dispersedly in many hands' (455) like the scattered pearls of the Queen's necklace, some stolen, some lost.

While Vivien functioned really as the agent of Merlin's melancholy, full blame lights on Guinevere, whose adultery is contrasted in the original grouping with the virginal passion of Elaine, and Enid's marital loyalty. The most sympathetic reading of *Guinevere* would recognize the positive feelings with which Tennyson offered its first lines (now the end of Arthur's speech, 575–7) as a birthday gift to his wife in 1857 – the year when new divorce laws made it easier for wives to separate from their husbands:

> But hither shall I never come again,
> Never lie by thy side; see thee no more –
> Farewell!

Enid represents early summer and the prime of life, the point of balance of Arthur's reign in the whole sequence of Idylls. Derived from Lady Charlotte Guest's translation of the Welsh *Mabinogion*, the story is told with some verve, though so long that it was divided in 1873 into *The Marriage of Geraint* and *Geraint and Enid*, forming then the third and fourth Idylls, to follow *Gareth and Lynette* (1872), the spring Idyll of initiation into manhood and marriage. Much simple pleasure in *Enid* comes from its natural images, which Tennyson's notes associated with home occupations, gardening or cliff-walking at Farringford. Enid is associated with hidden, shy, sudden presences, birds, fish, water. Sometimes this suggests her sensitivity, as in her fear of appearing a dull fish among the silver-tissues and cloth-of-gold creatures of the court (*The Marriage of Geraint*, 645–75); or her admiration of her husband's muscles, sloping like water over stones (73–8) – one of the few moments which suggest that the knights had bodies not to be ashamed of. The dress offered to Enid in the domain of Earl Doorm pays tribute to the qualities she gives the Idyll, the liquid shimmer and flow which Geraint in his sullenness tries to obscure:

> a splendid silk of foreign loom,
> Where like a shoaling sea the lovely blue
> Played into green, and thicker down the front
> With jewels than the sward with drops of dew,
> When all night long a cloud clings to the hill,
> And with the dawn ascending lets the day
> Strike where it clung: so thickly shone the gems.
>
> (*Geraint and Enid*, 686–92)

These descriptions have the fresh, homely, inward quality of the English Idyls, of waking to what is familiar and loved:

> and wings
> Moved in her ivy, Enid, for she lay
> With her fair head in the dim-yellow light
> Among the dancing shadows of the birds . . .
>
> (*The Marriage of Geraint*, 559–602)

A sparrow-hawk is the trophy of the tournament by which Geraint wins Enid; much less heraldically, he is twice imaged as a robin, sharp-eyed for something to pounce on in her (*The Marriage of Geraint*, 773–4; *Geraint and Enid*, 430–1). This petty preying is pursued downwards in the simile of Earl Doorm's courtesans:

> such the old serpent long had drawn
> Down, as the worm draws in the withered leaf
> And makes it earth . . .   (*Geraint and Enid*, 631–3)

This naturalist's precision, startling in a romance, and all of the imagery cited, of moments of sensitivity, awareness, attraction, suspicion, offer what D. H. Lawrence would have called a 'passional' underfeeling. *Enid* is really more concerned with the husband's bad behaviour than with the wife's exemplary submission; at the end she is aligned with Arthur for her simple nobility that imputes her own qualities to others. Geraint is studied as a 'case'. Attractively impulsive and sensual, he is aligned with Guinevere: both are late risers, left behind to watch the hunt from a distance; an insult to her sends him off on a quest; she promises that if he finds a bride, then she will dress her fine for their wedding even if the bride is a beggar; this then dictates his treatment of Enid. He wished Enid to be close to Guinevere, but at the rumour of the Queen's adultery takes her from the court; then is quick to construe her distress at his 'effeminate' absorption in her, as evidence of infidelity. His extremism, the difficulty he has with subtler interactions, is suggested in *Geraint and Enid*, 101–15, when he feels it would be easier to murder Enid than to speak his fears and have her answer him. His whole way of carrying on is condensed into a sharp little vignette as he sets off into the wilds of marital misunderstanding with Enid condemned to ride silently before him, and flings a purse of gold at an unwary watching squire:

> So the last sight that Enid had of home
> Was all the marble threshold flashing, strown
> With gold and scattered coinage, and the squire
> Chafing his shoulder . . .   (*Geraint and Enid*, 24–7)

Geraint's two final opponents are projections of himself: Doorm is his arbitrary will and Limours is 'amour', 'Half ridden off with by the thing he rode' (*Geraint and Enid*, 460). He needs to feel himself 'a rock in ebbs and flows, / Fixt on her faith' (*The Marriage of Geraint*, 812–13), but subjects that faith to continual unreasonable testing. Modern counselling as opposed to medieval morality would say that Enid's obedience is 'half the problem',

but her obedience is not the element in the marriage which Tennyson stresses. The original story has her repeatedly disobeying his
command of silence as they journey through the wilderness, in
order to save their lives; Tennyson dramatizes Geraint's blindness
to his own folly, with the tone of a bully on his dignity:

> 'Forward! and today
> I charge you, Enid, more especially
> What thing soever ye may hear or see,
> Or fancy (though I count it of small use
> To charge you) that ye speak not but obey.'
>
> *(Geraint and Enid*, 413–17)

Her reply is as patient as it can be while suggesting that she may
be quicker to see. But he knows what quick-sightedness is for; she's
not married to a fool; he's well able to look out for them both (*Geraint
and Enid*, 424–9). This is the wrangling of domestic comedy, with
Enid as foil to Geraint's absurdity; that Tennyson is capable of this
should be noted as a balance to Merlin's misogyny and Arthur's
blaming of Guinevere. With some psychological realism, he looks
critically at 'manliness' in relation to marriage.

Edyrn's speech near the end makes the point that an excessive
concern with being manly will lead to humiliation (*Geraint and
Enid*, 825–72). The echo of the clash of swords between Edyrn and
Geraint, at the initial tournament, is heard as a 'clapping as of
phantom hands' (*The Marriage of Geraint*, 566) – an acute aural
observation which also suggests that the man-to-man combat is
being mocked somewhere. Two passages of natural description
continue the argument:

> And here had fallen the great part of a tower,
> Whole, like a crag that tumbles from the cliff,
> And like a crag was gay with wilding flowers . . .
>
> *(The Marriage of Geraint*, 317–19)

> down his enemy rolled,
> And there lay still; as he that tells the tale
> Saw once a great piece of a promontory,
> That had a sapling growing on it, slide
> From the long shore-cliff's windy walls to the beach,
> And there lie still, and yet the saplings grew . . .
>
> *(Geraint and Enid*, 160–5)

The idea of some massive thing toppling, yet still able to bear
growth, reinforces the moral that Edyrn and Geraint can survive
the humiliations they bring upon themselves.

His honour rooted in dishonour stood,
And faith unfaithful kept him falsely true.

(Lancelot and Elaine, 571–2)

These heavy oxymorons define Lancelot as the lover of Arthur's Queen. Simple oppositions define Elaine in her song and in Lancelot's relation to her, dark maturity against morning glory. Their idyll reaches heights of frigid symbolism; its perspectives and deflections could be diagrammed, or illustrated with the aid of a prism. It is built on disguise and misrecognition, beginning with Lancelot's lie to Arthur and concealment of his identity, in consequence of his misreading a glance from Guinevere. The focusing image for the misdirections of light and sight is the prize of diamonds which Lancelot has won for Guinevere over nine years, which she climactically flings through a window as Elaine's funeral barge passes beneath:

> and down they flashed, and smote the stream.
> Then from the smitten surface flashed, as it were,
> Diamonds to meet them . . .
>   and right across
> Where these had fallen, slowly past the barge
> Whereon the lily maid of Astolat
> Lay smiling, like a star in blackest night.   (1227–35)

The effect is brilliant, as if some problem set in *The Lady of Shalott* had been worked out, but it is little more than a stage effect. 'A diamond is a diamond', Gawain says, meaning it purely materialistically. Just as Lancelot in his final review of his life remembers *his* mysterious birth, as if he could substitute for Arthur, so Elaine has wanted to be Guinevere, Lancelot's love, the one for whom the diamonds were destined. She stages her funeral barge like a bridal bed for a queen, on which she will make her debut at court, displacing attention from Guinevere: she wants to be seen and known (1045–54).

Yet the drive motivating Elaine's performances is innocent: the fixity of her diamond and lily emblems is in contrast to the epitaph for the cynical Gawain, 'blown along a wandering wind, / And hollow, hollow, hollow all delight' (*The Passing of Arthur*, 36–7). The first scene has her placing Lancelot's shield so that the light will strike off it and wake her every morning. She embroiders a fantastic case for it, a secondary working over of her feelings which she indulges while locking herself away from her household and her father to strip the shield bare again and tell herself stories of Lancelot fighting. Like the Lady of Shalott she is a kind of artist, dwelling on Lancelot's image to summon up a new story of legitimate love. Yet her love is also presented as very direct: she asks him to marry her as her reward for saving Lancelot's life after the Tournament of Diamonds, and in returning the shield strips it bare again (971–2). Elaine's love story, however, is secondary and instrumental, offering a perspective on the love of Guinevere and Lancelot, which is the real subject of this Idyll and of *Guinevere*; melodramas in marble of innocent and sinful love.

The ideal represented by Arthur and his Round Table (unwritten, like the code of the English ruling class, the Constitution, and the civilizing mission of Empire) is destroyed by the adultery of his Queen with his most famous knight. The rumour of it is blamed as the source of trouble in almost every Idyll, and this is finally confirmed by Arthur:

> Then others . . .
> drawing foul ensample from fair names,
> Sinned also, till the loathsome opposite
> Of all my heart had destined did obtain,
> And all through thee! . . .   (*Guinevere*, 486–90)

so that

> The children born of thee are sword and fire,
> Red ruin, and the breaking up of laws,
> The craft of kindred and the Godless hosts
> Of heathen swarming o'er the Northern Sea . . .   (422–5)

This ruinous sin is made central to the *Idylls*. Tennyson's handling of it is both too definite and too evasive. Arthur's tirade against Guinevere is not meant as a display of a distressed man's self-deceptions – it is the last word on the subject from an ideal authority, which moves the erring wife to love too late. A contemporary critic commented that Guinevere had been given into Arthur's keeping and that he had failed 'to keep her safely, by neglecting to understand her feelings and her character'.[1] This is not a response to which any of the *Idylls* are at all hospitable or alert, but once a breath of it is felt the last words of definition that Tennyson added to the *Idylls* in 1899, 'Ideal manhood closed in real man' (*To the Queen*, 38), are untenable.

It is worth comparing Malory's account of the final disruption since his work is a major source and one which is still easily accessible.[2] Malory is no moral allegorist: his several ladies of the lake are on no particular side; for example Vivien's original,

Nimue, is malign to Merlin but friendly to Arthur, while Merlin is just as ambivalent, foreseeing the love of Guinevere and Lancelot but not advising against Arthur's marriage. Arthur's tragedy in Malory is a political not a domestic one: once the affair is made public his alliance with the best knight in the world cannot be maintained. Mordred (here Arthur's son by his half-sister) has exposed the affair in order to weaken Arthur's power and usurp the throne. But it is plain that not even Lancelot's abduction of the Queen to save her from the proper punishment, burning, could have made a permanent breach; this requires additional motivation. Gawain, Mordred's half-brother but loyal to Arthur, had refused to attend the burning so as not to oppose the predictable rescue, but his younger brothers were there, unarmed, and were killed by Lancelot in the confusion. Because of this Gawain kept Arthur committed to war against Lancelot. Malory has a parting between Guinevere and Lancelot (which Tennyson omitted because he thought Malory's could not be bettered), and moving confrontations between Lancelot and Arthur. There is no comparable scene between Guinevere and Arthur because it is not their emotions for each other which matter.

The feelings of Malory's Arthur about male loyalty and brotherhood survive strongly in the Arthur of *Guinevere* – they are even suggested in the creaturely sympathy of his horse that 'neighed / As at a friend's voice', when Arthur pauses briefly in his denunciation of his wife. The great absence in the *Idylls* is a *Lancelot and Arthur*. Possible aspects of their relation are indirectly dealt with, fragmented and transposed into other stories: the fratricide of *Balin and Balan*; Gawain's seduction of Pelleas's love Ettarre, under the guise of brotherly assistance; Mark's murder of Tristram in *The Last Tournament*, stabbing his wife's lover in the back. The possibility of a revelation haunts *Lancelot and Elaine*, where Lancelot's feelings of guilt are juxtaposed with Arthur's criticism of him for rather lesser faults, played against the stormy misunderstandings of Lancelot and the Queen, each criticizing the other in comparison to Elaine and Arthur. In all this Lancelot is presented as the victim of the passionate woman, praying finally for annihilation. The eerie episode in which Arthur finds the diamonds which should be the emblem of true love (Tennyson added it to Malory's narrative) casts a dark light on brotherly love also: they were the relic of a mortal combat between 'two brothers, one a king' (*Lancelot and Elaine*, 34–55).

If Tennyson's Lancelot was falsely true to Guinevere he was

truly false to Arthur, but any direct facing of this is masked by the abstract terms, honour/dishonour, truth/falsity. As the relations of the three are developed through the whole narrative, it does look as though the condemnation of Lancelot should have been more bitter than that of Guinevere; but he is left to private remorse. In *The Last Tournament*, the last stage in Arthur's rule, 'pain was lord' in the hearts of both Queen and King (239, 485), a phrase which echoes Arthur's triumph in the battle which won him both Guinevere and the deathless love of Lancelot:

> And in the heart of Arthur joy was lord.
> He laughed upon his warrior whom he loved
> And honoured most. 'Thou dost not doubt me King,
> So well thine arm hath wrought for me today.'
> 'Sir and my liege', he cried, 'the fire of God
> Descends upon thee in the battle-field:
> I know thee for my king!' Whereat the two,
> For each had warded either in the fight,
> Sware on the field of death a deathless love.
> And Arthur said, 'Man's word is God in man:
> Let chance what will, I trust thee to the death.'
>
> (*The Coming of Arthur*, 123–33)

Guinevere's commitment to Arthur is far from being as personal and definite as this, though she echoes their vows at her marriage, 'with drooping eyes'. When Arthur fell in love with her she had not noticed him; all the doubt and decision as to whether she should marry him is her father's. At this point Lancelot's role as proxy is only briefly mentioned (*The Coming of Arthur*, 446–51), but she relives the experience just before Arthur's denunciation (*Guinevere*, 375–404). Her preference for Lancelot as her first love could have been presented as not unlike Elaine's unpersuadable passion; the same could not have been true of Lancelot, given his commitment to Arthur. Their ride together is not so much invented by Tennyson as stolen away from the story of Tristram and Iseult (which is then played in a much more cynical key), giving their love a fated quality, as if they also had drunk a love potion. But this narrative implication which could have lessened Guinevere's moral burden is not developed. F. J. Furnivall commented furiously on the blaming of Guinevere: 'If any one is to be blamed for men's lusts let it be *men*' – though he is right about Tennyson going easy on Lancelot, he chivalrously assumes that women are not lustful.[3]

What damns Guinevere is the high valuation put on the influence of the good woman, from within her proper sphere of the home, a Victorian value which survives hardily in the notion that women are nicer than men (but if they're not they're horrid). Given her story Guinevere never had a chance in this role, yet it is made part of the novice's story of Arthur's destiny:

> and could he find
> A woman in her womanhood as great
> As he was in his manhood, then, he sang,
> The twain together well might change the world.
>
> (*Guinevere*, 296–9)

Guinevere's social role in the *Idylls* is restricted to the dissemination of courtesy and of corruption by example; there is no work she is imagined as competent for, least of all motherhood, the heart of 'woman's influence'. Tennyson has not thought clearly or felt generously enough about the contradictions of using this medieval/Renaissance material in the nineteenth century. Guinevere's fault is like Merlin's, half-commitment, because she did not 'see' Arthur soon enough. It is also a characteristic of Tennyson's writing, that produces the most striking effects of the *Idylls*, the eerie pessimism that environs them:

> Beneath a moon unseen albeit at full,
> The white mist, like a face-cloth to the face,
> Clung to the dead earth, and the land was still.
>
> (*Guinevere*, 6–8)

The Queen's wish, too late, to see Arthur as she had failed to see him at first brings back this eeriness, as he is metamorphosed into the gray ghost of legend:

> but she saw,
> Wet with the mists and smitten by the lights,
> The Dragon of the great Pendragonship
> Blaze, making all the night a steam of fire.
> And even then he turned; and more and more
> The moony vapour rolling round the King,
> Who seemed the phantom of a Giant in it,
> Enwound him fold by fold, and made him gray
> And grayer, till himself became as mist
> Before her, moving ghostlike to his doom.
>
> (*Guinevere*, 592–601)

This is the end of Arthur's attempt to realize the ideal, according to Tennyson's final directions for reading the *Idylls*:

this old imperfect tale,
New – old, and shadowing Sense at war with Soul,
Ideal manhood closed in real man,
Rather than that gray king, whose name, a ghost,
Streams like a cloud, man shaped, from mountain peak,
And cleaves to cairn and cromlech still . . .

(*To the Queen*, 36–41)

Guinevere was much admired, and by readers as intelligent as George Eliot and the poet Arthur Clough. Possibly they admired the bravura display of agonized emotion, or the dignity of Guinevere's silence, not defending herself; Clough did say, 'He should have told her to get up.'[4] The scandal of the adultery makes a problem for the *Idylls* as a whole: is it to be read as the agent of a decline which the poem's view of history accepts as inevitable, like the cycle of a life or the seasons, or as a failure in commitment to a quality of life which could have been attained? Guinevere found Arthur too much of a Soul, too faultless, with no touch of earth – 'The low sun makes the colour' (*Lancelot and Elaine*, 131–4). If we reason from the Sense/Soul, ideal/real oppositions, it would be Lancelot who was real and ideal, as in Guinevere's metaphor of the sky and earth at sunset, while if Guinevere represented Sense, Arthur as Soul would be at war with his wife, a conflict hardly likely to fulfil his early hope:

'Then might we live together as one life,
And reigning with one will in everything
Have power in this dark land to lighten it,
And power on this dead world to make it live.'

(*The Coming of Arthur*, 90–3)

The confusion in Tennyson's oppositions derives from his pessimism, which makes ideal aspirations seem like ill-tempered complaints, if they are not realizable. *The Holy Grail* attempts to find a more adequate role for poetic idealism.

The Holy Grail (1869) is the story of quests after visions of the cup into which Christ's blood was said to have flowed when he was crucified; mythologists and theosophists like Bryant and Boehme interpreted this cup as a female symbol. Despite the largely negative representation of 'Woman' in the *Idylls*, Tennyson retained androgyny as an ideal: 'They will not easily beat the character of Christ, that union of man and woman, strength and sweetness' (Ricks, *Poems*, p. 1687). Hallam Tennyson thought

169

that this note referred to the close of *The Holy Grail*, where Arthur speaks of his visionary experiences and their relation to Christ as the divine made real and human. But just as the androgynous union preserves differences (masculine is strength, feminine is sweetness), so the spheres of vision and reality are distinguished in language. The side-effect is to suggest that 'vision' is a sort of leisure activity, as Arthur, like a Shakespearean monarch, compares himself to the peasant:

> Who may not wander from the allotted field
> Before his work be done; but, being done,
> Let visions of the night or of the day
> Come, as they will . . .   (*The Holy Grail*, 904–7)

The separation of spheres is typical of nineteenth-century discourse, some of whose major debates Tennyson addresses in this Idyll: the struggle for cultural and political leadership between traditional religious institutions and scientific reforming rationalism; the idea of historical development according to natural laws against a spiritual and ethical view of individuals and society; and how mysticism, and ideas of prayer and miracle, related to the practical working of society.

In the eighteenth century the Anglican Church had allowed the practice of offering prayers on special occasions to lapse. This was revived when special days of prayer were ordered to plead for divine intercession against rainfall threatening harvests, or against cattle plagues and typhoid fever. Charles Kingsley was one of those who resisted, refusing in August 1860 to offer prayers for fair weather, on the grounds that God worked by general laws and not by particular interventions; the sort of argument Arthur Hallam had used. What was at issue was the Church's authority, against the view that in so far as these things were controllable it was by human forethought and action in the light of scientific knowledge. Two views of the world and of human status within it were at odds. The monarchy in this case threw its weight behind the Church: when the Prince of Wales was dangerously ill with typhoid in December 1871, prayers were offered for his recovery; the service of thanksgiving for his recovery in February 1872 was felt to depreciate the part played by medical science. It was in this context that the Prayer Gauge debate arose: the challenge as to whether three years of prayer could be shown to improve mortality and recovery rates for a particular disease.[5] In *The Passing of Arthur* (1869) Tennyson had put a middle position, that prayer witnessed to human need:

> For so the whole round world is every way
> Bound by gold chains about the feet of God.   (422–3)

This is rather an odd, obstructive metaphor for human and divine entanglement. He deliberately wards off the precision of reasoning, since reason cannot prove the value he puts on reverent humility (*The Holy Grail*, 445–57).

The Holy Grail is also concerned to find a place for irrational and ecstatic intuition, an issue raised in the conflict between Protestantism and Roman Catholicism. Traditional mistrust of power, mystery and ritual was exacerbated by the re-establishment of the Roman Catholic hierarchy in Britain, in 1850. From the 1830s the Tractarian movement had been insisting on the apostolic authority of the Anglican Church, as a spiritual body enforcing its doctrines and as a power in Parliament; the Church had lost some bishoprics after the 1832 Reform Act. Tractarians opposed the broadening of Anglican doctrine to accommodate the findings of biblical scholarship and science. At this time the Church was the major professional opportunity for educated men, as the grandfather's expectations for the Tennyson brothers suggested. In 1845 Newman, the leading Tractarian, left the Anglican for the Roman Church, followed by others in the next decade. The Tractarian movement and High Anglicanism throve on the aesthetic and imaginative deprivations of the ultilitarian view of economic man. It also made conventional Anglicans query what it was they believed. The Anglican Church had prided itself on its rationality; this now seemed to lead to scepticism, as did the Evangelical stress on eternal punishment. The doctrines of the Fall, or Original Sin, and the Atonement, led to doubt as to God's morality – a major theme of working-class radicals. The Catastrophists' more or less cheerful acceptance of volcanoes, earthquakes and the extinction of species as all part of a providential plan led to similar doubts. The extremes of Evangelicalism and Tractarianism led to defections from formal religious observance; Tennyson was no churchgoer.[6]

Miracles were also called in question by the archaeology of knowledge itself, by German criticism. If the divine birth and resurrection of Jesus were doubted, as in Strauss's *Life of Jesus*, then so were the doctrine of Atonement and the promise of eternal life, which Tennyson would not relinquish. Biblical criticism had developed out of the collection and study of folk tales and traditions in Germany. The motive was less the old anti-clerical desire to expose the lies of priests, than positive curiosity about the construction and transmission of stories, as a collective human activity. The true interest of miracles was in how they came to be believed, and how stories of them were used. In the 1840s and 50s interest in Homer also contributed to fascination with narrative, bringing awareness of the use in oral poetry of set expressions and pre-fabricated passages, and raising the question of whether the Homeric poems were the work of one author, or compilations.

In these habits of thought Tennyson found the means to handle the legend of the Grail Quest in such a way that the value of religious symbols and the levels of experience to which they relate could be acknowledged without propagating superstition and without denying sceptical reservation. For the first time in the *Idylls* the story is told indirectly – although *Guinevere* had pointed the way, in using the innocent novice to animate the Queen's reveries with the stories she has heard from her father about the magical early days of Arthur's reign. The Grail story is told by Percivale, shortly before his death, to a fellow monk, Ambrosius, who has already heard some of it from a traveller he later realizes was Sir Bors; his homely speech and concerns help to define the story of the spiritual extremist Percivale as questionable. Five different accounts of the Grail vision are given, varying with the nature of the seers; this accords with the liberal Anglican notion of revelation as accommodated to the perceptions of particular eras, and with Tennyson's favourite dictum that 'every man imputes himself'. Percivale begins by insisting that the Grail was no phantom, but is finally glad that 'no phantom vexed me more'. Indeterminacy has invaded the position of the story teller: Percivale gives a new version of Merlin's disappearance, that he sat inadvertently in his 'Siege perilous' (the spiritual imagination, according to Tennyson's note, Ricks, *Poems*, p. 1666) and so was lost.

Once Tennyson had found this method he used it for *The Coming of Arthur*, written in February 1869, where stories of Arthur's doubtful origins and possibly miraculous birth are given by different speakers according to their dispositions. Leodogran, investigating all this in order to decide whether to marry Guinevere to Arthur, finally makes his decision on intuition, after a dream (*The Coming of Arthur*, 424–45). The writing of *The Holy Grail* between 9 and 14 September (Tennyson said, 'It came like a breath of inspiration', Ricks, *Poems*, p. 1660) made a way for the new idylls published with it in 1869, *The Coming of Arthur*, *Pelleas and Ettarre* and *The Passing of Arthur*, which incorporated the *Morte d'Arthur*. Tennyson made *The Coming* and *The Passing of Arthur* more archaic, partly to adapt to the earlier mode of the *Morte* but possibly also to suggest the uncertain legendary character of the 'gray ghost' emerging into the practical life of history, and dissolving again; the original titles were *The Birth* and *The Death of Arthur*. If *The Holy Grail* was finally a way through, it had long been a stumbling block. Tennyson had written in 1859:

I doubt whether such a subject could be handled in these days without incurring a charge of irreverence. It would be too much like playing with sacred things. The old writers *believed* in the Sangreal.

(Ricks, *Poems*, p. 1661)

His comment on the end of his poem values the figure of Christ without wishing to examine the grounds of belief:

There is something miraculous in man, and there is more in Christianity than some people think. It is enough to look on Christ as Divine and Ideal without defining more. (Ricks, *Poems*, p. 1687)

Intuition was enough; the quest for proof, miraculous or other, is deprecated, and in such areas the natural scientists agreed with him. He knew that he was stepping into a minefield of different beliefs, and this was the condition both for his tact and for his elated conviction of technical success in what was also 'one of the most imaginative of my poems' (Ricks, *Poems*, p. 1661).

Dwight Culler mocks Tennyson's concern to keep a 'thread of realism' so that all the potentially marvellous adventures and beliefs in the *Idylls* could be accounted for 'naturally':

In earlier years Tennyson did not feel a need to provide an alternative explanation for the Sea-Fairies or the Kraken or to assert that the Hesperides were three African ladies who had a pet lizard.[7]

This ignores the different scope of such poems, and Tennyson's sensitivity in the *Idylls* to how much contemporary life there was in questions of the nature and authority of a religious world view; it was not for him a purely academic or aesthetic question. The success of *The Holy Grail* is in the ingenuity of the structure in relation to its problems, in avoiding both mockery and superstition, and in the excitement of the apocalyptic quests of Galahad and Lancelot. Though the Quest is disastrous, Arthur rebukes the cynical Gawain, 'too blind to have desire to see'. His final speeches also confirm the significance of the poem's narrative–symbolic method, which respects different intuitions and is conscious of the fallibility of communication:

ALFRED TENNYSON

For every fiery prophet in old times,
And all the sacred madness of the bard,
When God made music through them, could but speak
His music by the framework and the chord:
And as ye saw it ye have spoken truth.

(The Holy Grail, 872–6)

This is a poem which wants to give mysticism its due, in the figure of Sir Galahad; not to do so would shred the shot silk of poetry. Galahad is inspired by Percivale's sister, who has the first vision of the Grail. Disappointed in love, she fasts to expiate the scandal of Guinevere's adultery and this produces her vision; her extreme piety begins the destruction of Arthur's credibility which is completed by Modred. Nevertheless, critics who see her, Percivale and Galahad as all motivated by a psychotic sublimation of sexuality travesty the poem's investment in Galahad's year of miracles, his experience of the sacrament as real (464–81) and his final entry after missionary crusading into the spiritual city, out of this world (515–32). The quest also has its Everyman in Sir Bors, modestly manly and also 'feminine' in his motive, to be of use to Lancelot in a spirit of waiting on God. His imprisonment by sun-worshippers symbolizes the dangerous range of options open to faith without specific form; his captors are materialists, like Vivien, Tristram, and Pelleas in his disillusionment. The vision of the Grail that brings Bors's release is the least sacramental and the most touching:

In colour like the fingers of a hand
Before a burning taper . . .

(690–1)

The image is of a commonly available experience suffused with wonder; different in feeling from Gawain's destiny, 'blown along a wandering wind', when the loading of all value on to natural delight has proved hollow in death (The Passing of Arthur, 35–7).

Idylls written after The Holy Grail exaggerate the extremes of opposition in the whole series, between idealism and sensual degeneration: the spring honeymoon of Gareth's initiation is to be contrasted to the violent swerve of Pelleas from naive faith to disillusion, so that he comes to prefer the 'great and sane and simple race of brutes' to Arthur's vows that distort the natural man (Pelleas and Ettarre, 471). He becomes the brutal Red Knight, intercut with Tristram of the Woods in The Last Tournament. Within The Holy Grail such mood swings are treated more critically, with Arthur representing a middle ground of ordinary action and satisfaction. Percivale begins his quest in an ecstasy of confidence which drops at once to despair and doubt; it becomes an allegory of contempt for the world in which 'wifely love and the love of the family' (Ricks, *Poems*, p. 1673), wealth as the reward of labour, glory and fame, one after the other fall

> into dust, and I was left alone,
> And thirsting, in a land of sand and thorns.   (389–90)

This myth of displaced desires, of the imaginative hunger which makes every gratification barren, leads towards the quests of Galahad and Lancelot; it is played out a second time under Ambrosius's ballad-style questionings – 'Came ye on none but phantoms . . .!', 'Saw ye none beside?' Percivale like Ulysses could have had the woman he loved most and a kingdom with her, but for the sake of the quest 'Cared not for her, nor anything upon earth'. Arthur stands out against this kind of not-caring, but it has its own kind of dignity in the poetry of Percivale's quest.

When the knights take their fatal vow to pursue the quest of the Grail, Arthur is absent chasing the attackers of an 'outraged maiden', returning hacked and grimed and seared in strong contrast to the bright faces full of the vision (264–7). Immediately before, Percivale's description of Arthur's hall had made clear the significance of its statuary and windows as representing history: action in a world with a beginning (Arthur's finding of the sword Excalibur) and an unknown destination (the window left blank), rather than the worldless eternity into which Galahad is to disappear. The point is repeated in a minor key in Ambrosius's apologetic account of his parochial concerns, his pastoral care rooted in gossip and curiosity. The moral is about both religious controversy and social action.

The writings of palaeontologists and geologists, Lyell and Buckland in particular, effected a radical change in the imagination of existence in time. Their images of flood, swamps and ancient bones are called up for Galahad's journey out of time and into transcendence. Simultaneously the bridge between the marvellous world of legend and spirit, and the world of evolutionary time, is destroyed:

> On either hand, as far as eye could see,
> A great black swamp and of an evil smell,
> Part black, part whitened with the bones of men,
> Not to be crost, save that some ancient king
> Had built a way, where, linked with many a bridge,

A thousand piers ran into the great Sea.
And Galahad fled along them bridge by bridge,
And every bridge as quickly as he crost
Sprang into fire and vanished, though I yearned
To follow . . .   (498–507)

Of this whole passage Tennyson noted: 'It was a time of storm when men could imagine miracles, and so storm is emphasized' (Ricks, *Poems*, p. 1676). The time when miracles could be imagined has gone; even Percivale when he sees the Grail confirms that 'never eyes on earth again shall see' it. The distraction of the mystical quest had destroyed whatever hope Arthur's world had of fusing ideal and real; matching Guinevere's lack of belief, the questers also have doomed Arthur to return to the mists of legend. At such points the *Idylls of the King* can be seen to be about the impossibility of their ambitions. The miraculous statuary falls from Arthur's halls; the knights return through the ruins of a marvellous construction, in an uncertainty enacted by the reader's hesitancy about the grammatical construction:

> our horses stumbling as they trode
> On heaps of ruin, hornless unicorns,
> Cracked basilisks and splintered cockatrices,
> And shattered talbots, which had left the stones
> Raw, that they fell from, brought us to the hall.   (713–17)

The many quests conclude in the shattering of fable. Set beside the everydayness of vision in Wordsworth's *The Prelude*, or Emily Dickinson's truth that 'must dazzle gradually', the language of *The Holy Grail* is too aesthetically fixed and pictorial. On the other hand it could be compared to Browning's *Bishop Blougram's Apology* (1855), which also attempts to rescue something of religious intuition from rationality. Tennyson's argument is that values do not come from idealistic searching but from getting the immediate business of the world done; but by comparison to Browning's monologue he does manage to give more substance to imaginative intensity than to knowing worldliness. The language of visionary intensity in Lancelot's quest suggests his heroic suffering of spirit, his desire for either redemption or annihilation. Some of his narrative is very badly done ('I have been the sluggard, and I ride apace', 642), with some Calvinistic crudities about weltering in slime and sin (767–79), but mostly it moves with the energy of the driven man, guarded between lions by either lunacy or faith to a moment of grace, preluding T. S. Eliot's *The Waste Land*:

> only the rounded moon
> Through the tall oriel on the rolling sea.
> But always in the quiet house I heard,
> Clear as a lark, high o'er me as a lark,
> A sweet voice singing in the topmost tower
> To the eastward . . .   (827–32)

Lancelot's vision of the Grail blasts and burns; or rather it is almost a vision, but for a stammering doubt, 'methought I saw'(843):

> I had sworn I saw
> That which I saw; but what I saw was veiled
> And covered; and this Quest was not for me.   (847–9)

His Romantic tragedy almost reaches the heroism of a confession to Arthur, but so indirectly that Arthur's reply remains in the realms of abstraction. The representation of Lancelot here releases Tennyson's Byronism: whereas for Guinevere the suffering she has caused to Arthur and all is dwelt on without remorse, Lancelot's sin is finally his private problem, a pain at the heart's core that sets the seal on his glamour.

The most important meanings of the *Idylls of the King* were achieved by 1869, with the publication of *The Holy Grail and other poems*, as six Idylls titled 'The Round Table' and framed between *The Coming* and *The Passing of Arthur*. The major imaginative effort of adapting the old material to the nineteenth century had been made. In this effort, it is repressive both about women's powers and about sexual love and pleasure, with the kind of repressiveness that makes sex exciting because it is bad and doomed; a far cry from both the English Idyls and *The Princess*. But in responding to the conflict between mystical–religious and humanist–rational accounts of the world it succeeds intelligently and imaginatively, because in this area it is sensitive to differences.

The *Idylls* are often technically brilliant. Tennyson was proud of his use of metre for imitative form; less predictable is the expressive use of cross-cutting in *The Last Tournament*, when the brutal massacre of the Red Knight and his men by Arthur's youngest knights is inset into Tristram's story of adulterous love and murder, so that the killing seems part of Tristram's dream in which the ruby necklace he has won seems like frozen blood, melting in the rivalry of his two Isolts (*The Last Tournament*,

406–88). The connection of sex and battle recalls *Maud*. Apprehension of a materialist view of the world produces some really impressive writing. Swinburne's *Tristram of Lyonesse* was written in response to *The Last Tournament*, but Tennyson's idyll was already, partly, an expression of horror at the sensuality and atheism of Swinburne's play *Chastelard* and his *Songs before Sunrise*. Swinburne and F. J. Furnivall (the defender of Guinevere) were in collusion to contradict Tennyson's use of Arthurian material: the *Athenaeum* for 14 March 1868, noted that Swinburne was 'composing a poem on Tristram and Yseult, and writing an Essay on the women of Arthurian Romances for the Early English Texts society, in which Tennyson's views will not be adopted'. In their view the story could only gain tragic human significance if Arthur's incest were acknowledged as the cause of his disaster; the idealization of Arthur was as unconvincing for them as it was for Tennyson's Vivien. On the other hand, Tennyson was still Hallam's 'poet of Sensation', so that the *Idylls* are alert to how the world feels to his materialists. Tristram as an observing creature, a hunter, is finely observed; his perceptions of a world that is only for survival and enjoyment are haunted by echoes of Genesis and *Paradise Lost*, of a Holy Spirit fleetingly present on the face of the waters and then distracted to chaos again:

> Before him fled the face of Queen Isolt
> With ruby-circled neck, but evermore
> Past, as a rustle or twitter in the wood
> Made dull his inner, keen his outer eye
> For all that walked, or crept, or perched, or flew.
> Anon the face, as, when a gust hath blown,
> Unruffling waters re-collect the shape
> Of one that in them sees himself, returned;
> But at the slot* or fewmets* of a deer,
> Or even a fallen feather, vanished again.
>
> (*The Last Tournament*, 363–72)

* *slot* – trail
* *fewmets* – droppings

Tennyson needed the world to return an image of man sustained by God; but his poetry could understand what Swinburne's was always conscious of, a material world that preceded and survived human purpose and desire.

Formalist approaches to the *Idylls* can show how their completed single line, extended through the discontinuities of individual idylls, is unified by repetition and recurrence: through the use of songs and dreams; through the symbolism of landscape, music, colours and heraldic beasts; through the parallelism of scenes and situations, not least the marital triangle, which is parodied by Pelleas, Ettarre and Gawain, and by Tristram, Isolt and Mark, as the Red Knight parodies the Round Table, and as Shakespeare is parodied in *The Last Tournament*, in the fool's loyalty to the divinely foolish king; through the analogies between Arthur's reign and the natural cycles of the seasons and of individual lives. Through this circling runs the possibility of providential progress, a line reaching beyond the inevitable decline of Arthur's order of things. That he may in some sense survive his death, as legend demanded, points toward the ultimate apocalypse or Ideal City of the world: far off, at last, as in *The Golden Year*, not now.

Yet this labour of cross-referencing does not of itself invest the poem with an aesthetic significance and status beyond query. Tennyson's art here does have the odour of death or at least, in William Empson's phrase, of mouldy wedding cake about it.[8] The nerve of feeling and thinking through was just about spent in *The Holy Grail*; even there, tact in not offending anybody may not deserve the highest praise, as Empson said of *Tintern Abbey*. Only one Methodist periodical took exception to it. This is the problem of the *Idylls*. If we engage with them without prejudice they can be taken in and spoken for on their own terms, only to feel dried blood in the mouth, grave-clothes on the body. Yet they exist and not negligibly either, as evidence both of Tennyson's astonishingly sustained mature work, and of nineteenth-century consciousness and its representations, in which the open explorations of *The Princess*, *In Memoriam* and *Maud* sink under idealization and the fear of sensuality. Security is sought in imperialism. Tennyson for all his individualistic recalcitrance had always been involved with the Broad Church, with people interested in a national idea uniting State, Church and People. The recovery of legend, romance and early texts had always been political, concerned to produce a sense of nationhood. This becomes explicit in the anxieties of *To the Queen* (1873). These were provoked by arguments that Canada, like other colonies, should secede from a 'Greater Britain' grown too large and too expensive:

> Is this the tone of empire? here the faith
> That made us rulers? this, indeed, her voice
> And meaning, whom the roar of Hougoumont*
> Left mightiest of all peoples under heaven?

What shock has fooled her since, that she should speak
So feebly? wealthier – wealthier – hour by hour!
The voice of Britain, or a sinking land,
Some third-rate isle half-lost among her seas?

(*To the Queen*, 18–25)

* Hougoumont – Waterloo

Arthurian values ('To do the good and right the wrong') were
as vague and comprehensive as those of Britain's civilizing mission to the world, to which the world could never take an English
attitude. Imperial value in *To the Queen* is a mystification of power,
scorning its crucial economic base. Self-respect and love of one's
own place do not need to be so bellicose and hierarchical. It is
chilling to find North American aesthetic academics expounding
the form and symbolism of the *Idylls* in terms which respond to this
imperial mood without reservation. Those who doubt Arthur's
power are called 'subversives'. With the quietist pessimism of the
literary man William Buckler, for example, scolds those who ex-
pect ideals to be realizable, but likes to see Leodogran welcoming
Arthur as 'wholly serviceable' to his problems of law and order,
and calls the celebration by the knights of Arthur's marriage 'the
Battle-Hymn of the Arthurian Republic'.[9] This goes hand-in-
hand with a sexual moralism which beats Tennyson at his most
harsh: Buckler's 'bestial couplings in the wild' is over-topped
when John Reed makes Guinevere responsible for the death of the
child Nestling. Tennyson handled this rather tenderly (*The Last
Tournament*, 20–9), but Reed, like one of Ibsen's husbands con-
founding 'moral' with physical disease, busily allegorizes: 'In
these arms where innocence no longer rests, no innocence can
live.'[10] There's strong sentiment there, but little compassion.
The yearning of Tennyson's writing towards power indistinguishable from 'the good' is compromised by its conviction that
people, like Lancelot, just aren't up to maintaining the necessary
commitment. This conflict however leads to no revaluation of
idealism itself: the kind of revaluation a confrontation between
Arthur and Lancelot could have entailed. The mood that
finally dominates the *Idylls* is the dread of a valueless world,
uncanny, utterly alien, an atmosphere powerfully evoked in
familiar constellations of images and cadences – the moaning sea,
the returning woe, the inarticulate void and vastness, the terrible
strangeness of there being voices in such a universe.
Sir Bedivere the average knight takes the place of Sir Lancelot,

as one of the first witnesses to Arthur and his last, who must 'go
forth companionless' as the days and years darken round him, to
tell Arthur's story 'Among new men, strange faces, other minds'.
'Comfort thyself', says Arthur, with proper harshness as in
Malory, 'what comfort is in me?' (*The Passing of Arthur*, 394–415).
Bedivere's task is to fling away the sword Excalibur, a precious
relic of Arthur that might have endorsed his mere stories. This
slinging away of an idol, a fetish, in a starry spectacle and a rush
of human energy, is one of the great moments of *The Passing of
Arthur*, where the level norms of the·metre and syntax lift to
splendour, miming, in the extra syllable of line 306, 'the rush of
the sword as it is whirled in parabolic curve':

> Then quickly rose Sir Bedivere, and ran,
> And, leaping down the ridges lightly, plunged
> Among the bulrush beds, and clutched the sword,
> And strongly wheeled and threw it. The great brand
> Made lightnings in the splendour of the moon,
> And flashing round and round, and whirled in an arch,
> Shot like a streamer of the northern morn,
> Seen where the moving isles of winter shock
> By night, with noises of the Northern Sea.   (301–9)

Tennyson's style itself can have the fetishistic quality of symbolist
poetry, when it lets go of the questioning indeterminacy of *In
Memoriam* to become a thing in itself, at odds with his Protestant
suspicion of forms. 'Style' is always a major presence in the *Idylls*.
Here it is used for the need to let go of comforting fixed presences,
of forms and idols, whether of Arthur himself or of the sword.
Excalibur's power is only fully realized in the moment of its loss.
The onomatopoeic display, ice-cold, metallic, stony, of Bedivere
bearing Arthur out of the world has the same paradoxical quality,
echoing with the strangeness of human language and presence in
the material world:

> But the other swiftly strode from ridge to ridge,
> Clothed with his breath, and looking, as he walked,
> Larger than human on the frozen hills.
> He heard the deep behind him, and a cry
> Before. His own thoughts drove him like a goad.
> Dry clashed his harness in the icy caves
> And barren chasms, and all to left and right
> The bare black cliff clanged round him, as he based
> His feet on juts of slippery crag that rang
> Sharp-smitten with the dint of armèd heels –

And on a sudden, lo! the level lake,
And the long glories of the winter moon. . . .

  and from them rose
A cry that shivered to the tingling stars,
And, as it were one voice, an agony
Of lamentation, like a wind that shrills
All night in a waste land, where no one comes,
Or hath come, since the making of the world.

      (*The Passing of Arthur*, 349–60, 366–71)

Notes

The place of publication is London unless otherwise stated.

Introduction

[1] Charles Tennyson and F. T. Baker, 'Some unpublished poems by A. H. Hallam', *Victorian Poetry*, Supplement, III, no. 3 (Summer 1965), pp. 10–11.

[2] O. Doughty and J. R. Walsh (eds.), *Letters of D. G. Rossetti*, Clarendon Press, Oxford, 1965, I, p. 245.

[3] P. G. Scott, 'J. A. Symonds and the reaction against Tennyson', *Tennyson Research Bulletin*, Lincoln, 2, no. 3 (1974), 85–95.

[4] J. F. Hagen, *Tennyson and his Publishers*, Macmillan, 1979, p. 122.

[5] Norman Page, *Tennyson: Interviews and Recollections*, Macmillan, 1983, pp. 87, 117.

[6] *Tennyson Research Bulletin*, Lincoln, 4, no. 1 (1982), 1.

[7] Lee Erickson, 'The poet's corner: the impact of technological changes in printing on English poetry 1800–1850', *English Literary History*, LII, no. 4 (1985), pp. 893–911.

[8] Martin Meisel, *Realizations*, Princeton University Press, 1983, pp. 56 and *passim*.

[9] Isobel Armstrong, *Victorian Scrutinies*, Athlone Press, 1972, for this and other reviews quoted, as well as a very useful discussion of critical attitudes.

[10] John Killham, 'Tennyson and the sinful queen', *Notes and Queries* (1958), 507–11.

[11] Ricks, *Tennyson*, pp. 161–3.

[12] Robert Bernard Martin, *With Friends Possessed: A Life of Edward Fitzgerald*, Faber and Faber, 1985, p. 193.

[13] Douglas Bush, *Mythology and the Romantic Tradition*, Harvard University Press, 1937 and 1963, pp. 198, 202.

[14] J. D. Jump (ed.), *Tennyson: The Critical Heritage*, Routledge and Kegan Paul, 1967, p. 12.

[15] A. J. Busst, 'The image of the androgyne in the nineteenth century' in Ian Fletcher (ed.), *Romantic Mythologies*, Routledge and Kegan Paul, 1967, pp. 1–95.

[16] Stephen Prickett, *Romanticism and Religion*, Cambridge University Press, 1967, pp. 67, 246–7.

[17] Unpublished paper by Gareth Stedman Jones, King's College, Cambridge, 1986.

[18] E. S. Shaffer, *Kubla Khan and the Fall of Jerusalem*, Cambridge University Press, 1975, pp. 246–7.

[19] Gillian Beer, *Darwin's Plots*, Routledge and Kegan Paul, 1983.

[20] Tess Cosslett, *The Scientific Movement and Literature*, Harvester, 1982.

[21] W. F. Cannon, 'The problem of miracles in the 1830s', *Victorian Studies*, IV (1960), 5–32.

[22] Walker Gibson, 'A distinction between poetic and scientific language in Tennyson, Lyell and Darwin', *Victorian Studies*, II (1958–9), 60–8.

1 English Idyls

[1] Ricks, *Poems*, p. 914.

[2] E. F. Shannon, *Tennyson and the Reviewers*, Archon Books, 1967, p. 120.

[3] Robert Pattison, *Tennyson and Tradition*, Harvard University Press, 1979, p. 161.

[4] Christopher Ricks, 'Tennyson's methods of composition', *Proceedings of the British Academy*, LII (1966), 226.

[5] For information about the Alexandrian idyll I am indebted to Pattison's book and to A. Dwight Culler, *The Poetry of Tennyson*, Yale University Press, 1977.

[6] Quoted by J. R. Watson in *Encounters: Essays on Literature and the Visual Arts*, J. Dixon Hunt (ed.), Studio Vista, 1971, p. 109. See also Mordecai Omer, *Turner and the Poets*, GLC, 1976.

[7] Norman Page, *Interviews and Recollections*, p. 138.

[8] D. S. Hair, *Domestic and Heroic in Tennyson's Poetry*, University of Toronto Press, 1981, p. 32.

2 Monologues and metonymy

[1] Ricks, *Poems*, p. 354.

[2] Martin Meisel, 'Half sick of shadows: The aesthetic dialogue in Pre-Raphaelite painting' in U. C. Knoepflmacher and G. B. Tennyson (eds.), *Nature and the Victorian Imagination*, University of California Press, 1977, pp. 309–40.

[3] Pattison, *Tennyson and Tradition*, pp. 154, 157.

[4] John Killham, *Tennyson and The Princess*, Athlone Press, 1958, p. 13.

[5] J. T. Sherry, 'Tennyson and the paradox of the sign', *Victorian Poetry*, XVII (1979), 204–16.

[6] Pattison, p. 161.

[7] Robert Langbaum, *The Poetry of Experience*, Penguin Books, Harmondsworth, 1974; Alan Sinfield, *Dramatic Monologue*, Methuen, 1977. See also W. E. Fredeman, 'One word more – on Tennyson's dramatic monologues' in Hallam Tennyson, *Studies in Tennyson*, Macmillan, 1981, pp. 169–85.

8 W. E. Fredeman, 'A sign betwixt the meadow and the cloud', *University of Toronto Quarterly*, XXXVIII (1968), 69–83.
9 Henry Kozicki, *Tennyson and Clio*, Johns Hopkins University Press, 1979, p. 156.

3 *The Princess*: mimicry and metamorphosis

1 P. F. Baum, *Tennyson Sixty Years After*, Chapel Hill, New York, 1948, p. 101.
2 Note by Christopher Ricks, *Tennyson Research Bulletin*, 2, no. 2 (1973), 68–72.
3 Lee Holcombe, 'Victorian wives and property', in Martha Vicinus (ed.), *A Widening Sphere*, Indiana University Press, 1977, pp. 3–28.
4 Barbara Taylor, *Eve and the New Jerusalem*, Virago, 1983, pp. 33, 96, 220.
5 Killham, *Tennyson and The Princess*, p. 167; other material about Kemble is also drawn from chapter 5.
6 Pattison, *Tennyson and Tradition*, pp. 101–2; Anita Draper, 'The artistic contribution of the "weird seizures" to *The Princess*', *Victorian Poetry*, XVII (1979). Stevenson's article is reproduced in *Critical Essays on the Poetry of Tennyson*, John Killham (ed.), Routledge and Kegan Paul, 1960, pp. 126–36.
7 Eric Griffiths, 'Tennyson's Idle Tears', Tennyson Conference, Lincoln, July 1987 (to be published by Macmillan).
8 Carol Christ, 'Victorian masculinity and the angel in the house' in *A Widening Sphere*, Martha Vicinus (ed.), pp. 146–62.

4 *In Memoriam*: 'some wild Poet'

1 Terry Eagleton, 'Politics and sexuality in *The Princess* and *In Memoriam*' in *1848: The Sociology of Literature*, Francis Barker, *et al.* (eds.), University of Essex, 1978, p. 99.
2 Timothy Peltason, *Reading In Memoriam*, Princeton University Press, 1985, p. 119.
3 Alan Sinfield, *The Language of Tennyson's In Memoriam*, Basil Blackwell, Oxford, 1971, p. 93.
4 D. R. Dean, 'Tennyson and geology', *Tennyson Society Monographs* X, Lincoln, 1985, pp. 9, 13.
5 Harold Nicolson, *Tennyson*, Constable, 1923, p. 233.
6 Susan Shatto and Marion Shaw, *Tennyson: In Memoriam*, Clarendon Press, Oxford, 1982, pp. 26–32.
7 Hallam Tennyson, *Alfred Lord Tennyson – A Memoir*, vol. I, Macmillan, 1897, p. 210.
8 Peter Dale, '"Gracious lies": The meaning of metaphor in *In Memoriam*', *Victorian Poetry*, XVIII (1980), 147–67.
9 Shatto and Shaw, p. 209.

[10] Elaine Jordan, 'Tennyson's *In Memoriam*: an echo of Goethe', *Notes and Queries*, n.s., XV (November 1985), 414–15.

[11] Shatto and Shaw, p. 222.

[12] Humphry House, *All in Due Time*, Hart-Davis, 1955, p. 129.

[13] Peltason, pp. 139, 153.

[14] Peltason, p. 176.

5 *Maud*, or the madness

[1] Norman Page, *Interviews and Recollections*, p. 115.

[2] Goldwin Smith, 'The war passages in *Maud*', *Saturday Review*, 3 November 1855, in John Jump (ed.), *Tennyson: The Critical Heritage*, Routledge and Kegan Paul, 1967, pp. 186–90.

[3] Hallam Tennyson, *A Memoir*, vol. I, p. 408.

[4] A. Dwight Culler, 'Monodrama and the dramatic monologue', *PMLA*, XC (1975), 366–85.

[5] *Suggested by Reading an Article in a Newspaper* (line 54), Ricks, *Poems*, p. 1006.

[6] Hallam Tennyson, *A Memoir*, vol. I, p. 343.

For information on the Crimean War see:
Asa Briggs, *Victorian People*, Pelican Books, 1965.
Olive Anderson, *A Liberal State at War*, London and New York, 1967.
James R. Bennett, 'The historical abuse of literature: Tennyson's *Maud: A Monodrama* and the Crimean War', *English Studies*, LXII (1981), 34–45.

6 *Idylls of the King*

This chapter is indebted throughout to Kathleen Tillotson's 'Tennyson's serial poem', in G. and K. Tillotson, *Mid-Victorian Studies*, Athlone Press, 1965, pp. 80–109. For the Arthurian revival see Mark Girouard, *The Return to Camelot*, Yale University Press, 1981.

[1] J. M. Ludlow, *Macmillan's Magazine*, November 1859, quoted by Ann Gossman and George Whiting in *Notes and Queries* (1959), 446–8.

[2] I have used *The History of King Arthur*, Thomas Wright (ed.), 1858, which Tennyson used as well as earlier editions.

[3] *La Queste del Saint Graal*, Roxburghe Club, 1864, pp. vi–vii.

[4] Quoted by Rachel Trickett in *Tennyson's Craft*, Tennyson Society Occasional Paper, Lincoln, 1981, p. 12.

[5] F. M. Turner, 'Rainfall, plagues and the Prince of Wales . . .', *Journal of British Studies*, 1974, 46–65.

[6] J. W. Burrow, 'Faith, doubt, and unbelief' in L. Lerner (ed.), *The Context of English Literature: The Victorians*, Methuen, 1978, pp. 120–38.

[7] A. Dwight Culler, *The Poetry of Tennyson*, p. 230.

[8] *Tennyson Research Bulletin*, Lincoln, IV, 3 (November 1984), 107.

9 W. E. Buckler, *Man and his Myths: Tennyson's Idylls of the King in Critical Context*, New York University Press, 1984, pp. 32, 34.
10 J. R. Reed, *Perception and Design in Tennyson's Idylls of the King*, Ohio University Press, 1969, p. 115.

Index

INDEX